CHRISTIAN-NATIONALISM AND THE RISE OF THE AFRIKANER BROEDERBOND IN SOUTH AFRICA, 1918–48

Charles Bloomberg

Christian-Nationalism and the Rise of the Afrikaner Broederbond, in South Africa, 1918–48

Charles Bloomberg

Edited by Saul Dubow

MACMILLAN

First published 1990

Published by
THE MACMILLAN PRESS LTD
Houndmills, Basingstoke, Hampshire RG21 2XS
and London
Companies and representatives
throughout the world

Printed in Hong Kong

British Library Cataloguing in Publication Data
Bloomberg, Charles
Christian-Nationalism and the rise of the
Afrikaner Broederbond in South Africa.
1. South Africa. Afrikaners. Nationalism.
Religious aspects, history
I. Title II. Dubow, Saul
291.1'77
ISBN 0-333-48706-0

Contents

Friends of Charles Bloomberg

Foreword: Charles Bloomberg and the Broederbond

The publication of this book is the best tribute his friends can pay to the late, much-lamented Charles Bloomberg. It represents the life's work of a man dogged for twenty years by a severe heart condition which killed him in 1985, a man we knew as a delightful friend, brilliant journalist and talented artist. But behind all these qualities, lay a deeply serious researcher and historian, grappling with one of the most important themes in South African history, the development of the beliefs and organisations which lie at the heart of Afrikanerdom. The work is the more astonishing because it was written under conditions which were totally inimical to serious research, harassment, poverty, and perpetual insecurity.

Charlie's friends were entranced by a personality which combined friendliness and lack of aggression with enormous talent and charm, a perpetual fascination with new sights, new people and new experiences, and an uncomplaining acceptance of an uncomfortable and stressful way of life. He was the ideal person to understand South Africa. Lacking any preconceptions based on race, colour or creed, he was blessed with that subtlety of perception which sometimes accompanies a sweetness and openness of nature.

Charlie, and his younger sister Ada, were the children of Willy Bloomberg. By trade he was a dental mechanic, but by nature he was a true Jewish intellectual: somewhat solitary, self-taught, immensely knowledgeable, free-thinking, radical, a man who had accumulated a famous library. By contrast Charlie's mother, who had formerly been her husband's assistant, was deeply religious.

After High School Charlie took an arts degree at 'Wits' – the University of the Witwatersrand in Johannesburg – before studying law in the early 1950s. He was involved in liberal student politics. Charlie was no orator, but an inspired observer and reporter. As an editor of the student magazine, the liberal 'Wits Student', he had his first taste of the complexities involved in South African journalism. Student leaders at the University of Pretoria, who supported apartheid, had privately agreed to accept whoever the

vii

Wits students nominated, black or white, in any joint student organisation. Charlie published the promise, a revelation which provoked an anti-liberal reaction at Pretoria and prevented any further collaboration.

After university Charlie naturally became a journalist. His chance came in the years after 1958 when he became a political reporter on the Johannesburg *Sunday Times*. Its editor, Joel Mervis, had brought a new dynamism to the paper, concentrating, like its British namesake, on bold headlines backed by well-documented political exposés, creating an atmosphere which appealed to Charlie. His gentle approach worked wonders with people as different as Nelson Mandela and a number of Afrikaner ministers.

So he was the natural recipient of the material which formed the base for the single most important exposé in South African journalistic history – the series of articles, starting on 25 April 1963, which revealed the existence, and explained the workings and enormous influence, of the Afrikaner Broederbond, the hitherto unknown organisation whose members dominated the spiritual, political and economic life of the Afrikaner people.

Charlie's revelations were based on the spiritual agonies of one of the most remarkable Afrikaners of his generation, Dr Beyers Naudé.[1] A brilliant 'Moderator' in the Dutch Reformed Church, the NGK, Naudé was born into the heart of Afrikanerdom. His father had been a founding member of the Broederbond, of which he naturally became a member. Naudé himself was one of the NGK delegation to a conference organised by the World Council of Churches in December 1960 at Cottesloe, a former university residence at Wits. The conference was held to consider the increased racial tensions which followed the killings at Sharpeville earlier that year. After Cottesloe Naudé became increasingly isolated within the NGK, and found his ideas totally repudiated at the NGK's first national synod in October 1962.

In early 1963, convinced that the Broederbond had a stranglehold on the NGK, he broke his vow of silence. He discussed the agonies he felt with Professor Albert Geyser, a close friend, not himself in the Broederbond. In Randall's words: 'Naudé asked for Geyser's advice and left a number of Bond documents for him to study.' Geyser decided that 'public exposure was the best means of countering the "quasi-biblical arguments" used by the Bond to cloak its clandestine political activities'. Without consulting Naudé, Geyser photographed the documents and gave the negatives to Charlie, a natural recipient given his paper's mass circulation and reputation. With a colleague, 'Hennie' Serfontein, Charlie used the documents as the basis for a long series of articles. Naudé subsequently founded the Christian Institute, and, as a former insider, became one of the government's most feared adversaries and one of the most important symbolic figures in the anti-apartheid movement, revered by black and white alike.

Now that the Broederbond has been discussed in a number of books (including one written by Charlie's former colleague) it is difficult to recreate the impact of the articles, which were both sensational and authoritative, revealing in detail the full extent of the Broederbond's influence throughout Afrikanerdom.

The Broederbond, helped by the Special Branch of the South African police, immediately made feverish attempts to trace the source of the leaks. Dr Piet Koornhof, then the secretary of the Broederbond, and later a cabinet minister, told members of the Bond that the disclosures were part of 'the Communist pattern of suspicion-sowing' aimed at 'subverting Afrikanerdom and its holiest spiritual possessions' – an attitude reflected by the Afrikaner press.

The mere mention of 'Communism' and 'subversive forces' provided enough justification for action by the Special Branch. On 1 October 1963 the offices of the *Sunday Times* were raided and searched and all the copies of the Broederbond documents were removed, on the flimsy pretext that the documents had been stolen. Six weeks later a special meeting of the executive council of the Broederbond was convened to announce that the source of the leak had been identified as Beyers Naudé.

Charlie's situation soon became impossible. Laws passed after the Sharpeville massacre provided for detention without trial, and some of Charlie's political contacts were arrested. He was led to believe that he himself might also be taken into custody. In addition he (as well as Geyser and Naudé) began to receive death threats. Not surprisingly he decided to leave South Africa, a wrenching decision, for it remained his spiritual home for the rest of his life.

By then he had determined to transform the material, not simply into a history of the Broederbond, but into a much more ambitious study tracing the Bond's roots back to Holland and the rise of Christian-Nationalism. Before he left he copied hundreds of documents covering the Bond and its links with Christian-Nationalism. Working against time, in an atmosphere of increasing tension, he stored the material in several secret hideouts. In the middle of 1964 he left South Africa for England and friends arranged for his documentary hoard to follow, a precursor of the devious means he had to use to protect his work for the rest of his life.

The two traumatic years preceding his departure permanently marked Charlie, making him eternally suspicious. From then on he separated his life, his friends (and the material he had accumulated) into separate compartments. His obsessive secrecy meant that none of his friends grasped the full range of his contacts or activities. Charlie was fully aware that he could have been accused of paranoia, indeed once consulted a psychiatrist – who told him that he could do nothing, for Charlie was not suffering from a persecution complex but from the real thing.

His problems were medical, not psychological. Throughout the last twenty years of his life, Charlie suffered from hypercholesterol-aemia, a genetic predisposition to high levels of cholesterol in the blood. This resulted in coronary artery disease, and necessitated a series of heart operations. His smoking resulted in emphysema, a debilitating condition which restricts the ability of the lungs to absorb oxygen and which made it increasingly difficult for him to cope with any physical effort.

Charlie had been promised a scholarship at Oxford to pursue his research, though he was eventually guided to Edinburgh, where it was hoped he would complete a thesis based on the documents he had accumulated. Unfortunately he found life at the university unsympathetic, and he found the problem of coping with the mass of material he had accumulated almost insuperable. A work he had originally hoped to complete in the time taken for a normal doctoral thesis became the basis of a struggle which was not resolved when he died twenty years later.

Charles Bloomberg then led a marginal and haunted life. In the last fifteen years of his life he alternated periods in which he earned a meagre living as a journalist and scriptwriter – he wrote the haunting commentary to the episode on the Holocaust of the television series *The World at War* – with periods in which he worked on his book, at the Free University in Amsterdam, where he found some good friends, or in people's spare rooms, in Britain and in South Africa. Sometimes he took a room in a lodging-house. He was about to leave one of these rooms when he met his replacement, a young American, Hope, whom, years later, he married on his death-bed. Towards the end he also earned some money from the bright and vivid sketches, many of the scenery of his beloved South Africa as he saw them through a railway carriage window.

His friends naturally tried to get his book published and it was provisionally accepted by at least one publisher. Unfortunately, following his unhappy time at Edinburgh, Charlie had grown suspicious of virtually every academic authority on the subject. He resolutely refused to compromise, and reacted violently to any suggestion which, he felt, resulted from a lack of sympathy with his work or attitudes. Moreover none of the possible publishers had anyone with the academic skills or depth of knowledge of South Africa required to turn what was by then an impossibly unwieldy mass of material into publishable form.

After his death his widow and a group of his friends determined that the work must be published, even, as seemed inevitable, in a much shortened form. A mass of material was uncovered from an astonishing variety of hidey-holes. An appeal to Charlie's many friends world-wide provided sufficient funds to enable a young South African historian, Dr Saul Dubow, to spend a year shaping it into publishable form – a task many of us, including those who had wrestled with the material during Charlie's lifetime, secretly feared was impossible.

As Dr Dubow explains in his preface, he has concentrated on the history of the Broederbond, as Charlie himself had anticipated in at least one of the many synopses he prepared. Through a combination of hard work, thorough knowledge of the historical background, scrupulous scholarship – and a surprising degree of empathy with someone he had never known – Dr Dubow was able to fashion a book which does full justice to Charlie's research and perceptions.

NICHOLAS FAITH

Preface

This work is a condensed version of the vast manuscript on Christian-Nationalism and the Afrikaner Broederbond which Charles Bloomberg researched and wrote during the 1960s and 1970s. In a note to a publisher dated 1977 he said, 'My first draft manuscript is 600 000 words. This will have to be drastically shortened for publication, edited, and where necessary, rewritten; the entire work has to be updated; a large number of footnotes and many thousands of translation, from three languages, checked. To round out the work for publication, I need a year, free from TV and journalistic commitments.' Unfortunately, Charles Bloomberg never had this clear period of time to complete his work and, following his death in 1985, the project outlined above was undertaken by myself.

In its original form the manuscript fell into three main parts: a study of the origins and development of Christian-Nationalism (1652–1920); an outline of the anatomy of the Afrikaner Broederbond; and an historical account of the rise of the Broederbond as a Christian-National organisation (1920–48). A final – but uncompleted section – was to analyse the Broederbond and the crisis in Afrikaner ideology from the accession to power of the Nationalist government in 1948, to the Soweto uprising in 1976. For the purposes of publication the sheer scale of this project rendered it impractical. Thus, in November 1979, Bloomberg wrote a synopsis of a single-volume work on the Broederbond and its Christian-National doctrine covering the period from its inception in 1918 to the Nationalists' victory in 1948. I have used that outline as a guide in the process of editing this book.

Charles Bloomberg first became interested in Afrikaner nationalism during the 1950s when, as a student at the University of the Witwatersrand, he began research on the Afrikaner Economic Movement. The progress of his MA degree was interrupted, however, and in 1958 he became a political reporter on the Johannesburg *Sunday Times*. In 1963, in collaboration with J.H.P. (Hennie) Serfontein, he wrote a major series of articles for that newspaper on the Afrikaner Broederbond. He writes:

I was the reporter who cracked open the AB . . . Very little was known about it – even about its very existence – when I broke a long series of disclosures in 1963. These were the most extensive ever printed. They were supported by photostats of current AB documents. The exposé revealed that the AB was exceptionally active – and operating in all spheres of life. Attempts were made to stifle the reports, threats [were made] to assassinate me. Mr Vorster asked the Chief of Security, Major General van den Bergh to investigate into the source of my information. Police officers raided the offices of [the] *Sunday Times*, Johannesburg, looking for documents . . . Premier Verwoerd appointed a judicial commission of inquiry into charges against the AB, arising from my reports. Three Afrikaans Churches were also forced to hold inquiries.

I decided to collate, analyse and write up the material on the AB as in-depth study. This was impossible to do in S. Africa. So I attempted to do so at a British University. Persistent harassment and poverty slowed me down; but after 10 years I completed the length[y] manuscript, the most comprehensive study of the AB and its doctrine. A series of heart attacks – coupled with harassment by S. African and British police, and a denial of protection in the United Kingdom, decided me that I would go back home: I returned to SA after 11 years in June 1974.

It is important to appreciate the context in which this book was originally conceived. In the aftermath of the 1960 Sharpeville massacre and the declaration of a state of national emergency, the South African regime rapidly reasserted its authority. In 1961 Verwoerd defiantly led South Africa out of the Commonwealth and proclaimed it a Republic. By 1963 the state had succeeded in driving the liberation movements underground and imprisoning most of its leadership. Moreover, the economy recovered swiftly from the politically-induced crisis of 1960–1 and for the rest of the decade – aside from a blip in 1964–5 – grew at the remarkable annual rate of between 5 and 8 per cent. Under these circumstances the dominance of Afrikanerdom reached unprecedented heights and the doctrine of apartheid was implemented with unparalleled intensity.

The apparently monolithic hegemony of Afrikaner nationalism during the 1960s is clearly reflected in Bloomberg's interpretation of the Broederbond, though he was also highly sensitive to the conflicts within Afrikanerdom which culminated in the 1969 extreme right-wing split away from the ruling Nationalist Party. Thus he stresses the (now discredited) view that, from its earliest days, Afrikaner nationalism has been powered by the messianic, prophetic doctrine of Christian-Nationalism which was subsequently formalised into a systematic ideology in the early twentieth century. Likewise, Bloomberg emphasises the notion of South Africa as a confessional state in which Calvinist ideology serves as the major determinant of political action.

As Bloomberg explored the secret machinations of the Afrikaner Broederbond, he became increasingly aware of the Christian-Nationalist ideology which informed it. He believed that little serious attention had been given to the white (Afrikaner) protagonists in the South African conflict, or to the ideas which motivated them. And he suggested that some Afrikaners would be prepared to die fighting rather than 'surrender values which, in their view, constitute the essence of the Afrikaner being'. In view of the resurgence of millenerian, neo-fascist Afrikaner organisations like the Afrikaner Weerstandsbeweeging during the 1980s, this prediction strikes a chord today.

It was Bloomberg's interest in the internal development of Afrikaner ideology which led him to investigate the nature of neo-Calvinism. In particular, he became convinced that the links between Dutch and South African neo-Calvinism were of crucial importance to an understanding of modern Afrikanerdom. For Bloomberg, the development of Christian-Nationalism in South Africa mirrored its progress in Holland, and he stressed the 'towering influence' of Dr Abraham Kuyper on Afrikaans political theory and theology. Throughout this work Bloomberg emphasises the inherent contradictions within Kuyperian thought, whose legacy is at once democratic and authoritarian. This theme is pursued with special attention to the ambivalent attitudes displayed by Afrikaner and Dutch neo-Calvinists towards Nazi-Fascism.

When Charles Bloomberg began his academic research at Edinburgh University, there was a relative paucity of secondary material on the Afrikaner Broederbond and on Afrikaner ideology in general. He insisted that the organisation's influence was greatly underrated and that the literature which did exist on the subject was inadequate. The works with which he was most closely acquainted were Sheila Patterson's *The Last Trek* (1957); W. Vatcher's *White Laager* (1965); Alexander Hepple's *Verwoerd* (1967); Brian Bunting's *The Rise of the South African Reich* (1964 and 1969); Pierre van den Berghe's *South Africa: A Study in Conflict* (1967); Leo Marquard's *The Peoples and Policies of South Africa* (1952); Colin and Margaret Legum's *South Africa: Crisis for the West* (1964); and Gwendolen Carter's *The Politics of Inequality* (1959). Bloomberg was variously critical of most of these works – either on empirical or interpretative grounds – though he declared himself impressed by the objectivity and balanced judgements in the books by Carter and Patterson. Nevertheless, he contended that all these works neglected the vital importance of the Broederbond. On this score the one exception was the book by Vatcher, though Bloomberg was wary of its uncritical reliance on 'popular but unproved speculation'.

Since Bloomberg's survey of the secondary literature dealing with the Broederbond two full-length exposés of the secret organisation have been published. The first, by J.H.P. Serfontein, entitled *Brotherhood of Power* (1978), was based largely on materials collected together with Bloomberg (an association which is described in some detail in Serfontein's introduction). The second book, by Ivor Wilkins and Hans Strydom, entitled *The Broederbond* (1978), utilised further revelations to the *Sunday Times* about the secret organisation. As works of investigative journalism backed by copious documentation, both these books are extremely valuable, though they seem to me to lack the analytical insights or historical perspective that characterises Bloomberg's writings.

The academic debate about Afrikaner nationalism has advanced considerably since the 1960s. Two works in particular should be mentioned: *The Rise of Afrikanerdom* (1975) by sociologist Dunbar Moodie, who examines the notion of an Afrikaner 'civil religion' from a Weberian point of view; and Dan O'Meara's *Volkskapitalisme* (1983), whose subtitle, 'Class, Capital and Ideology in the Development of Afrikaner Nationalism, 1934–48', indicates its historical-materialist orientation. Despite methodological differences, both these books are complementary. Moodie provides the most detached and systematic interpretation to date of Afrikaner ideology, while O'Meara ridicules the idealist conception which portrays 'Afrikanerdom' as a unified, immanent, ethnic category. Attacking both nationalist and liberal commentators, O'Meara argues that Afrikanerdom should be analysed as an historically specific and contradictory set of class alliances rooted within the development of South African capitalism.

Further challenges to the idea of Afrikanerdom as a timeless people bound by archaic tradition have been mounted in recent years by Hermann Giliomee and André du Toit. In one of a brilliant series of articles du Toit has demonstrated, for instance, that Afrikaners have not regarded themselves as 'God's Chosen People' since the time of the Voortrekkers; nor have they always had a clear vision of themselves as an integrated entity, charged with the fulfilment of a divinely inspired historical task. Thus it emerges that many of the mythologies associated with Afrikanerdom (which Afrikaner nationalists have assiduously cultivated and for which they have been relentlessly lampooned by critics) are the relatively recent creations of late nineteenth and early twentieth century theoreticians. The implications of these discoveries are considerable, for they suggest that Afrikaner identity is the product of an historically contingent process, rather than an embalmed and static political tradition.

Where Charles Bloomberg would have stood on this debate is a matter for speculation. One wonders too how he would react to claims that the Broederbond's power over the Nationalist Party was never complete and that regional differences within Afrikanerdom (especially between the Cape and Transvaal) exacerbated the unevenness of its influence. Arguably, Bloomberg's concentration on the pronouncements of Potchefstroom-based intellectuals obscures many of these divisions and suggests a greater degree of unanimity than actually existed. In many respects his work reflects the traditional view of Afrikanerdom as an encapsulated offshoot of seventeenth-century Calvinist Holland. Bloomberg was, however, also keenly aware of the internal divisions within Afrikanerdom, of its increasing secularisation during the 1960s, and of its pragmatic ability to adapt to political and social realities. Notably, he was acutely conscious of the significance of the Afrikaner economic movement during the 1930s and 1940s. Indeed, he commented, in advance of later writers, that a full-length study of its development was desirable and went some way to researching this topic.

Inevitably, recent political developments in South Africa prompt important questions about the past. The split within the Nationalist Party in 1981–2 which led to the creation of the Conservative Party under the leadership of Andries Treurnicht (who figures prominently in this account as a leading Kuyperian theologian) suggests that the Christian-Nationalist tradition is now the legacy of the far right. This impression is strengthened by the fact that the ruling Nationalist

Party has, over the past decade, increasingly distanced itself from the ideology of Verwoerdian apartheid. In attempting to disguise the nature of racial domination it has promoted a somewhat inchoate technocratic ideology of reform based on adherence to 'neutral' free-market principles and an unremitting hostility to the 'total onslaught' of international communism.

The response of the Broederbond to these developments is not yet entirely clear. However, it is apparent that the organisation has been left divided and severely disabled following the resignation in June 1984 of Andries Treurnicht. In the month preceding this event a rival 'cultural' organisation, the Afrikaner Volkswag, was established in Pretoria. Reports claim that three out of five former living chairmen of the Broederbond were amongst its founder members. Carel Boshof, the first Chairman of the Volkswag (and a former Broederbond Chairman) 'contended that such an organisation had become vitally important because of a "cultural crisis" in the ranks of the Afrikaner nation brought about by "liberal influences."'[1] In February 1987 a secret Broederbond document was leaked to the press by the far-right Herstigte Nasionale Party. Headed 'basic constitutional conditions for the survival of the Afrikaner' it apparently envisages the possibility of 'black majority rule' – though with mechanisms to ensure white minority protection.[2] If this document is indeed reflective of contemporary Broederbond thinking, it seems likely that the organisation has settled for a more restricted role as an informal 'think tank' with close links to influential elements within the state.

In revising and editing this work for publication I have at all times sought to retain the arguments, perspective and tone of Bloomberg's full manuscript. Inevitably, choices about what to include and omit have had to be made. In this, I have attempted to preserve what is most relevant to contemporary discussion and interest. For example, I have downplayed the 'scoop' value of Bloomberg's disclosures about the Broederbond, partly because they are no longer newsworthy but also because many of the revelations have already been published by others. Conversely, I have endeavoured to highlight the distinctive aspects of Bloomberg's ideas, such as the influence of Dutch neo-Calvinism on twentieth-century Afrikaner nationalism, the ambivalent relationship of Afrikaner nationalists to various forms of totalitarianism, and his historical treatment of the Afrikaner Broederbond. Although I have cut certain sections very substantially, I have not attempted to distort Bloomberg's individual interpretation so as to accord with the views of contemporary scholarship. Quite aside from cutting down the manuscript to one-sixth of its original length, it has been necessary to correct factual errors, elucidate certain points, check sources and fill in sketchy bibliographical references. (The translations, it should be noted, are Bloomberg's own.) However, the length of this project has been limited and, as a result, it has been impossible to fulfil all these tasks to my own full satisfaction. In particular, I have not been successful in tracking down all of the references to which Bloomberg alludes.

In undertaking this work I have at all times been supported by those who initiated the project: trustees Nicholas and Roz Faith and Jeremy Isaacs. I have also benefited greatly from discussions with John Lazar, whose recent Oxford doctorate on Afrikaner nationalism in the 1950s is an important contribution to our understanding of this period. Aart Wildeboer discussed with me the nature of the Dutch–Afrikaner connection at the beginning of this century. Dunbar Moodie very kindly read the full manuscript and suggested a number of important changes. However, in order to retain the integrity of Charles Bloomberg's distinctive vision, I have elected to incorporate only some of these.

SAUL DUBOW

Introduction

This is an attempt to shed light on the anatomy, character and doctrine of the Afrikaner Broederbond (Afrikaner Brotherhood), and to trace the secret society's role in the rise of twentieth-century Afrikaner Nationalism. In so doing, specific reference is made to the formulation and propagation of the doctrine of Christian-Nationalism which underpins the Broederbond's range of activities. The setting for our story is the dramatic resurgence of Afrikanerdom from the dust and ashes of its defeat in the Anglo–Boer War of 1899–1902. It was a revival which established Afrikaner hegemony within the privileged white elite, ended the paramountcy of English settler culture and ideology, and eliminated the British imperial factor from South Africa.

Today, the dominant fact about South Africa is the struggle for the redistribution of wealth, political power and status between the established white ruling class and the dispossessed black majority. It is a conflict born of the challenge from blacks who are excluded by law from a share in power, the benefits of which have been a white monopoly for over 300 years. It is primarily a colour conflict, but this should not be allowed to obscure one important fact: the whites are not a homogenous, uniform and monolithic ruling class. On the contrary, they are also subject to deep rifts and conflicts. Consisting of two Western European colonial settler populations, one stemming from seventeenth-century Holland, the other from nineteenth-century Britain, they are split on cultural–linguistic lines as well as by differing political–economic interests.

Conflict between the two groups first broke out when Britain occupied the Cape in 1806, replacing Holland as the European metropolitan colonial power. For the next 150 years, Boer and Briton struggled for hegemony over Southern Africa. It was essentially a contest between two white nationalisms, and bore the character of a white civil war, but it also reflected a fundamental clash between two world views. Influenced by the liberal doctrines of 1789 and spurred on by missionaries and the anti-slavery lobby in Britain, the first British administration tended towards a relaxation of the traditional colour bar and accepted the principle that 'civilised' non-whites could share – to some extent – in the hitherto white monopoly of political power. The Boers, on the other hand, clung tenaciously to their concept of a divinely-fixed hierarchy headed by a privileged aristocracy of white-skinned rulers.

The first stage in this battle was the mass emigration of Boers after 1835 from British liberal rule at the Cape into the interior. After conquering the African kingdoms in the north the Voortrekkers, as they were known, established independent Boer Republics, constitutionally and economically divorced from Europe and metropolitan rule. Rich discoveries of diamonds and gold on Boer territory in the late nineteenth century aroused Britain's interest in the interior and led directly to two Anglo–Boer wars (1881–2 and 1899–1902) for military and political control over Southern Africa.

By the Treaty of Vereeniging in 1902 the Boer Republics surrendered to Britain and were incorporated into the Empire. This led, in due course, to the amalgamation of the four British colonies into the Union in 1910, and the creation of institutions to integrate Boer and Briton into a single nation with dominion status within the Empire. The establishment of Union enhanced the country-wide influence of the local English population and reduced the Boers to a subject nationality – much like French Canadians – within the Empire.

It was resentment over the unequal distribution of status, wealth and political control, as well as the fear of cultural absorption into an English oriented binational society, which roused the Afrikaner Nationalists in 1913–14 to renew the Anglo–Boer struggle by political means. Their remarkable recovery from defeat has been a decisive fact in twentieth-century South African history, with far-reaching consequences not only for the composition and character of the white elite, but also for those excluded from ordinary civil rights.

The story of Afrikanerdom's regeneration from the ashes of its 1902 defeat to undisputed mastery of South Africa is a remarkable one, elaborately romanticised by Afrikaner publicists as a modern version of a minuscule Afrikaner David slaying the British Goliath. It is the story of how the Afrikaners, a small offshoot of a segment of European culture, asserted their separate identity and consolidated themselves into a new and distinct Western European nationality. Moreover, it is the story of the defeat of efforts to blend Boer and Briton into a single South African culture, and the replacement of the ideal of white partnership by exclusive Afrikaner rule.

These themes were played out against the background of an industrial revolution and the rapid proletarianisation of a predominantly rural people. The trek to the cities, coupled with the Boers' defeat at the hands of the British, were the two forces that decisively moulded Afrikaner Nationalism. Beginning with the mineral revolution at the end of the nineteenth century, industrialis- ation turned the Boers into an urban proletariat in the employ of a foreign, capitalist class. The fact that English speakers monopolised finance, commerce and mining persuaded Afrikaners that their national and class enemy was one and the same. Consequently the Afrikaners' struggle for a redistribution of power, for cultural autonomy and economic liberation, was fused with a struggle to overthrow the influence of English speakers.

Afrikaner Nationalism launched a three-pronged struggle – cultural, economic and political – for an autonomous Afrikaner existence and ultimate mastery within the white group. There was nothing fortuitous or sudden in the victorious resurgence of the Afrikaners; certainly, they did not turn the tables on their conquerors in a single, spectacular event. This was only achieved after the tireless and systematic conversion of Afrikanerdom by self-conscious ultra-Nationalist elements who had never reconciled themselves to defeat in the Anglo–Boer War.

When the Nationalists finally converted South Africa into a Republic in 1961, the wheel of history had turned full circle. At a single stroke the jubilant Afrikaners had liquidated the consequences of the 1902 Treaty of Vereeniging and the constitutional legacy of defeat. A dynamic, united and supremely confident Afrikanerdom ruled over the whole of South Africa and all but eliminated the last traces of British influence in the Union. Dr Verwoerd's withdrawal from the Commonwealth in that year finally severed South Africa's 150-year link with Great Britain. The Boer martyrs had been avenged. On the eve of the Republic's inauguration on 31 May 1961 the leading Nationalist paper, the *Transvaler*, exultantly proclaimed: 'Our republic is the inevitable fulfilment of God's plan for our people . . . a plan formed in 1652 when Jan van Riebeeck arrived at the Cape . . . for which the defeat of our Republics in 1902 was a necessary step.'

With the advent of the Republic in 1961 the National Party (NP) commanded an overwhelming parliamentary majority. Nationalists were also consolidating their grip upon the administration. By 1962 every branch of the state apparatus – the Civil Service, judiciary, police and army – was controlled and staffed by Afrikaners. Of the 46 top civil servants, 42 were Afrikaners; of the country's 318 diplomats, 315 bore Afrikaans surnames; of the 11 Appeal Judges, only two were of English-speaking descent; and no English names at all were to be found in the senior military and police lists. Moreover, Afrikaner businessmen were strategically eroding the last bastion of English-speaking power: the commanding peaks of finance, commerce and industry.

In an attempt to understand the dramatic success of Afrikanerdom, I propose to examine the role of the Afrikaner Broederbond or AB, a tightly-knit secret brotherhood of Afrikaner Nationalists, formed in 1918 to 'promote all the interests of the Afrikaners' and to fight for the Afrikanerisation of South Africa's state on Christian-National lines. As the champion of Afrikaner autonomy, the Broederbond worked to consolidate all Afrikaners into a single *laager* (encampment). Wrapped in a veil of secrecy, the Broederbond has been an enigmatic factor in South African politics, its precise character and role obscured by a cloud of rumour, speculation and myth.

What distinguishes the Broederbond from other twentieth-century political, ethnic or patriotic societies is the wide range of its activities, the extent of its influence, the high calibre of its members and its religious-confessional basis. From its ranks have come virtually all the top Nationalist leaders in the political, economic, religious and cultural fields. All the heads of government in South Africa from 1948 until the present have come from its ranks. Members have included Cabinet ministers, party leaders, church moderators, university principals, Civil Service chiefs, captains of industry, theologians and academics.

The AB has played the role of Afrikanerdom's elite vanguard. It has been the invisible cement holding the structure together; the central arterial core of the Christian-Nationalist movement and the agency *par excellence* for propagating the Christian-Nationalist creed in South Africa. This doctrine blends the theology of orthodox, classical seventeenth-century Calvinism with the Afrikaner's racial and Nationalist consciousness, and has attempted to reconcile the Bible with apartheid. Largely as a result of the Broederbond's tireless propaganda, Christian-Nationalist ideas permeate Nationalist thinking and constitute the ideological basis of the Republican state and the theology of the Dutch Reformed Churches (DRCs).

The overall aim of this study is to trace the role of the Broederbond in the rise of twentieth-century Afrikaner Nationalism, taking into special account its Christian-Nationalist character and tradition.

Only in this way, I believe, can the story of the AB be told meaningfully and to the best advantage. The relationship between the Broederbond and Christian-Nationalism is of crucial importance both to the secret society and to the doctrine. Neither can be fully understood without the other.

One of the striking facts of the South African Republic is that it rests on an explicitly religious foundation. This is laid down in the Constitution's preamble which makes all governments subordinate to 'the sovereignty and providence of God in guiding the affairs of nations'. Unlike other Protestant states with similar constitutional conventions (that is, which politely recognise the traditionally established church, although religion plays little part in determining governmental policy), this is no ornamental hangover from the Reformation. On the contrary, it expresses the dynamic Calvinist spirit of the ruling NP.

Internationally, the Nationalists are seen as the apostles of white mastery and the most determined contemporary champions of racial segregation; certainly the Party is the organ of Afrikaner ethnicity and power. But a less well-known feature – of critical importance to those who would understand the Nationalists – is that, at least until recently, it has been a confessional party, faithful to the strict sixteenth-century doctrine of Jean Calvin, and similar in many respects to Holland's two Calvinist confessional political parties.[1] What the party stands for is not merely white rule based on race: it also stands for a society modelled on Christian norms. It thus justifies all policies, including segregation, in terms of the Christian-Nationalist Protestant ethic.

The NP of D.F. Malan, established in 1934, formally embraced Christian-Nationalism. Article 1 of its Constitution states: 'The Party acknowledges the sovereignty and guidance of God in the destiny of countries and seeks the development of our nation's life along Christian-National lines.'[2] in education (according to Article 24), 'the Christian-National basis of the state should be taken fully into account'.[3] Furthermore, all black people must be kept 'under the Christian trusteeship of the European race'.[4]

All Party officers and officials must swear the following Christian-National pledge:

> I hereby solemnly and sincerely declare that I acknowledge the sovereignty and guidance of God in the destiny of countries and peoples, and that I will in a spirit of brotherhood together with

my fellow party members seek the development of South Africa's life along Christian-National lines.[5]

The NP's leaders have frequently proclaimed the Party's subordination to God, and their own personal fidelity to the DRC's creed. Dr Malan, the ex-pastor who founded the Party and who was the first Nationalist prime minister (1948–54), pithily summed up the Christian-Nationalist outlook when he repeated the Voortrekker maxim in 1937: 'Believe in God! Believe in your Volk! Believe in yourself!'[6] Malan's successor, J.G. Strydom – Party leader and prime minister from 1954–8 – declared in a radio broadcast on the night of his election:

> Mindful of the fact that we acknowledge the sovereignty and guidance of God in the destinies of countries and nations, and that we seek the development of our national life along a Christian national road, I want to ask the nation to think of me and the new government in their prayers. It is on this foundation that our forefathers built, and this is the basis on which we must continue to build if we are to survive.[7]

A similar pledge on taking office was given by Strydom's successor, Dr Hendrik Verwoerd (a Stellenbosch sociology professor), who had once planned to enter the DRC's ministry. Immediately on his surprise election by the NP caucus, Verwoerd commented: 'I believe that the will of God was revealed in the ballot.'[8] In a national radio broadcast he declared:

> It must be stated at the outset that we, as believing rulers of a religious country, will seek our strength and guidance in the future, as in the past, from Him who controls the destinies of nations . . . In accordance with His will, it was determined who should assume the leadership of the Government in this new period of the life of the people of South Africa.[9]

In these utterances Verwoerd was not expressing megalomania but merely acknowledging the role of divine providence. As the architect of the bantustans and an Afrikaner Republic, his outlook was rooted in 'the Christian ideals of his volk'. Verwoerd's race policies in particular were 'born out of the nation's Christian life and morals', said Dr P.J. Meyer in October 1967, when paying tribute to the late premier.[10]

Balthazar John Vorster, who succeeded Verwoerd as prime minister and leader of the NP in 1966, originally espoused an extreme pro-Nazi form of the Christian-Nationalist creed. 'We stand for Christian Nationalism', he said in 1942, 'which is an ally of National Socialism. You can call the anti-democratic principle dictatorship if you wish. In Italy it is called Fascism, in Germany National Socialism and in South Africa Christian Nationalism.'[11] Later, having joined the NP, Vorster somewhat modified his extreme position but nevertheless remained a firm Christian-Nationalist. Throughout his premiership he invoked God to endorse the government's political policies.

The original NP, founded in 1914, acknowledged God's guidance and pursued a policy of Christian-National education. For its founder, General Hertzog, the term Christian-National did not denote a well worked-out philosophy, but was an attempt to capture an important truth about the Afrikaner ethos, and to stress the Party's links with religious life. These were concessions to confessionalism in the Afrikaner cultural and religious movements, rather than the expression of a philosophy or an affirmation of the Party's religious basis. But when Dr Malan broke away with 17 dissidents in 1933 in protest against Hertzog's decision to collaborate with the South African Party (SAP) under Smuts, he explicitly based his new party, the Purified Nationalist Party (forerunner of the present regime), on Christian-Nationalist precepts. This was in direct contrast to Hertzog's view that Afrikanerdom had accomplished its historical mission as a separate entity.

In 1941 the Christian-Nationalists split into two camps: the Nazi-style Ossewa Brandwag (OB) and the NP. Essentially, it was a power struggle between two bodies for Afrikanerdom's allegiance, but the battle was fought out within the Christian-National ideological framework. Thus, although their chief difference was over the tactics and techniques for attaining a Christian-National Republic, these differences were fought out in terms of Calvinist teaching regarding democracy, hierarchical authority, the form of state power, and parliamentary versus extra-parliamentary methods.

The conflict in the late 1960s between *Verligtes* (enlightened thinkers) and *Verkramptes* (narrow thinkers) which ultimately led to the breakaway of the extreme right-wing Herstigte (reconstituted) National Party (HNP) in 1969, further illustrates this point. On the face of it the dispute was only about political strategy and had nothing to do with God, Christ or Calvin. The real debate was between traditionalists and modernisers, isolationists and expansionists, and it arose in large part out of a need to escape total international isolation. Yet the conflict was expressed in religious terms. Dr Andries Treurnicht, then editor of the daily *Hoofstad* (and now leader of the right-wing Conservative Party which split away from the Nationalists in 1982 on the question of political reform) questioned whether *Verligte* Nationalists were still 'standing by God and His Word'. He accused the groups around the then Prime Minister Vorster of 'rejecting the Christian-National basis of our whole social, educational and political way of life' in their attempts to broaden the basis of Afrikaner rule.[12]

The great significance of this attack was that it was the first time that NP leaders had accused each other of subverting Christianity and Christian-Nationalism. In response to the right-wing onslaught, Piet Cillie, editor of *Die Burger*, criticised those 'elements' who, when 'thwarted in their political ambition and cornered in their intrigues pose as knights of Christianity'.[13] P.W. Botha, then leader of the Cape NP, told its 1969 provincial congress that the Party did not make religious dogma a condition of membership and could not allow a 'church battle' to develop within its ranks. Botha said that the highest loyalty of Christians was to God and not to a sovereign national state, even if it was controlled by the NP.[14]

The NP has traditionally been backed by a vast network of Afrikaner confessional-Nationalist bodies, which collectively constitute the Nationalist movement. All, like the Party, have been based on Christian-Nationalism. This network, embracing boy-scout, kindergarten, youth, student, labour, finance, business, recreational and leisure-time, cultural and educational bodies, is similar to the galaxy of interlinked organs of the 'Gereformeerde volksdeel' in Holland: a Calvinist society within a society. There, Abraham Kuyper created in the 1880s a society within a society containing not only a political party, but bodies to cater for everything from cradle to grave. The NP has therefore been the political arm of a mass movement based on a theocentric culture, whose organs in the cultural, economic and intellectual fields are based on Christian-Nationalism. Of these extra-parliamentary bodies the two most important have been the Federasie van Afrikaanse Kultuurvereni-gings (Federation of Afrikaans Cultural Organisations or FAK) and the DRC.

Historically, the FAK has been one of the main watchdogs over Afrikanerdom's Christian-Nationalist character. Founded in 1929 by the Broederbond, it is a central liaison body to which nearly 3 000 cultural, youth, religious, educational and other bodies are affiliated.[15] If the NP is Afrikanerdom's political organ, the FAK is its cultural front, keeping a watchful eye over confessionalism in all aspects of Afrikaner life. Office-bearers of the FAK have included Verwoerd, Dönges, Hertzog, Koornhof, Diederichs, Meyer and many political leaders whose names feature prominently in this work.

Inevitably, the three DRCs play a pivotal role in furnishing the Christian-Nationalist creed. The Afrikaner churches are practically coterminous with the Afrikaner people, claiming as members more than 80 per cent of Afrikaners, and about half of the white population*. If the DRC's social role has always been important, its ideological role has been of crucial significance in the development of Afrikanerdom. Despite its autonomy from the state the DRC is not divorced from politics or concerned purely with prayer, meditation, ritual and spiritual purity. Peculiar to its brand of Calvinism is its 'this worldliness': the notion that the creed should play a role in history and become involved in political, cultural and economic conditions. The creed is 'totalist' and 'universal', claiming every sphere of life for the Gospel.

As the sole settler institution of any kind with an unbroken 300-year connection with the Afrikaners, the DRCs have participated in their setbacks and triumphs. As the Afrikaner's prime religious institution they have a stake in the community's survival and welfare because if the Afrikaner disappeared, so would the Church. In particular, the DRC is committed to preserving the Afrikaner's tongue and cultural identity. It worships God in Afrikaans, using an Afrikaans Bible, catechism and psalm book. The DRC has become deeply rooted in Afrikaner ways and customs, involving itself in every aspect of cultural life to promote God's glory and ensure the primacy of the confessional element. Politically, the Afrikaans churches hold that state policy should rest on Christian-Nationalist foundations. The state has been seen as a divine creation, its authority deriving from God, not the electorate. The franchise is therefore not an automatic right for everyone, but a privilege entrusted to those who are capable of exercising it with responsibility to God.

---

* Figures drawn from the Department of Statistics suggest that in 1930 the three white constituent churches of the DRC had over 2 million adherents, about 45 per cent of the white population.

The DRC has not only been an ideological powerhouse of Christian-Nationalism; it has also supplied a high proportion of Afrikanerdom's political leaders from D.F. Malan to N.J. van der Merwe and Andries Treurnicht. Both General Hertzog and Dr Verwoerd originally intended to be theology students. The common ideology of the DRC and the NP is, in part, due to the fact that each is an exclusively Afrikaner institution: the one an expression of Afrikaner political life, the other the manifestation of Afrikaner religious life.

The claim by the South African state and the NP to be Christian is remarkable for two reasons. First, since the French Revolution, secular doctrines have replaced theology in the West as explanations of government, rights, nationalism and so forth. Thus it is unusual, to say the least, for a twentieth-century state boldly to embrace and model itself upon a doctrinal orientation and style which the rest of Western Protestantism has long discarded. Twentieth-century South Africa is unique in that both state and governing party have been openly faithful to seventeenth-century Reformed concepts regarding the nature of political authority, and thus have stubbornly rejected the triumphant wave of anti-clericalism which swept Europe after 1789. The Enlightenment dethroned God; but Afrikanerdom crowned Him as the sovereign of their Republic.

Second, in a world strongly opposed to white supremacy and all vestiges of open colour discrimination, South Africa is the only state which is formally organised on a racially segregatory basis. Whites, who monopolise all power, privilege and wealth in some 86 per cent of the country and in the central government, form a ruling caste based on pigmentation. The inferior treatment which is given to blacks is not subtly camouflaged or covert, as in Britain, but it is proclaimed as a cardinal principle of the social structure, and embodied in statutes which are enforced with the might of the state. The fact that whites monopolise all power, productive resources, land and social status, makes South Africa the only country in the post-colonial era to uphold rule over a black majority by a minority white caste. Notwithstanding the criticisms of world Protestantism the Nationalists have defended this system as flowing from God's word, insisting that it meets the higher criteria of Christianity.

1 The Precepts and Tenets of Christian-Nationalism

The Afrikaner's Christian world outlook belongs to two traditions: one nearly 2 000 years old, the other a product of the modern Age of Ideology. The older one dates from the fourth century, when Constantine made Christianity a state religion, turning the church into a pillar of the status quo and Christianity into a cloak for the emperor. Every single Christian European nation has, at least once, painted the cross on to its banner and claimed to be a holy nation with a sacred mission, civilising or Christianising. Christian-Nationalism is merely a heightened form of religious ethnocentricism; it is a species of theological fancy dress dedicated to self-aggrandisement.

A systematic body of closely-woven ideas, Christian-Nationalism incorporates (a) the idea of the 'chosen-people-with-a-sacred-mission', and (b) the Right's stress on authority, hierarchy, discipline, privilege and elitist leadership, as well as glorification of God, nation, family, blood and the cult of force. It couples this with a rejection of liberalism, Marxism, 'sickly sentimental humanism' and the equality of humankind regardless of race.

In essence, Christian-Nationalism is a *theological* defence of Afrikaner Nationalism, and of Afrikaner hegemony in politics. It proposes the structural subjection of blacks and their surgical separation from whites and power. Key terms are 'diversity of nations' (approved), and 'equalisation' (disapproved). Like other all-embracing, prophetic, messianic doctrines, Christian-Nationalism contains a definition of Utopia (Paradise, Fall, Redemption) and designates instruments for salvation. The main such vehicle is the chosen people and its elitist fighting organ, the Broederbond.

The term 'Christian-National' comes from the nineteenth-century counter-revolutionary, pro-authoritarian, anti-modernist movements which sought to restore the status quo that prevailed before 1789, with its ordered, hierarchical, monarchist structure. The French Revolution dethroned God as well as King; disestablished church as well as aristocracy. Patriotic and nationalist, the Christian-Nationalist movement rejected 1789's anti-God, anti-clerical, anti-Church challenge. 'God, King, and Nation' was its watchword. The

1

term Christian-National was already in use in 1834. (In Holland, the slogan was 'God, Oranje, Nederland'.) Its prophets – such as de Bonald, le Maistre, del la Garde, von Stahl, Stocker and van Prinsterer – used God, Christianity, nation and aristocracy as weapons against the 'no God, no master' egalitarianism associated with the French Revolution.

All the concepts of Afrikaner Christian-Nationalism can be related to the once-powerful, but today greatly weakened, anti-liberal and authoritarian religious tradition in nineteenth- and twentieth-century Europe. The Afrikaners are perhaps the last surviving representatives (who still exercise actual power) of the radical right-wing backlash to 1789, urbanisation, industrialisation and secularisation. These ideas fed directly into late twentieth-century radical rightist ultra-Nationalisms (including Nazi-Fascism); and they were lavishly scooped up by Afrikaner Christian-Nationalists during the war years.

A fascinating illustration of the synthesis of 'Christianity' with the counter-revolutionary syndrome comes from Dr P.J. Meyer, Chairman of the South African Broadcasting Corporation (SABC) from 1958 to 1976 and doyen of twentieth century Afrikaner theorists. In 1972 Meyer resigned as Chairman of the AB after a marathon 12-year term of office. During the Second World War he was a general in the paramilitary, pro-Nazi OB. Previously, he studied at the Nazi anti-Comintern school in Berlin. He wore a Hitler toothbrush moustache, and named his son Izan (Nazi spelt backwards). Meyer pictured Afrikaners as an 'army of God' whose ancestors concluded a 'Covenant with the Almighty' and had a mission to 'carry the light and spirit of Christianity into Africa from the South to the North'.[1]

In Meyer's view Afrikaners, as Africa's 'first Calvinist nation', have been concerned to attack all modern 'de-christianising' and 'denationalising' doctrines: the false gods of liberalism, communism, rationalism, materialism and internationalism. They have fought the 'degenerate elements in European philosophy', especially the idea of equality. Meyer rejected the intellectual fathers of the nineteenth and twentieth centuries (like Kant, Freud, Darwin, Marx, Hegel, Comte and Bergson), who paved the way for the de-Christianising of Western thought. Surrounded by foes – Soviet Marxism, Chinese communism, American capitalism, West European liberalism, Mohammedanism and African Nationalism – the Afrikaner single-handedly tackles them, in the confidence that God is with him.

Ultimately, his task was to liberate Europe itself from secularism, decay and confusion.[2]

Meyer's radical rightism contains both racism and Christianity. The result is a monolithic consolidation of all ideas antipathetic to 1789 and its ideological offspring. Meyer symbolises the hidden link between the Broederbond and Christian-Nationalism. He was a member of the Broederbond's secretariat from 1935 to 1942, and between 1960 and 1972 he was re-elected three times as Chairman. As an outstanding prophet of the Christian-Nationalist creed it is no accident that Meyer should have been the Broederbond's leader, for the two are inseparable. Meyer was no lunatic crackpot, and neither was he a paranoid delusionist. Not only was he re-elected by Afrikanerdom's elite several times to lead the AB; but he was also chairman of the Rand Afrikaans University and headed the SABC from 1958 to 1976. In the 1960s he was, next to Dr Verwoerd, the most powerful Afrikaner, and certainly the most authoritative voice of Christian-Nationalism. His views accorded closely with those of the Afrikaner establishment's core at the time.

Meyer's brand of Christianity claims to be rooted in the past, in the seventeenth-century origins of the Afrikaners and their nineteenth-century covenant with God. Like him, modern Christian-Nationalist theoreticians point out that the original settlers came from seventeenth-century Reformed Holland. Their nineteenth-century descendants married race and religion, proclaiming Afrikaners as a chosen nation with a sacred mission. Afrikaner culture has for 350 years been permeated by Reformed notions of divine providence, predestination and election. On this level, Christian-Nationalism is an outgrowth of Afrikaner folk experience; it systematises the informal union of Christianity and Nationalism into a sophisticated, ordered ideology.

In view of its influence, there has been surprisingly little study of the Christian-Nationalist creed. One reason is the English-speaking world's blind spot on ideology; another is that Christianity has only very recently discovered the 'blasphemy of racism': the stinging phrase coined by the World Council of Churches in 1968. Outside South Africa, there has been an even slower realisation of Christian ideology's relevance to the Nationalist regime and the significance of the rapidly spreading internal Christian challenge to it. In any event, one cannot fathom Afrikanerdom's highly motivated messianism or its ideological and cultural cohesion without examining its sustaining world view.

Christian-Nationalism first flowered during the nineteenth-century Great Trek, a flight away from the egalitarian and emancipatory ideas injected by Holland and Britain into the Cape. Rebelling against the end of slavery, the Boers saw themselves as a metaphoric reincarnation of Old Testament Israel fleeing from the yoke of a British Pharoah. The analogy was grotesque, but the well-armed ex-slave-owners trekking into the black interior to re-establish states with the 'proper Christian relationship between master and servant' saw themselves as a chosen people with a sacred mission.

The Trekkers were certainly not the first conquering Western European Christians to wrap themselves in this mystique. They articulated an informal Dutch colonial folk tradition which, stretching back to 1652, bequeathed a potent mythic legacy to their twentieth-century Afrikaner descendants. The doctrine of Christian-Nationalism was formulated as a single, systematic body of ideas only in the 1930s. But 300 years of history had already woven Christian-Nationalism's two components together. Thus Dutch Reformed concepts have long served to bolster Afrikaner Nationalist ideas: for example, the Calvinist notion of 'election' has become synonymous with that of a racial elite; 'vocation' with a superior mission; priesthood of believers with an aristocracy; power deriving from a sovereign God with authoritarian rule. These syntheses germinated, evolving in the crucible of Calvinism's gradual colonisation of black South Africa.

THE KUYPERIAN HERITAGE

In Holland, the effects of the French Revolution in 1789 ended Calvinist domination of the state. Dutch Patriotte, aided by French troops, overthrew the monarchy and established the Batavian Republic in 1795. Holland's new regime promptly disestablished the DRC, formally ending the favoured position it had held since the seventeenth century. Although the Batavian Republic was short-lived, even the restoration of the House of Orange-Nassau could not extinguish the new ideas and demands for reform. In Dutch Reformed circles a compromise theology, which tried to reconcile rationalism and liberalism with orthodox faith, became fashionable. Among the new approaches which found support were Deism, which held that God, having created the world, then withdrew to leave humankind to cope alone. There were attempts to explain religious claims and miracles in rational terms and the literal validity of the Bible came into question.

Changes in the status of the Protestant church angered its ultra-orthodox members, especially those in the countryside who remained faithful to the letter of the 1619 Canons of Dort, with their emphasis on Providence, Predestination and the Fall of Man. The first signs of the fundamentalist revolt came in 1834 when the Reverend de Kock objected to the singing of hymns and formed a splinter church, the Kristelik Afgeskeie Kerk. As the orthodox protest swelled, an intellectual, Groen van Prinsterer, emerged in 1842 as the focal point in the counter-attack against liberalism in church and state. In that year van Prinsterer outlined the principles of what later became the Gereformeerde (re-reformed) Kerken van Holland. On his election to the Lower House of the States-General in 1849 he formed the nucleus of Holland's first modern political party, appropriately called the Anti-Revolutionary Party (ARP). Van Prinsterer was also responsible for introducing the term 'Christian-National' into Holland, equating it with conservatism.

During this period, Abraham Kuyper (1837–1920) emerged as the charismatic leader of the awakening orthodox protest movement in succession to van Prinsterer. The son of a preacher, Kuyper trained in literature and theology at Leiden University. After a brief flirtation with modernist teachings, he was converted to old-fashioned pious Calvinism while serving as a minister in a small rural village during 1863–7. Far from shrinking into fundamentalist obscurantism, Kuyper updated traditional Calvinist propositions while preserving their original flavour. He led the orthodox into ideological battle with rationalism and humanism, turning van Prinsterer's sketchy ARP into a cohesive political machine, and popularising the term 'Christian-National'. Under his leadership the hard-core orthodox Calvinists separated from the Hervormde Kerk in 1886 (now allegedly compromised with liberal and rationalist theory) to form the Gereformeerde Kerken. To supply ministers for the new church he founded the Amsterdam Vrij Universiteit (Free University) – that is, free from secular control – which was in turn ringed by Christian-Nationalist schools.

Kuyper believed that Calvinists formed the *kern der natie* (core of the nation), and had to bring all life under God's canopy. He built a Calvinist society within a society, an inner circle of the pure, with its own trade union, leisure-time organisations, welfare bodies, a radio listeners' club, daily newspapers and a weekly journal. As a founder of the ARP (which he led for 40 years) and the Free University (where he taught as theology professor), editor of the daily *De Standaard*, author of 200 books and 2000 meditations, and Prime Minister from 1901 to 1905, Kuyper dominated *gereformeerde* life for nearly 50 years. One might call him the leader of Holland's second reformation. He has, indeed, been admiringly referred to as 'a second Calvin' and the 'Dutch Pope'.

Kuyper became a potent force amongst twentieth-century Afrikaner intellectuals, and his theological influence became all-important for the biggest church, the Nederduitse Gereformeerde Kerk (NGK), and the Gereformeerde Kerk (GK), which was a direct offshoot of his own Gereformeerde Kerken. He idealised the Boers, strongly feeling the 'pull of blood' towards his God-fearing Dutch kith-and-kin. Kuyper befriended President Paul Kruger of the Transvaal Republic and championed its cause during the two Anglo–Boer wars. He led a vigorous pro-Boer campaign in Europe during the second Boer War (1899–1902) and wrote *The South African Crisis* (1900), which set out the Afrikaner's case against Britain. Despite their defeat Kuyper remained optimistic, proclaiming that South Africa would eventually come into Boer possession provided that they never abandoned the Reformed faith of their fathers.

According to Kuyperian thought God is sovereign, transcendent and absolute, permitting no rival idols, such as state or people, Liberalism, modernism, humanism, Marxism, individualism, rationalism; all are creeds which deify anthropocentric entities, such as humankind, class or human reason (rather than revelation). Openly or covertly, they deny God as centre of all life. They challenge the theocentric watchword of the orthodox, 'I am the Lord thy God.' To counter the new insurgent philosophies, Kuyper formulated the 'Christian world and life view' which (a) stated that God's light fell on all aspects of life, and (b) defined the Calvinist position of humankind, society, nation, history, family, economics, sex, social class, culture, colonialism, monarchy, education, and so on. It was a meticulous and totalist world view, capable of confronting all competing secular ideologies.

According to Kuyper, God's special grace fell on believers; but he also loved the profane world and non-believers, who could enjoy divine grace ('common grace'). Kuyper thus abolished the barrier between sacred and secular. Calvinists did not need to shun the sinful world; they should go out and rescue it. For the glory of God they should consecrate and redeem politics, culture, economics, and so forth. Indeed, Kuyper strongly resented 1789's exclusion of Calvinists from state and politics. He maintained that Calvinists had a positive duty to let their influence be felt everywhere as the salvationist and fertilising core of the nation.

Kuyper insisted that all authority – including that of government – came from God. The state and the church were divinely created, the former enjoying common, the latter special, grace. But each occupied different fields and fulfilled different functions. The church was totally separate from the state, and vice versa. The church was an institute; Calvinists collectively formed an organism. As such, they operated freely in politics and could participate in government to ensure that God's word was obeyed, though without involving the church itself. In this regard, Kuyper seemed to open the way to Christian totalitarianism: an authoritarian state and ideologically monolithic society, obedient to a single uniform set of Christian norms.

Against this tendency, Kuyper's key pluralist principle of 'sovereignty in own circle' gave every human association a form of corporate autonomy, suggesting extreme decentralisation with maximum freedom of conscience and a state reduced to functioning as a regulatory mechanism. Patently, Kuyper's immediate object was to protect the minority Gereformeerde Kerken and gereformeerde circle from interference by an anti-Christian or 'neutral' state, while permitting Calvinists maximum political scope and religious freedom. Later, extending this side of his views, he added that Calvinism favoured democracy and equality and would not rest until every person was respected as a creature in God's likeness. His theories can, therefore, sustain a democratic as well as an anti-democratic interpretation.

Kuyper's son, Professor H.H. Kuyper, for example, a noted right-winger who supported Afrikaner Nationalism and colour racism, eventually became a wartime Nazi collaborator. Kuyper's grandson died fighting with the SS on the Russian front in the Second World War. A one-time protégé, Professor Hugo Visscher, became adviser to the Dutch Nazi Party in 1937. Others, however, like Dr. J.J. Buskes (one of the student pallbearers at Kuyper's funeral), became socialists and early critics of apartheid. Notably, Dr Bruins Slot, hailed in his obituary as 'Kuyper's successor', was editor of *Trouw*, the Calvinist daily newspaper which has consistently expressed its opposition to apartheid.

A patriot and monarchist, Kuyper appealed to Nationalist pride, past grandeur and sentiment. He referred to the nation as a 'moral organism'. But, despite occasional chauvinist flashes, he did not absolutise the nation; he was too rooted in the Old Testament and Calvinism's injunctions against idolatry for that. Just as counter-revolutionary thinkers in France and Germany did, he designated the Jews as aliens, carriers of the liberal and socialist virus, and he attacked their financial influence. Once converted, however, they became fully Dutch. His anti-Semitic phase was therefore religious rather than racial. Admission to the nation was by way of baptism, not blood. However, he occasionally waxed lyrical about the Dutch race's qualities, and its mystical blood ties with Boers.

According to Kuyper, God created a diversity of races, colours and cultures which humans should recognise as part of reality. His views on race were conventionally conservative, though they varied to the point of self-contradiction. On the one hand, he praised the superiority of the white northern 'civilisers' over black 'primitiveness', and he scared white American audiences with hints of a coming black uprising. He once declared that 'the life of the coloured races on the coast and in the interior of Africa [is] a far lower form of existence, reminding us not of a lake, but rather of pools and marshes'. In his writings, Kuyper is nowhere critical of the Boer race attitudes, tacitly accepting them as part and parcel of Calvinist democracy. On the other hand, he felt – referring presumably to Europe and Asia – that intermarriage could improve the human stock. Groups who contributed most to human development were not those who remained isolated – such as Scandinavians, Slavs and Mongolians – but those who 'commingled' blood, and so developed into a richer type. Calvinism, he believed, encouraged and provided conditions for 'the mingling of blood'.

This lack of consistency suggests that Kuyper shared in popular white European racism, though he was no fanatical white supremacist in the Gobineau/Chamberlain mould. It should be noted that one of Kuyper's justifications for 'pluriformity' (as opposed to Catholic uniformity) is the concept of racial diversity, and this became central to the Afrikaans churches' defence of rigid ethnic segregation of believers. Yet Afrikaners have agonised over Kuyper's apparent endorsement of 'commingling' and have decided, probably correctly, that he was not referring to South African conditions when he uttered it.

Starting off as a theological opponent of 1789, Kuyper drifted into the counter-revolutionary camp; the step from religious to political opposition was a short one. Politically, he opposed the champions of those who sought humankind's liberation both from God and monarchy, but he was not opposed to human emancipation, regarding God as a liberator. He was anti-revolutionary rather than counter-revolutionary, seeing revolution as sinful; and he always equated religious orthodoxy with the politics of the right. Yet Kuyper supported democracy (provided that it was based on Calvinism) which 'condemns not merely all open slavery and systems of caste, but also all covert slavery of women and the poor', as well as hierarchy and aristocracy of birth. Unlike the spirit of 1789, which asserted humankind's equality in united rebellion against God, Calvinism's equality was of men kneeling together before the Creator. Despite an aversion to socialists (he mourned 1917 as an even bigger catastrophe for mankind than 1789), Kuyper was aware of urban poverty, criticised capitalism and proposed social reforms which, for their time, were progressive. Kuyper's legacy, while rightish-leaning, is therefore equivocal, with signs of compassion for the human condition, absent in many contemporary Christian theorists.

Committed as he was to the Dutch Empire, Kuyper felt that the Dutch were not in Indonesia as ruthless profiteers, but should uplift their subject natives and, having done so, ought to withdraw. There was no moral basis for naked exploitation of colonial peoples. This contrasts strikingly with Afrikaner supremacist attitudes of the period, and perhaps foreshadows the 'tribal homelands' policy of the 1960s. Yet his nationalism often sounded like neo-imperialism. He favoured a Pax Hollandia, a commonwealth of Dutch expatriates living in former overseas possessions, which foreshadowed the Dutch Nazi 'Dietse Volk' (Pan-Dutch) of the 1930s and 1940s.

To conclude: Kuyper bequeathed a double heritage of both right- and left-wing; authoritarian and libertarian; racist and anti-racist; elitist and democratic. His teaching was an intricate balance of paradoxes. One set of his ideas made him vulnerable to Nazism; another set inspired the *gereformeerde* illegal resistance to Nazism. One set made him sympathetic to Afrikaner identity and hegemony; another turned his successors into anti-racist crusaders. What Afrikaners have done is not only to embrace his theological orthodoxy, but also his right-wing legacy.

All Afrikaner theorists in this study have been followers of Kuyper; and all Kuyperians are Christian-Nationalists, whether promoting its tenets secretly or publicly. Most top Afrikaner theologians from 1890 to 1960 and beyond did their postgraduate work at Amsterdam's Free University. Coming from the NGK and GK, and returning to run the leading theological schools, they included: J.D. du Toit, E.P. Groenewald, A.B. du Preez, L.J. du Plessis, H.J. Strauss and N.J. van der Merwe. Others graduated from Potchefstroom University for Higher Christian Education (established in 1905) which was modelled on the Free University and served as a bastion of Kuyper's teachings. Although there was disagreement over the correct policies to be pursued at specific moments, Potchefstroom always propagated the Christian-National world view and carried on its internal debates within that framework. One of its most prominent graduates was Dr Koot Vorster, Moderator of the NGK, who wrote his PhD while serving a wartime gaol sentence for passing secrets to the enemy.

Potchefstroom graduates who later joined its staff included the eminent Afrikaans philosopher Professor H.G. Stoker, who was interned during the War for supporting the pro-Nazi OB, and also S. du Toit, J.C. van Rooy, D.W. Kruger and L.J. du Plessis. Other leading theologians, such as F.J.M. Potgieter (Stellenbosch), and Andries Treurnicht, Chairman of the Broederbond from 1972 to 1975 and now leader of the far-right Conservative Party, are Kuyperians, although not graduates of the Free University or Potchefstroom.

From Kuyper Afrikaner Nationalists have developed a core set of ideas. They have articulated an all-embracing theocentric view of the nation, society and politics, which claims (a) that the national principle must always be under the guidance of the Christian principle, (b) that Calvinism is 'totalist' or 'universal' so that all public affairs fall within its domain, and (c) that Calvinism is a 'this worldly' and 'open' creed which, while anchored in God's eternal truths, can adopt valid features from other doctrines. This 'openness' has made possible Calvinism's alliance with Nationalism (which it 'Christianised'). It has also enabled the Christian-Nationalist structure to incorporate concepts and techniques from, for example, Nazi-Fascism, on account of their apparent relevance to God in promoting his sovereignty.

Christian-Nationalists subscribe to the key Kuyperian notion that Calvinists are the 'kernel of the nation' and the guardians of its Christian heritage. Just as Calvinists founded the Dutch nation, so they founded the Afrikaner nation in 1652. They are custodians of the nation as a Christian entity and must ensure its continued fidelity to Christian norms, the illumination of God's word over everything, and the Bible as the source of truth for all political life.

A further link between Afrikaner Christian-Nationalism and Kuyperian thought is the equation of Calvinism with political conservatism. P.J. Meyer's writings exemplify the transposition of religious orthodoxy into political thought: since the Enlightenment smashed the world of classic Christianity – whose legatees the Afrikaners are – its libertarian political ideas are total anathema. 'Liberalism' is therefore often used in the context of South African political and religious life as a theological swear word.

From Kuyper, Afrikaner theorists have also derived a strategy for confessionalising society by a network of Calvinist bodies in the secular arena. The spearhead and high command of this movement has been the AB, whose aim is 'the Afrikanerisation of South Africa on Christian-National lines'. Started in 1918, the Broederbond was taken over by Kuyperians and transformed into a tightly-knit, clandestine, confessional organ which penetrated all spheres of Afrikaner life. Until the 1970s at least, all the Broederbond's chairmen have been top Christian-Nationalists: J.C. van Rooy and L.J. du Plessis were chairmen in the 1930s; Diederichs was Chairman in the 1940s; H.B. Thom of Stellenbosch University was Chairman in the 1950s; P.J. Meyer in the 1960s; and Andries Treurnicht in the 1970s. All were, or are, followers of Kuyper. Prominent Christian-Nationalist theoreticians in the AB have included J.D. du Toit, Dr H. Verwoerd, H.J. Strauss, A.B. du Preez and E. Groene-wald, Gericke and J.D. Vorster.

Christian-Nationalism has no single prophet, and its tenets are not set out in any single work. Whenever expounded, however, Kuyper's figure hovers luminously in the background in the shape of concepts like common and special grace, the diversity of races, the organic nation, pluriformity of the church, Calvinists as an organism, the church as an institution, the disaster of 1789, 'Sowereiniteit in Eie Kring' (sovereignty in own circle), and so forth. All expositions of Christian-Nationalism in South Africa have, directly or indirectly, referred to Kuyper.

Examples abound indicating the impact of Kuyperian thought on Afrikaner Nationalist thought. The South African Reformed Churches' report to the 1963 Reformed Ecumenical Synod (a small ultra-orthodox ecumenical body) defending racially segregated churches quoted extensively from Kuyper. Kuyper is clearly seen as the ultimate arbiter on questions of reformed theology and is quoted far more frequently than all other theologians combined, including Calvin. J.C.G. Kotzés noted work (1964) on the Afrikaans churches and race also relies heavily on Kuyper in its account of the origin and development of nations.[3] Dr Vorster's seminal (1961) essay on the biblical foundations of apartheid quotes Kuyper six times, Calvin not at all. He uses Kuyper as his sole theological authority for justifying racially segregated churches.[4]

The first major religious defence of apartheid from the DRC, a book by the noted Pretoria theologian A.B. du Preez and intended mainly for overseas consumption, quotes frequently from Kuyper and his followers to show the divine origin of nations.[5] In 1958 Potgieter, another leading NGK theologian of Stellenbosch, quoted Kuyper 38 times in a 15-page essay, 'Veelvormige Ontwikkeling: Die Wil Van God' ('Pluriform Development: The Will of God'). In this basic work Kuyper is the sole Western European theologian to be cited in footnotes.[6] Andries Treurnicht, the theologian and politician, wrote his doctoral thesis at the University of Cape Town on Abraham Kuyper.[7] Examples of Kuyper's influence reach back to the keynote address to the 1929 foundation conference of the Kristelike Nasionale Bond, delivered by J.D. du Toit ('Totius'), perhaps the greatest intellectual force in the twentieth-century Afrikaner revival.

The Afrikaner intellectual love affair with Kuyperian thought flourished for most of this century, tapering off in the mid–1960s, when Reformed Netherland's ardour cooled because of apartheid. On the Dutch side, it ended in 1975, when the Free University severed a long-standing teacher exchange agreement with Potchefstroom after conferring an honorary doctorate on the Reverend Beyers Naudé, the severe Afrikaner critic of Christian-Nationalism. Whether Kuyper would feel at home in present-day South Africa is a more difficult question, depending on how one juggles with his quotations. Kuyper was the product of a specific epoch and a peculiar Dutch situation. He revitalised Calvinism in the struggle against a liberal, secular society. He was hypnotically fascinated by the Afrikaners. He also lived at a time when Western Europe, at the peak of its imperial glory, was disinclined to question the superiority of its institutions, civilisation and religion. What he would say about a struggle over human rights in South Africa between white Christians and subject black Christians is a matter of sterile conjecture. Sufficient to note that, just as he became a hero of the Dutch religious right, so he is deeply relevant to Christian-Nationalism.

During the late 1930s and the Second World War, the Dutch Nazi Party appropriated Kuyper, posing as the executor of his teachings. But the vast bulk of Gereformeerdes fought Nazism and denounced Hitler for falsely idolising race and state. Changing posture in the 1960s they swung to an anti-racist position, bombarding the Afrikaans churches for practising apartheid, and backing black Christians. The Free University awarded an honorary doctorate to the Reverend Martin Luther King in 1965 and in 1972 to Beyers Naudé, already an outcast from the DRC. In 1968 a top Free University theologian, J. Verkuyl, told shocked Afrikaner theologians; 'You worship a different God.'

THE TENETS OF CHRISTIAN-NATIONALISM

The Christian-Nationalist views God as 'Hammadibil', the original divider or separator of things. The key words are 'diversity', 'pluriformity', 'multiformity', 'variety', 'distinctions', 'differenti-ations': a vocabulary preoccupied with differences, obvious or hidden, between races, colours, nations, languages and cultures. Creation's chief hallmarks are (a) the diversity of forms, shapes and species; and (b) this diversity's divine origin and compliance with an invisible divine order, unchangeable by humankind. The insistence that differentiation is fully endorsed by the scriptures is an enduring theme. Consider, for example, the claim by Nico Diederichs, a pioneer exponent of Christian-Nationalism, and later President of South Africa:

> God willed there should be nations so as to enhance the richness and beauty of His creation . . . Just as He decided that no dreary uniformity should rule in nature, but that it display a richness and variety of plants and animals, sounds and colours, so, too He willed the existence in the human sphere of a variety of nations, cultures and languages.[8]

The argument that God institutes national division among the children of Adam and Eve draws on a number of Old and New Testament sources. A number of texts are frequently quoted to demonstrate that the Lord separated people into language groups, encouraged them to crystallise into nations, and intends nations to exist until the end of time. It may be useful to refer to some of these.

In Genesis, Chapter 10, following the Flood, each of Noah's sons becomes a progenitor of a new nation and language group. Shem, Ham and Japhet are classified by their families, their languages and their nations'. Listing their family trees, the text concludes, 'These are the families of the sons of Noah, according to their genealogies in their nations: and from these, the nations spread abroad on the earth after the flood.'

The following chapter, Genesis 11, is perhaps the most often quoted. Here, all mankind – significantly, speaking the same language – gather in force on the plains of Sinear in order to erect the Tower of Babel. This represents a revolutionary attempt to overthrow or replace God.

> And the Lord came down to see the city and the tower which the sons of men had built. And the Lord said, 'Behold, they are one people and they have all one language; and this is only the beginning of what they will do; and nothing that they propose to do will now be impossible for them. Come let us go down and confuse their language, so that they may not understand one another's speech'. So the Lord scattered them abroad from there over the face of all the earth, and they left off building the city.

Two passages are held to indicate that God demarcated territories for each nation and decided how long they should live there.

> When the Most High gave to the nations their inheritance when he separated the sons of man, He fixed the bounds of the people according to the number of sons of God.
>
> (Deuteronomy 32:8)

> And He made from one blood every nation of men to live on all the face of the earth, having determined allotted periods and the boundaries of their habitation.
>
> (Acts 27: 26)

Two further texts (Genesis 15:18 and Amos 9:7) are taken to show that God gave nations their time and place of habitation.

In Matthew 24:7, it is said that 'Nations will endure forever.' This is apparently the implication of the New Testament prediction that Christ would gain adherents from every tribe and language group at the close of our era. Foretelling that 'nation will rise against nation, and Kingdom against Kingdom', it underscores the permanence of nations. Matthew 24:15 repeats the same point: 'And this gospel of the Kingdom will be preached throughout the whole world, as a testimony to all nations, and then the end will come.'

In Colossians 3:11 and Galatians 3:28, Paul asserts that in Christ there is neither Greek nor Jew, barbarian nor Scyth, man nor woman. Clearly, this refers to the transcendence of temporal distinctions in the all-encompassing unity offered by Christ. However, Christian-Nationalists interpret it as follows. Unity in Christ is invisible only, and does not annul practical and visible differences of race or nationality on earth. Biological, physical and psychological differences between men and women do not vanish when they become believers, and neither does Paul intend these to disappear. Although 'Christ is all and in all', national differences persist, just as sexual ones do.

Of the above texts, perhaps the most important is the passage in Genesis which describes the fateful moment when nations were created. All the key theoreticians, like J.D. Vorster, A.B. du Preez, J.D. du Toit and F.J.M. Potgieter agree that by suddenly breaking up people into language groups, God revealed his will that they should live in separate cultural–ethnic units. A confusion of tongues will persist until the end of time. This means that, in one guise or another, races, cultures and nations will also persist as discrete entities.

According to Dr Vorster, 'God intervened, confused their language and thwarted their plan . . . God broke the threatened uniformity and allowed people to separate into races, which were again divided into mutually different peoples or groups.'[9] This is taken as evidence of God's determination to smash a sinful plot and to deny opportunities for sin. But it also expresses God's care and mercy: a 'deed of grace to curb sin'.[10] Nations should therefore be seen as a divine manifestation of grace rather than the mere consequence of sin. They are a revelation of His will. Potgieter draws the same conclusion: 'God according to the Scriptures, mercifully intervened, with the Babelist confusion of tongues, and revealed that His will for this dispensation was pluriformity . . . in the ethnic field.'[11]

In his book on Christian ethics and autogenous development, published in English as *Inside the Crucible*, du Preez goes to considerable lengths to explain that nations, despite their roots in the Babel rebellion, are not sinful. They are precious objects of divine grace, to be cherished by all God-fearing people. Races will persist as long as people are divided into different language groups. Du Preez quotes Kuyper on this point: 'The significance of the

Confusion of Tongues consists in the fact that God Himself used this means to divide the human race into peoples, nations and states: God almighty intervened in human life to cause this division. Both the idea and its realisation came from Him, not from sinful man.'[12]

A number of important conclusions follow from the scriptural basis of nations and their sacred differences. One of the most important relates to the notion of biological races. Regardless of humankind's common blood (a proposition which, in any case, some Christian-Nationalists challenge) and God's common fatherhood, terrestrial differences between white and black are held to be fundamental and ineradicable. Most extensively differentiated are those by the 'deeply ingrained difference' of skin colour, in the words of S. du Toit.[13] According to Vorster, race differences are 'biological in character' and show themselves in 'peculiar characteristics which are inherited'.[14] Colour, indeed, is the exteriorisation of inner differences. The black man's 'otherness' is stressed by Abel Coetzee, a prominent Afrikaner anthropologist:

> Both a white man and a kaffir have certain common properties or qualities. Both have, for example, two ears, one nose, two eyes, two legs, two arms, etc., but this does not permit one to say that the white man is a kaffir or a kaffir is a white man. They are two separate peoples.

According to Christian-Nationalist thought, talents, virtues, aptitudes and intelligence are unequally distributed among nations. Some are stronger, more efficient and more creative than others. Just as there is great inequality of character, temperament and capacity amongst individuals in one group, so there are superior and inferior nations. Since these alleged differences are held to be God's will, races do not alter their positions in the superior–inferior hierarchy, and each must accept its place in the global scheme. While Christian-Nationalists often warn Afrikaners against the dangers of denationalisation, assimilation, Anglicisation and kaffirisation – all of which imply possible decay and degeneracy – in general their viewpoint is that nations do not alter their cluster of genetic–cultural characteristics. (Presumably, denationalisation would constitute a disfigurement of profile but not a change in essence.)

Dr (later Prof.) G. Eloff, a biologist and leading exponent of race genetics, cited Afrikaner physical characteristics – such as arm length

– to show they were a superior breed, and expounded on qualities of Afrikaner blood. Writing on race improvement he stated, 'society today cannot be without a number of inferiors . . . to provide for its physical needs'. Because of their strong muscles and capacity for continuous work, 'the non-highly-civilised persons' had to be society's drawers of water and hewers of wood. Church and state should therefore encourage marriage and procreation among 'superior persons'.[15]

Eloff, who was once the AB's Assistant Secretary, was dazzled by Nazi genetics, which his thinking imitated. Christian-Nationalism never explicitly adopted his ideas of race improvement, but the Aryan premise – a biological elite caste heading a race hierarchy, composed of master and servant races – remained covertly part of its creed long after Nazism's eclipse. Like many Christian-Nationalist ideas these underwent a semantic change in the 1960s as Christian-Nationalism, no longer defending race hierarchy, retreated to its final line of ideological battle: the more ambiguous (and euphemistic) notion of 'pluriformity'.

Just as God diffuses abilities unequally, so He is said to assign each nation its own particular mission. Though some carry a more glorious or responsible earthly mission than others, each must obey the divine role in which they are cast. In so doing, they serve God, their maker. Out of this gradation of the worth of missions comes the idea of the Afrikaner's leading role. In the words of L.J. du Plessis, their vocation is 'to rule, to Christianise, to civilise'.

Christian-Nationalism regards any subversion of nationality to be a subversion of God; the marriage of a black Adam to a white Eve violates the divine law of nationhood. Inter-marriage (also called 'bastardisation' or 'hybridisation') rejects God's gifts, takes the first steps towards restoring pre-Babelist unity and re-enacts sinful rebellion against God. Esperanto, cosmopolitanism, internationalism, world government and so on are therefore held to be anti-Christian and lead also to the unaesthetic condition of 'monotonous uniformity'.

Attempts to destroy the variety of nations or to amalgamate what God has distinguished offend the sacredness of diversity. Thus, according to J.D. du Toit, 'What God divided, man must not join; what God joined, man must not separate.' He adds, 'God's plan is realised in pluriformity. Higher unity lies in Christ and is spiritual in character; consequently we desire no equalisation and also no bastardisation.'[16] Obviously, if inconsistently, this does not apply to whites. The Afrikaners, for example, are made up of marriage between Dutch, French, Scottish, English and German colonists, as their surnames indicate.

Christian-National theory holds that God's gift of nationalism obliges the recipient to honour eternally and with gratitude this expression of grace. Nationalism is therefore a religious obligation. Services to the nation express service to God; loyalty to nation manifests loyalty to God. Working for the fulfilment of national calling is work for the realisation of God's plan. To maintain the *volk* (the people) is to accept God's will and disposition. 'Indeed', argues Vorster, 'a person glorifies God by helping to develop his own national culture'.[17]

According to B.F. Nel, it is God's will that every individual becomes fully developed within the structure of his nation, and it is through Nationalism that people attain authenticity and maximum self-fulfilment: 'A person cannot become a full person unless he develops within a definite community – namely the nation, and on condition that he stands in the correct relationship to God.'[18] In practice, critics argue, Christian-Nationalism commits the ultimate abomination of idolatry by making a fetish of the nation. However, its proponents argue that by equating the terms 'Christian' and 'Nationalism' the tension between them is abolished. Thus, according to Nico Diederichs, 'nationalism is necessarily religious because it regards every nation as a product of the Highest Creator, destined to fulfil a calling and contribute to the realisation of the universe's Divinely determined purpose'. Diederichs is concerned to stress that, although the nation is 'the highest and most total of all human associations', it is always subordinate to God and is but a 'means in his hand'.[19] This formulation ignores the fact that Christian-Nationalist formulations often come close to making nation a God-substitute and nation-worship a replacement for God-worship.

The Afrikaans churches are segregated. Their African, Coloured and Asian adherents worship in segregated premises and have segregated church organisations. Ecclesiastical apartheid flows from the church's conformity to the divinely ordained diversity of races, cultures, nations and language. The visible church – as distinct from its heavenly form – must reflect racial variety on earth. Separate churches do not reflect schisms created by human beings, but divinely-shaped entities. They are a positive, not a negative, phenomenon.

According to the Reverend L.J. Hugo, a variety of ethnic churches exist simply because of language and cultural differences: 'These differences are willed by God and cannot thus be sinful . . . that languages have led to a diversity of churches is generally accepted.'[20] According to Potgieter the fact that 'there should be a distinct church formation for whites, coloureds and Bantu, is, in principle, the will of God for this dispensation'.[21] Thus, although the church is united in its own being – that is, in the body of Christ – the church as an institute manifests itself multiformly. The real church is an invisible, mystical and supernatural unity of believers drawn from all nations; by contrast, the visible Protestant Church is doctrinally and racially pluriform.

There is only one Church of Christ which is, in its profoundest being, invisible because only the Lord knows His own. The division into visible and invisible does not imply two churches: it is but one inseparable church seen from two sides. In its visible form, the Church of Christ manifests itself in particular as an institute in which it finds fixed form, a time and place, and generally a community of believers as an organism. Unfortunately there is no church as institute which can claim to be the only Church of Christ. This is due to the tragic fact of humankind's inadequacy. Race and class differences among believers are not annulled by unity in Christ. Indeed, this unity can co-exist with a structural stratification of Christians into first- and second-class persons, just as the Gospels condone slavery.

Complementing the religious view of the nation as a divine creation, with a divinely-given personality and mission, is the Christian-Nationalist claim that the nation has an organic structure and character. While the religious perspective explains the nation's origin, assigns it a moral value and determines its role and calling, the organic principle explains its intrinsic cohesion and enjoins inner solidarity. The religious element sanctifies the nation and makes nationalism a holy duty; the secular view insists that individual self-realisation is only possible within the nation, to whose interests the individual must be subordinate.

The view of the nation as an organism first appeared in Christian-Nationalist thought during the rise of Nazi race theory, though it can be traced back to Abraham Kuyper. Kuyper speaks of Calvinists ('the pith and kernel of the nation') as an organic whole, and also of the nation as an organism. Theoretical articles by Christian-Nationalists in the 1920s, such as F. Language's attempt to justify Nationalist consciousness, do not mention the organic theory.

H.G. Stoker was the first to use this concept (in 1931), to which he gave both a Kuyperian and a Nazi slant.[22]

Far from being an arithmetical, atomistic collection of individuals, the nation, says Stoker, forms an organic entity: it 'is more than the sum total of its parts, namely its volk citizens just as a tree is more than the sum total of its roots, plus stem, plus branches, plus leaves, plus blossom', because 'an organism is an original entity and not a loose association of parts'. What integrates all the parts is their common blood, ethnic and biological identity, common culture and common faith. 'The organic unity of the nation', claims Stoker, 'flows from two parallel and related roots: (a) the vital–organic blood tie, and (b) the spiritual–organic tie'. The first gives members their distinctive physical constitution and characteristics; the second finds expression in their culture, tongue, traditions and spiritual endowment.

As a genuine organism, each part is also held to be dependent upon the others, even though functions and usefulness differ. Afrikanerdom, despite its internal class and status differences, constituted a whole, Dr E.G. Jansen told the Moedertaal (mother-tongue) Congress in December 1943:

> Just as a collection of different limbs comprise the human body, so do persons in various professions and occupations make up the volk's body. . . . one part cannot exist without the other and all parts together build up the culture of a volk. There is thus a central task for every Afrikaner, whether he is rich or poor, educated or uneducated. Everyone in his own field of work, must accept the essential unity of the Afrikaner volk . . . and all sectors should co-operate harmoniously.

The *volk*'s interests transcend those of each of its members (who have no real existence outside or apart from the *volk*), so it claims their undivided loyalty. 'As the embodiment of the real interests of the private members', writes Stoker, all *volks*-citizens separately and collectively must love the *volk* and serve it with their best energies and be willing to make the supreme sacrifice. In *Ons Republiek* (1941), Diederichs proposed a *volk*-state whose 'core and content must be the Afrikaans volk as an organic unity, which finds external expression in this state'. For Diederichs, the Afrikaans *volk* was not the sum total of individuals living in South Africa. Rather, it was the organic natural and cultural community which was born in this Fatherland, has suffered for it and acknowledges in it as its one and only Fatherland; that organic whole which developed here into a new volk with its own language and spiritual life and with a new sense of destiny. The state's task will be to ensure that all forces with a formative effect on the spirit of the volk must be true to the Christian National character of the volk . . . the machinery of the State will also have to be so constituted that it is used in the service of the organic volk and not of private groups or individuals.[23]

Like any evolving organism, the nation, according to Christian-Nationalism, passes through inevitable stages as it grows from infancy to adulthood, from a simple entity to a complex and specialised one. J.C. van Rooy has listed four distinct phases wherein the Afrikaner nation is portrayed as a historically-conditioned entity, moving inexorably from youth to maturity. In the highest stage of its development (the twentieth century), the *volk* acts as a mature adult, spurning imitative behaviour, rejecting foreign tutelage and casting off the restrictions of a foreign ethos and foreign hegemony. It systematically and consciously seeks to control its internal and external life.

Christian-Nationalists do not believe that Afrikanerdom's inevitable development justifies a fatalistic or passive posture or that it relieves members of responsibility for the *volk*'s welfare and destiny. The *volk*'s growth depends on its members' energy; the manner of growth depends on how intelligently and purposefully it plans and applies its resources. Forces of free will thus operate within the broader deterministic framework as the nation develops. Will, self-mastery, self-confidence and goal-directedness all play a great part.

The theory of nation as organism and the theory of nation as a divine creation reinforce each other. Both reject the nation as merely an arithmetical collection of individuals. Both see the nation as the central form of human association, as a pivot of the individual's existence which provides the only community in which he or she can find meaningful self-realisation, as well as being the authority to which supreme loyalty is owed. Finally, both see the nation's emergence and development as the result of inevitable supernatural or metaphysical forces which operate independently of the wishes of its members.

Taken together, these theories extract from Calvinism and

Nationalism the features which emphasise the nation's prime importance, its distinctive character, unique vocation and 'right' and 'duty' to exist. The combination of the two theories also has moral implications; while God creates individuals as well as nations, He chooses the nation, an organic entity composed of individuals, as His instrument, and it has the highest claim on the individual's loyalty. The organic nation cannot be, like a plant, morally neutral; it must be Christian and all members must uphold its Christianity. Coupled with the organic theory, the notion that the group's distinctive characteristics are of an immutable biological or genetic type, and are transmitted through blood to succeeding generations, is a frequent theme. This is a racial doctrine in virtue of the fact that it equates the group's temperamental characteristics with its internal genetic make-up.

During the 1930s and 1940s, many Christian-Nationalists were strongly influenced by the Nazi approach to race. An example is the application by Eloff of Nazi physiology and eugenics to Afrikaners. But a number of Calvinist-oriented theological writers – such as S. du Toit and A.B. du Preez – rejected the concept of different bloods on the basis of Acts 17:26, 'And He [God] made of one blood all the nations of mankind.' Scripturally, all people were therefore of one blood, even though divided into nations. This did not, however, lead them to reject the notion of race, a term which is used by all Christian-Nationalists.

The contemporary view – as revealed in the volume *Grense* (boundaries), and particularly in Dr Vorster's essay – is that genetic factors determine the quality of a race or nation. The meticulous ethnic separation of blood banks in South Africa according to the donor's race indicates how Afrikaner Nationalists (and, indeed, most whites) regard 'blood' as containing mystical properties, as being related to pigmentation and as something which determines the superiority or inferiority of a race. Advanced Christian-Nationalists have more recently come to accept that the human race is 'of one blood', but nevertheless maintain that genetic differences between races are immutable. S. du Toit specifically rejected the blood argument in 1954, but was still able to argue in the same document that race and colour differences were ineradicable, eternal and gave rise to different temperamental qualities.

THE CHRISTIAN-NATIONALIST THEORY OF STATE AND CHURCH

Christian-Nationalists view the state as an authoritarian institution responsible only to God. Its main functions are therefore little different from those of a police force. The ethical basis of the Christian-National state is neither Rousseau's 'sovereignty of the people' nor Hobbes' contract, but God's direct delegation of authority. This concept has clear authoritarian implications and helped wartime Christian-Nationalist theoreticians such as du Plessis and Meyer to accept the authoritarian Christian-National state.

In the ideal Christian-Nationalist state, the government, the political system, all parties and the electorate must be Christian. One could call this a totalist Christocracy. It differs from a theocracy (church-dominated government) or a Caesaro-Papist system (government-dominated church) by virtue of a strict separation of state and church. According to J.A. du Plessis, one of the early leaders of the Kristelike Nasionale Bond, church and state differ in origin, method and purpose, and each is 'sovereign' in its own sphere. Any mixing of their functions is against God's ordinances and must lead to conflict: 'Both State and Church are divinely willed and established institutes, to each of which God by sovereign decree granted its own sovereignty to serve his will for the temporal and natural, and the eternal and spiritual.'[24]

According to Treurnicht's interpretation, the state has certain obligations towards religion. It is bound to acknowledge the existence of God, to protect the church as an institution and guarantee its freedom to fulfil its calling. The state should also maintain public morality in the light of scriptural principle.[25] Treurnicht's formulation is a summary of Article 36 of the Netherlands Confession of Faith which obliges the state to uphold the true religion and root out heresy. However, the power of the state could endanger individual freedom of Christian conscience. Kuyper therefore distinguished between the church as an institution which did not interfere in politics, and Calvinists who, as a community, were called to Christianise the state and society. Kuyperian Calvinists expressed reservations over Article 36. Was it not dangerous to delegate to a secular organ – the government – the right to decide which was the true religion? Did this not amount to a licence for the state to interfere in religious affairs? Du Plessis himself stresses the danger of a 'democratic dictatorship which tyrannises with force over the freedoms of the Church and exerts duress on the individual's conscience'.[26]

The Afrikaner Calvinist's concern for freedom and opposition to absolutism or totalitarianism must be viewed in a religous context. That the Christian-Nationalists' desire to check totalitarianism or absolutism is designed to protect the church from interference is clear from two key notions. The first is the right of resistance to a state which rules in a manner contrary to divine ordinances and so forfeits its right to govern. In such a case, as Calvin pointed out, the magistrates, as spokesmen and watchdogs over the people's freedom and the state's loyalty to God, had the right to disobey a government which itself had disobeyed the Sovereign of the Universe. The second is Kuyper's pluralist doctrine of 'sovereignty in own sphere', which envisages a corporate organisation of society. All communal spheres, such as home, school, economic life and church, should have maximum freedom to conduct their own affairs without state or other outside interference. Each sphere has its own authority which, like that of the state, is derived from God. Common Afrikaner phrases such as 'in every sphere', 'in all circles', 'on every terrain', 'in every realm' or 'in its own area' are directly taken from Kuyperian thought.

Stoker, in his classic work *Stryd om die Ordes*, manages to reconcile the notion of 'sovereignty in own sphere' with a Christian dictatorship. In the concept of 'sovereignty in own sphere' he sees 'divergence and cohesion'; each human association is independent and can only fulfil its calling as received from God, but they all have the same purpose which is 'ultimately synonymous with the honour and glorification of God'. The community is pluralist in structure but uniform in outlook. Stoker stresses the God-given authority of the government and says:

> the specific State organisation (monarchy, aristocracy, triumvirate, republic, dictatorship, Fuhrer-state, etc.) is determined not by principle but by practical circumstances . . . any one of them can be good, provided that it honours God's ordinances, formulates and maintains law according to His will and allows every individual and human association to be independent in its own area and to realise its God-given destiny.

It is perhaps difficult to see the practical application of this doctrine to Afrikaner life. But in the context of Dutch Calvinism's battle in the nineteenth century for autonomous existence, especially in education and ecclesiastical affairs, the doctrine makes sense. It has also been useful to the Afrikaner Christian-Nationalist because it provides a doctrinal basis for defending the church's formal autonomy from the state. The 'separate spheres' idea conceives the church as a private institution which does not interfere in politics: since it does not have a prophetic calling towards government, it can in turn claim immunity from interference by the state.

Although this precept protects Calvinists from an anti-Calvinist authoritarian regime, it is doubtful whether liberal opponents of the Christian-National authoritarian state, the constitution of which was drafted in 1942, would have enjoyed the right to resist. Indeed, the draft republican constitutions make it clear that no opposition would be tolerated and that all political parties would have to accept the basic premises of Christian-National political criticism. Yet the draft set out in the *Declaration of Volks Organisations* contained a curious proviso which respected the theocratic right of freedom of conscience. Such a proviso could never have appeared in a Nazi constitution, and its appearance, however meaningless, can be traced to Kuyper's autonomous spheres and his concern for freedom of conscience.

The very term 'Christian-National' envisages a nation with Gospel-based political, social and economic norms; its guardian is not, formally, the church but extra-ecclesiastical confessional Calvinist groupings. Afrikaner Calvinists have distinguished (as does Kuyper) between the church as a private institution and Calvinists as an organic spiritual community. Afrikaner Kuyperians, in rejecting 1789's divorce of religion from politics, believe themselves to be called upon to purify every aspect of the Afrikaner nation's life. This is in accordance with the doctrine of common grace, which invites true believers to be active in all spheres of ordinary life (however profane or secular), to curb sin and to prevent the misuse of God's gifts of culture and nationality.

Like their Dutch counterparts, South African Christian-Nationalists insist that no single church should run the state. Nevertheless their object, according to du Toit, is to ensure 'the complete subjection and total obedience of everyone under all circumstances' to God's word. The role of Calvinists is, therefore, to organise themselves into extra-ecclesiastical confessional bodies (one for every area of existence) and to penetrate the Gospel's spirit into every 'sovereign sphere' of human association, from household to government. Their ideal is in fact a Christocracy: a Christian government controlling a Christian political–economic–cultural system and ruling over a Christian nation.

The principles of Christian-National education have been a fundamental aspect of Afrikaner political thought and action. A comprehensive blueprint for Christian-National education was drawn up in 1948 by a committee of the FAK including van Rooy, Dönges and Jansen. The document's declared object was the 'propagation, protection and development of the essentially C. and N. character of our Nation'. The Christian foundation of this attitude was to be based on the Holy Scripture and the Articles of Faith of the three Afrikaans churches. The National principle (which remains subordinate to the Christian principle) was defined in terms of the love of 'everything that is our own, with special reference to our country, our language, our history, and our culture'.[27]

This remarkable document specified strict compartmentalisation in educational matters according to language and colour and it outlined the role of teachers, the church, the home and the state. It was believed that 'the welfare and happiness of the Coloured man rests upon his realizing that he belongs to a separate racial group' and that he should be 'educated along Christian and National lines in accordance with this conception'. Similarly, the document stated that 'the teaching and education of the native must be based on the European's attitude to life and to the world, more particularly that the Boer nation is the senior European trustee of the native'. Moreover, 'native' education should 'lead to the development of a native community on Christian-National lines which is self-supporting and provides for itself in all ways'.[28]

Christian-Nationalists claim that God created the Afrikaner nation for a special mission. Their history is predetermined rather than fortuitous. Thus there was nothing accidental in the landing and evolution of the Dutch settlers in 1652; it was not a chance by-product of the Dutch East India Company's trade with India, but a central part of God's master plan. Afrikaner history is seen in terms of two Calvinist notions: divine determination and the manifestation of God's will in history. D.F. Malan, who led the NP to victory in 1948, said in 1937 that Afrikaner history was 'nothing other than the highest work of art of the centuries. We have a right to our nationhood because it was given to us by the Architect of the universe.[29]

According to Christian-Nationalist doctrine God was responsible for the Boer victories in the wars against the Khoi people (1653–70), the San (1700–50) and the Bantu (1750–1890). The most dramatic of God's interventions was the Battle of Blood River on 16 December 1838, when a few hundred Boers, after praying for victory, defeated the Zulu empire, killing some 12 000 soldiers in the process. The day of the battle is celebrated as the 'Day of the Covenant': the day when God made known his covenant with his 'chosen people'. The Boers were saved from almost certain extinction on account of God's protection. Being divinely inspired, Afrikaner history is sacred. The past is therefore the guarantee for the future.

As recipients of this awesome divine mandate, Afrikaners were empowered, as trustees, to exercise authority over the heathen. The objective was to help blacks to become self-supporting and themselves bearers of Christian civilisation. The NGK's Federal Council defined Afrikanerdom's vocation in 1935 as the evangelisation of all Africa.

> The Church is deeply convinced of the fact that God, in His wise counsel, so ordained it that the first European inhabitants of this southern corner of darkest Africa should be men and women of firm religious convictions, so that they and their posterity could become the bearers of the light of the Gospel to the heathen races of this continent, and therefore considers it the special privilege and responsibility of the DRC in particular to proclaim the Gospel to the heathen of this country.

Importantly, this vocation also justifies Afrikanerdom's insistence on maintaining its separate identity and creating conditions for its dominance. Self-preservation is a paramount duty and a sense of identity must be maintained in all aspects of Afrikaner life.

According to Christian-Nationalist thought the Afrikaner nation's spiritual unity is threatened by various forces. These range from socio-economic systems (capitalism, socialism) which divide Afrikanerdom into classes or link certain sections of Afrikanerdom (capitalists, bourgeoisie, workers) with corresponding sections among the English or Africans, to ideologies which weaken the racist, Nationalist, or ideological foundations of the Christian-Nationalist world view.

During the first four decades of this century capitalism was regularly denounced as an evil force. But, since the emergence of a successful Afrikaner capitalist class, it is no longer regarded as foreign, selfish, un-Christian or internationalist. Communism is still seen as a potent danger to the cohesion of the nation because it divides mankind into world-wide classes and ignores divisions of race and colour (the charge that used to be levelled against capitalism). Moreover, communism encourages the breaking down of national divisions by offering salvation through a proletarian revolution and the redistribution of property rather than through national self-realisation. Finally, communism is irreligious and is therefore the antithesis of Christian-Nationalism.

Liberalism has been seen by Christian-Nationalists as communism's ally, handmaiden or precursor. It attacks the primacy of nations by making the individual absolute, and it sees society as an aggregate of different coloured individuals, rather than an organic national unity. It is more concerned with the individual than the group. Moreover, liberalism is seen as theologically antagonistic because of its rationalistic assumptions. By claiming that reason can solve problems, it dispenses with revelation and the need for God's grace and intervention. Thus one of the most abusive words in Afrikaner vocabulary has been 'liberal' or 'liberalist'. Indeed, to be called 'liberal' (as Prime Minister Vorster was accused of being by an anonymous member of the Nationalist extreme right in 1969) is akin to being libelled or defamed.

The systematic and compulsory segregation of groups becomes a holy duty for Christian-Nationalist theorists. According to M.D.C. de Wet Nel, who served as Minister of Bantu Administration under Verwoerd and was a leading exponent of apartheid:

> The calling of this small white nation is to give the world the basis and pattern on which different races can live in peace and safety in future, each within its own national circle . . . Western civilisation and particularly Christian civilisation is one of the great powers in the world. In this southern corner of Africa we are one of the strongholds of that Western civilisation. It is our duty to see that civilisation is not destroyed. Therefore we should legislate in such a way that our civilisation will be preserved and that it will be a source of power not only to the White people but also to the Bantu population.[30]

The traditional Christian-Nationalist policy of 'Christian white guardianship' had always meant 'horizontal' apartheid, with whites above and blacks below. But, as a corollary of guardianship, there developed the idea of separate ethnic development as an ethical alternative to hierarchic separation. Under pressure in the 1950s the Nationalists extended the right to self-government to eight black 'nations' in South Africa. Segregated tribal territories had been debated within Christian-National circles from as early as the mid-1930s. In 1934 the journal *Koers* carried an article advocating the establishment of separate territorial homelands. Writing in 1935, H. du Plessis warned that, given a share of authority 'in our own life', Africans would 'kaffirise' the whole of social and economic life. 'The variety of races is biologically and historically determined by God', du Plessis wrote. 'We must acknowledge the unity in diversity and attempt to maintain it.' Christians should therefore preserve Bantu identity while consecrating it, for Christianity had to be a bulwark against assimilation, denationalisation, and Europeanisation. In this article du Plessis stresses autonomous development, fostering a national mother-tongue, preservation of cultural customs and recognition that Africans have their own 'volks souls'. He urges the reform of their value system on the basis of Christian norms.[31] Other Christian-Nationalist theoreticians argued in favour of giving 'Christian-Nationalist territorial units'.

The Broederbond-inspired 1942 draft Republican constitution proposed the granting of self-government to segregated race groups (under the management of the central government) in accordance with their fitness for the role. From 1944 onwards, a small group of scholars led by Pretoria's G. Cronje and including Stellenbosch's Nic Olivier and B.I.C. van Eeden, explored and propagated the idea of self-governing African reserves. By far the most articulate of this group was the Broederbond's Cronje, who published key works outlining the direction that apartheid should take. The key Tomlinson Commission (1955), which prepared the first blueprint for 'tribal homelands', bears the strong imprint of Christian-Nationalist principles. In the Commission's view, 'it was by no mere accident that European Christianity established itself at the southern point of Africa, but that a high and exalted purpose was intended'. It noted that the sovereignty and omnipotence of God was accepted as an article in the Union Constitution and also in the 'Christian conscience of the vast majority of its citizens'.[32] Moreover, South Africa had a special vocation to spread Christianity throughout Africa. Europeans were therefore obliged to:

> remain in Africa as the principal bearers of the Christian religion and Christian civilisation. The European *must* be here for the sake of the aborigines of Africa as well . . . in consequence of the principles of the Christian Religion and Ethics it is the duty of peoples who stand on a higher level, to watch over the interests of underdeveloped peoples. Christian guardianship rests upon biblical grounds.[33]

The Tomlinson Commission urged the creation of independent homelands in terms of Christian-Nationalist theory. It was necessary that 'the churches should be deliberately associated with the entire development programme for the Bantu Areas, especially in what relates to the development of the Bantu as human beings'.[34] Thus the aims of church and state were essentially linked: 'Good mission policy is good government policy in South Africa, and forms the basis of a sound racial policy.'[35]

To summarise: whereas Christian-Nationalism purports merely to recognise observable pluriformity, diversity and variety in life, in fact it magnifies disparities, boundaries, divisions and barriers, thereby rejecting all doctrines of humankind's common solidarity or unity. Extolling natural barriers between groups, it fights any form of supra-nationalism. As weapons, it employs extreme biological, genetic, racial and scriptural arguments. Boundaries between races, cultures and nations are sanctified because (a) they are 'natural' (organic) and (b) they are part of the eternal order (divinely ordained). Segregation is therefore seen as a normal, common-sense recognition of visible differences between nations. Since it is apparently in accord with the divine will, the glorification and reinforcement of distinctions becomes a holy duty.

Christian-Nationalism has been presented as an ethical and workable formula for peaceful co-existence in a multinational society. The alternative, seen as an integrated or egalitarian society, is castigated as an 'unnatural' and sinful rebellion against the divine will. The Afrikaner is designated as the chosen vehicle for implementing true compartmentalisation and stratification. Implicit in 'white guardianship' is the Afrikaner's leading role and special, national mission. The salience of Christian-Nationalist thought is in the way that it meets Afrikaner aspirations for self-determination and political supremacy in South Africa. Its electrifying power lies in the way similar aspects of Nationalism and Calvinism have been coupled together to produce a potent weapon against any doctrine of integration or denationalisation.

2 The Anatomy of a Secret Society: An Overview

The AB is a secret, oath-bound male fraternity of Afrikaner Calvinists over the age of 25 which strives for 'the ideal of the everlasting existence of a separate Afrikaner nation with its own culture', and subscribes to the doctrine of Christian-Nationalism. All its members are co-opted, drawn from the top echelons of their occupations and localities and pledged to work for the 'Afrikanerising of South Africa in all its spheres of life'. The Broederbond is thus more than a Nationalist, patriotic or cultural pressure group: it is the repository and executor of a specific ideology, which marries Afrikaner Nationalism with the seventeenth-century doctrines of the Genevan reformer, Calvin. Composed of hand-picked zealots, it is a religious order as well as the elite vanguard corps of the Nationalist struggle. It maintains the nation's religious character as well as acting as the watchdog over all its interests.

The Broederbond fights for 'the glory of God and the welfare of the volk'. Its 'cause is the volk's struggle to continue existing for the fulfilment of our God-given volks-calling'. Claiming to be 'founded on the rock of Jesus', the AB only admits practising Calvinists and is, in effect, restricted to members of the three sections of the DRC. A recruit must be 'one hundred per cent Christian', and show 'the highest degree of religious conviction', for the organisation is 'founded on Godly love and justice'. As the self-appointed and self-perpetuating guardian of all the interests of the Afrikaners, the Broederbond is not responsible to any electorate: it is not appointed and neither can it be dismissed from positions of influence by any external force. Brethren hold themselves responsible to God alone, believing that the organisation 'will have to account to God for its actions'. Strong support is given to the DRC 'in order to perpetuate the Afrikaner volk as a Protestant Christian community'.

The Broederbond regards Afrikanerdom as a divinely created nation with a sacred mission. Much stress is laid on the Afrikaner's special Christian identity and the notion that they are key actors in a divine plan for Southern Africa. Their glory is God's glory. They stand for something infinitely greater than themselves, and fight for

31

a cosmic cause which transcends and gives profound meaning to their temporal existence. The burden of this historical task is to spread the light of God in a barbaric continent. To this end, the Broederbond designates itself as supreme watchdog of Afrikaner-dom's Christian-National character and as the chosen core of 'mission conscious Afrikaners', who will propel the *volk* towards realisation 'of their God-given calling'.

Although the AB has never been proscribed or persecuted, a cloak of absolute secrecy enshrouds all its activities.[1] All members swear a solemn vow never to divulge the organisation's secrets during their lifetime, even to their wives. The penalty is expulsion and social ostracism. No public statements are issued except in rare emergencies. Elaborate security precautions conceal its proceedings, operations, names of members, the venue of its meetings, the whereabouts of the administrative headquarters and the identity of its secretariat. This secrecy is a 'cardinal principle' and is strictly maintained. Since the usual reasons for underground activity (illegality of aims, fear of victimisation or persecution) are lacking, it must be assumed that the AB operates clandestinely because of the freedom of manouvrability this confers. The Broederbond's usual defence is that secrecy protects its members and helps efficiency.

What distinguishes the AB from most twentieth-century secret societies or modern, cultural, patriotic or Nationalist pressure groups is the wide ambit of its interests, the unlimited field of its operations, and the vigorous pursuit of power in the political, economic, cultural and ideological fields. It discusses and formulates programmes for 'the moral, intellectual, communal and political advancement of the nation'. Were it not for its secrecy and limited membership, the AB would be akin to a political party or an all-embracing nationalist movement. It shows, in any event, the strong influence of the Christian-National confessional-political movement built by Abraham Kuyper, the neo-Calvinist Dutch theologian.

Historically, the AB has had three objects: to unite all Afrikaners who have the welfare of their people at heart; to foster national awareness; to implant a love of language, religion, tradition and fatherland; and to promote all of Afrikanerdom's interests. Within the purely domestic Afrikaner arena, it acts as a secret co-ordinating council to weld Afrikaners into a single integrated insulated *laager* and as the guardian of the Nationalist spirit. Within state and society as a whole, it spearheads the struggle for Afrikaner dominance in

Parliament, the administration, business, finance and industry. The Broederbond is therefore concerned with the Afrikaner nation as a totality, and with advancing all its interests. Internally, it enhances the spiritual and material quality of Afrikaner domestic life. Externally, it intervenes on Afrikanerdom's behalf in society as a whole with the object of bringing all facets of state and society under Afrikaner sway.

The Broederbond is composed of about 6 800 individual members. It is divided into a country-wide network of 450 branches, comprising between five and fifty members, each with its own executive.[2] Every branch aims to be representative of the local community and to contain a representative cross-section of the classes, occupations and professions in the area. Once a year there is a congress attended by one delegate from each branch. This elects a 13-member Uitvoerende Raad (Executive Committee), the Bond's 'highest executive organ', also sometimes known as the Apostles. A full-time secretariat operating from a camouflaged headquarters in Braamfontein, Johannesburg, runs its affairs.

Seeking 'quality not quantity', the AB has always been small and compact. Started by 14 individuals in 1918, its membership grew to 2 000 in 1935, 2 627 in 1944, 3 500 in 1949 and 6 768 in 1963. In this period some 8 000 have belonged. Like a club, admittance is only by sponsorship, internal election and invitation. New members cannot apply. Potential recruits are screened for up to two years before being nominated. Sponsors must affirm that the recruit believes in 'the never-ending existence of the Afrikaner nation'. The whole brotherhood votes on each nomination. Approval must be *nem. con.*, one adverse vote constituting a blackball.

Only those belonging to the white Afrikaans ethnic/cultural group are eligible. As well as being staunch Nationalists and Calvinists, new members must also be leaders, potential leaders, experts or authorities in various fields. The society's motto is 'Be Strong', its badge a masonic-type triangle pierced by a cord to symbolise brotherhood. Members identify themselves with hand signs and black dress is worn at meetings. Brethren, who are called 'friends', are divided into various categories. These are not hierarchic or seniority groups as – in theory – all members are equal. But certain brethren, usually those in important governmental posts, are exempt from the obligation to attend branch meetings or to perform routine work. Such individuals may be reclassified as External or Released Brethren. A member who, for reasons of age or illness, can no longer be active, is placed on the list of Retired Brethren.

All members are expected to show 'brotherly' feelings to their colleagues. Stress is laid on comradeship, solidarity, service to the community and living an exemplary life according to 'the traditional Christian virtues'. The Broederbond is a fraternal order in that it provides companionship, sociability and mutual benefit. This includes a confidential employment service, study loans for members' children and token donations to families of deceased members. In a broad sense, it also distributes top posts in Afrikaner life among its membership. But, despite this internal patronage, the AB stresses that it is 'a service organisation and not an interest organisation', and that individuals join 'to give and not to receive'. It is thus an ideological fraternity made up of mission-conscious Afrikaners rather than a mutual benefit society in the material sense.

Discipline is tight. All executive orders must be obeyed without hesitation although these are couched as 'cordial requests' and not as military-style commands. The AB tries to be the Brains Trust to the nation. It sees itself as a network of consultatative study circles who evolve projects and policies for the nation. One of its major preoccupations is to prepare details and specialist programmes, projects and schemes for strengthening the Afrikaner cause in every sphere. Much work revolves around the formulation and initiation of policies for 'what is best for the moral, intellectual, social, and political progress of the Afrikaner people'.[3] Draft policies are prepared by 14 standing expert Study Commissions which are then debated by the whole membership. Composed largely of intellectuals and clergymen, the AB feels that it has a didactic mission to give expert guidance to Afrikanerdom. Its public statements talk more of 'programme formulation' than of 'programme execution'. Like a society of philosopher-kings, it sees itself as the wise, studious and responsible guardians of the *volk*.

Claiming to be the 'executive organisation' of 'chosen men' who embody 'the best in our volk's life', the Broederbond is an elitist body of leaders and prospective leaders from all walks of life. Amongst its members have been five prime ministers, three state presidents, two governors-general, university principals, DRC moderators, provincial administrators and Civil Service heads. Every elite – political, cultural, religious, economic, intellectual – is milked for recruits, choosing those who already occupy positions of power, or else enlisting and grooming promising young men at an early stage in their careers.

Being secret, the Broederbond is unable to realise its programmes itself. If these are not to be academic pipe dreams, the AB must secretly gain a sufficient foothold within public organisations which possess the machinery and influence to translate its projects into reality. Thus the Broederbond secretly forms caucuses within public organisations with the object of gaining control of their bureaucratic machinery, media, resources and mass following. On account of its cross-sectional membership the Broederbond has operatives in organisations ranging from farmer co-operatives, village management boards and the Afrikaner equivalent of the boy scouts, to the parliamentary Cabinet. In politics, the Broederbond works through the NP; in cultural affairs, the FAK; in religious matters, the DRC; and in the economic field, through the FAK's Economic Institute. It is heavily entrenched in the top echelons of all these bodies.

Like a conventional political party, the Broederbond possesses a basic programme of principles, and works out policies to meet specific circumstances. Moreover, it aims to gain control of government and the state machine. Like an integrative party, it operates in non-political fields in order to build up a mass movement based on its Christian-Nationalist doctrine. In each case it rallies its supporters and forms them into confessional-nationalist bodies. There is a close connection between the Broederbond's neo-Calvinist confessional-nationalist outlook and composition, and that of Abraham Kuyper's ARP in Holland. But its scope, select membership and secrecy distinguish it from a political party. The AB does not seek a mass following, and restricts membership to hand-picked leading personalities. It does not compete in its own name and neither does it contest in open with other parties for an electoral mandate to form a government. Moreover, although the attainment of political power is essential in order to attain its ends, the AB does not – like conventional political parties – restrict itself to the narrow field of party politics. Indeed it scorns the label 'political', preferring to be known as interested in all aspects of Afrikaner national life.

To assess the precise position or role of a public body is difficult enough; the problems are greatly magnified in the case of a *secret* society. While the AB's structure, doctrine and strategy have remained relatively constant, the extent of its actual influence has varied. In general, however, it has been for most of its history the leading group within the Afrikaner Nationalist movement, or what Pierre van den Berghe has called 'a secret executive committee of the Nationalist Party, and hence, of the government'.[4] Research indicates that the Broederbond has been Afrikanerdom's unofficial (and self-constituted) central policy-making organ, co-ordinating the entire mechanism of the Nationalist movement in its parliamentary and extra-parliamentary forms. It has acted as a General Staff (planning, guiding, directing) and as the front-line shock troops (taking the initiative, setting examples, and forming the vanguard) of the struggle which led to the Nationalist victory in 1948, and has helped to maintain that regime ever since.

The AB defies easy characterisation because its character and goals are, in many respects, unique products of the South African situation. It is distinguished from most twentieth-century right-wing Nationalist or patriotic societies by a combination of several unique factors. These include its strict Calvinist character and composition, the unbounded sphere of its interest, its assumption of the role of the nation's guardian, its total and absolute secrecy, its membership (which comprises a substantial cross-section of the Afrikaner elite), and the backroom formulation of policies designed for implementation by public organisations. It is probably the only twentieth-century secret society to have actually exercised decisive power over the legislative, executive and administrative organs of government in a modern, industrialised state. Unlike most secret societies the AB was not forced underground because of persecution or proscription, but submerged entirely voluntarily. At no point in its history have its objects been declared illegal.

Like masonic groups the AB has special hand signals, a distinctive dress, and appears to have different degrees of membership. But the Broederbond is fiercely anti-masonic for Calvinist religious reasons and is not primarily interested in charity or mutual benefit. What differentiates it from conventional contemporary masonic lodges are its aims to lead the nation and gain control of government, its doctrines on racialism and nationalism, and its opposition to the internationalist spirit of freemasonry. As with the semi-secret Opus Dei or Orangemen, the Broederbond has a religious basis to its aims. But whereas most twentieth-century closed religious orders or lodges are only semi-secret the Broederbond attempts to submerge itself totally from public view. There is no precedent in Dutch Calvinist history for a secret society (notably, the Kuyperian tradition stresses the need for 'open politics'). Holland's Calvinists have operated clandestinely only in conditions of religious or political persecution in the sixteenth century and again in the 1939–45 War.

Like the Maquis or other anti-Fascist resistance groups, the Broederbond fought until 1948 an underground struggle against what it regarded as the dominant power (British-Jewish Liberalism), but the Broederbond does not have an internal sealed 'cell system'. While these other groups were formed to resist military invaders, the Broederbond's struggle is against other sections of the peaceful local population.

The Broederbond has been a highly disciplined underground and vanguardist organisation aiming at state control similar to Lenin's Bolshevik Party. But, in contrast to the Bolsheviks, the AB has never publicised policies in its own name or made appeals to the public. It has preferred to operate in complete anonymity, using public organisations as its vehicles. Like many American immigrant ethnic secret societies, the aim of the Broederbond has been to preserve a minority culture from being swamped. But the Broederbond's aims, while displaying a strong conservatism and defensiveness, are aggressively oriented, imposing Afrikaner culture and values on all aspects of life. In any event, it is plausible to argue that the Afrikaans language and culture are safely entrenched. The AB undoubtedly shares common features with secret, National-ist, religious, mutual interest and political fraternities but, in the final analysis, it is *sui generis*, its meaning specific to the political, ideological and religious context in which it operates.

CHRISTIAN-NATIONALISM AND THE AB

The Broederbond is both a product and the champion of the Christian-National *weltanschauung*, an understanding of which is essential in order to grasp the inspirational concepts which propel it forward and govern its view of the universe. Indeed, no proper understanding of the AB's motivations, objectives, style or general orientation is possible without reference to Christian-Nationalist tradition. The hyphen which links 'Christian' and 'National' stresses that these are not autonomous or disparate elements, but that they are interlaced into a single synthesis. To separate the 'Christian' from the 'Nationalist' component is to perform an artificial act of analytical surgery since, fused together, they form a single organic whole. But in order better to understand the Broederbond's ideological make-up, and for analytical purposes alone, the two branches require separation into their individual parts.

The religious element in the AB's composition is neither an afterthought nor a footnote to its Nationalism. In the first place, one may note the existence of a religious admission test. Broederbond meetings are held in a religious atmosphere; the Broederbond fights to strengthen the Afrikaner's Dutch Reformed heritage, to strengthen the theocentric elements in Afrikaner culture, and it holds itself responsible to God alone. Although the Broederbond's statutes nowhere define 'Christian' or 'Protestant', the context makes it abundantly clear that these are synonymous with the Dutch Reformed tendency in Western Protestantism. A potential recruit must belong to the Protestant faith and show the highest degree of religious conviction. All meetings open and close with a prayer, whether they be gatherings of the Executive Council or ordinary village branches. These enjoin the Lord to bless the organisation's efforts and to advance the interests of the nation. They frequently entail the reading of psalms.

Dr Nico Diederichs, a former Broederbond Vice-Chairman, reportedly opened an Executive Meeting in 1945 by 'reading a portion of the Bible . . . [and offering] a long and fervent prayer wherein [he] depicted the Executive Committee as an instrument appointed by the Almighty to sit in council and to show Afrikaners the way'. The language and spirit of austere Calvinism permeates proceedings. All brethren are expected to attend meetings wearing dark clothing. Although the Broederbond does not go so far as to claim to be the Afrikanerdom's Elect, the spirit of a chosen religious elite or aristocracy prevails within the organisation. It justifies its unaccountability to the public in religious terms, holding itself answerable to God alone. To God it gives thanks for successes and on God it relies for the future. The Broederbond's religious character is both a cause and a result of the important role played by clergymen in its affairs. Clergymen were prominent in Broederbond affairs from the start. Preliminary meetings were held at the Krugersdorp parsonage of the Reverend J.F. Naudé and Johannesburg meetings were held in the DRC's Irene Church Hall by permission of the Reverend W. Nicol. Naudé was elected the Bond's first President at its inaugural meeting in June 1918, and Nicol became Chairman in 1925. The leading founder, Henning Klopper, has been described as 'a staunch Calvinist who neither drinks nor smokes'.

At its first meeting the Broederbond resolved that 'the foundation of the whole organisation must rest on the Rock of Christ', a 'clean and moral life should be led', and 'self-sacrifice should be their

watchword'. Professors and teachers from the neo-Calvinist Potchefstroom University for Higher Christian Education played a key
role in the Broederbond's history after the society – in a unique
public gesture – gave open support to the formation of the Kristelike-
Nasionale Bond in 1929 when South Africa's first Christian-
Nationalist programme was formulated. Between 1931 and 1933 the
Broederbond's Chairman was L.J. du Plessis, a lecturer and later
professor at Potchefstroom University, who was also Secretary of
the Kristelike Unie (or KU: Christian Union) and Kristelike
Nasionale Bond van Calviniste (Christian National Calvinist Bond).
His successor was J.C. van Rooy, who led the Broederbond between
1932 and 1938 and from 1942 to 1951.

Most of the staff of the Calvinist Potchefstroom University belong
to the Broederbond. These have included the great 'Totius' (J.D. du
Toit), Hennie Coetzee and, of course, L.J. du Plessis and J.C. van
Rooy. E.P. Groenewald, a leading figure in Pretoria's DRC
theological school, and A.B. du Preez, author of a major theological
defence of apartheid, are both said by authoritative sources to be
brethren. In addition to leading clergymen and theologians, the
Broederbond also contains virtually all the most important theoreticians of Christian-Nationalism. These include men like Diederichs,
J. de W. Keyter and P.J. Meyer, who all held high office in
Broederbond satellite organs.

The Broederbond could be compared to a lay, but confessional,
arm of the Church, a group of Calvinists who carry out religious
work in fields where the institutional church prefers not to operate.
When advising brethren on how to celebrate the Day of the Covenant
(celebrating the 1838 victory of the Voortrekkers over the Zulu
nation at Blood River), the Executive Committee in 1962 urged
them to 'give this year particular emphasis to the religious background
to our volk'. This advice took note of the fact that the anniversary
that year fell on a Sunday and at a time of threatening circumstances
for the *volk*.[5] As in past years the Broederbond proposed subjects
for speakers at Day of the Covenant celebrations. Another 1962
informational circular shows the Broederbond's efforts to unite the
three Afrikaans churches. Entitled 'Towards a more Positive Dutch
Reformed Church Understanding', it warns against conflicts among
the three sections of the DRC, stressing that they are one church
in creed, language, descent, territory and fatherland, despite
organisational divisions.

In its statement to the 1963 NGK Synod, the AB was careful to avoid giving the impression that it operated as an unofficial arm of church members in the political, cultural or economic fields, and emphatically denied any undercover activities within the DRC itself. Faithful to the ultra-orthodox Calvinist position, the Broederbond combats Catholicism, communism, liberalism, atheism and agnosticism wherever these tendencies manifest themselves. It espouses and subscribes to a variant of Calvinism which glorifies the nation, race and culture, upholds apartheid, regards the colour bar as sacred, and extols Nationalism. When, in the 1950s and 1960s, dissident DRC theologians such as the distinguished professors Ben Marais, Ben Keet, Albert Geyser and the Reverend Beyers Naudé challenged the biblical foundations of apartheid, it was the Broederbond which was the organising core of the counter-attack. This is well borne out in the 1962 circulars and in the Broederbond-sponsored book *Grense*, which undertook a theological defence of apartheid.

In practice the AB is not a religious society for the propagation of the gospel. The immediate object of its fervent religious impulses is the nation, which is seen as a divine creation. As sincere Calvinists, Broederbonders would be the first to deny the charge that they idolise race, culture or nation, an accusation repeatedly levelled against Christian-Nationalists both from within the DRC and by international Calvinism in the 1960s. But, in practice, the doctrine amounts to a glorification of the nation. Whereas God is abstract, the nation is real; it is both the embodiment and the proof of divine will and intentions. Nationalism does not negate but actualises and realises belief in Christ. The Afrikaner's dedication to the nation is therefore regarded as a mark of his loyalty to God. Thus the Broederbond extols the virtues of Afrikaans traditions and history, demands absolute service and loyalty to the nation, fosters a narcissistic love for the nation's cultural symbols, draws clear boundary lines between the nation and other groups, and insists that the nation has the right and duty to assume power in every field of life in South Africa.

Originally, a recruit had to prove an Afrikaner ancestry going back to before 1820 (the date of the first British civilian settlement), but this rule was later relaxed to permit admission of Netherlands-born Nationalists, of whom Dr Verwoerd is a notable example. In recent years, the stress has been on dedication to the struggle, readiness for sacrifices, and a capacity to contribute to the Nationalist cause. The AB probably adopted the Christian-National outlook in the closing years of the 1920s, at a time when there was a revival of Voortrekker-type religious-based Nationalism in opposition to the increasing pragmatism and watering down of Nationalist principles by General Hertzog, the Nationalist Prime Minister. The basic Christian-National principles were formulated not by the Broederbond itself, but by two bodies with which it had close links: the KU and the Kristelike Nasionale Bond. Both attempted to give form to the idea of the chosen people and set out, in public, the first full-scale exposition of Christian-National principles. N.J. van der Merwe and L.J. du Plessis were Chairman and Secretary respectively of the Kristelike Nasionale Bond, and later became Broederbond leaders. Thus, although it did not originate the doctrine of Christian-Nationalism, the Broederbond became its most influential defender, interpreter and propagator.

In the eighteenth- and nineteenth-century era of informal scriptural Nationalism, the Boers plundered the Bible for justifications of their conquest and enslavement of blacks and produced the claim that they were the chosen people, the Israelites of South Africa. Such crudities have been avoided in the apartheid era. Contemporary DRC theologians deny that the story of God's curse on the children of Ham is a justification for the permanent servitude of black people. In accordance with orthodox Calvinist theology, they now accept that the Elect will not be confined to white-skinned believers, and they have abandoned the untheological notion (which Calvin himself rejected) that God could ever create another chosen nation on the Hebrew model of antiquity. Nevertheless, modern Christian-National theory contains 'chosen people' undertones, although the concept is camouflaged as one of 'special divinely-ordained vocation'. The justification for an Afrikaner monopoly of power is provided by the notion of a divinely-bestowed responsibility to act as guardians for the 'backward' peoples. Similarly, the justification for apartheid is sought in the concept of divinely fixed and immutable boundaries between different races, nations and cultures.

Two key official declarations of AB policy illustrate the view that Afrikaners have a divine origin and a divinely-given vocation. The first comes from the Broederbond's founder secretary, I.M. Lombard, who endeavoured to explain the Broederbond's character in the face of General Smuts' threat to ban it as a political body during the Second World War:

> The Afrikaner Broederbond is born out of the deep conviction that the Afrikaner nation was planned by God's hand in this country and is destined to continue existing as a nation with its

own character and calling. Of every member is expected that he will live and behave in the firm belief that the fortunes of nations are determined by a divine hand.

A similar sentiment is expressed in the AB secret handbook of 1956, *Principles of our Aspirations*:

> As unswerving Afrikaners we believer that the Afrikaans people were brought into existence in the southern part of Africa by God with an individual vocation of worshipping in His name. We believe that the special vocation of the Afrikaner as a distinct self-contained community with its own character and nature is founded in the Protestant-Christian conviction that God at all times controls their destiny.

Contained in the claim that God gave the Afrikaners 'an individual vocation of worshipping in His name' is perhaps the implication that the Lord merely brought Afrikanerdom into being so that there would be in darkest Africa a Christian religious community to bear witness to the divine presence and to glorify and worship Him. But this is not the full extent of Afrikanerdom's vocation and calling. Its real purpose is apparently to spread Christian civilisation and rule in South Africa. As the Broederbond's Chairman said at the twenty-fifth anniversary conference of the organisation, 'The Afrikaner nation was founded by God to bring the faith of the Dutch Reformed Churches to the dark continent.' In the organisation's view, the struggle for identity and power is not aimed at purely material ends. Nationalism does not covet power, glory or material wealth for its own sake, but in order to provide the means to better glorify God and spread Christ's Kingdom.

Earlier, attention was drawn to Abraham Kuyper's technique for spreading the Christian-National *weltanschauung* throughout secular Holland. Attention was drawn to the fact that he considered Calvinists and those who had been 'called' to be the 'core of the nation'; an organic, disciplined and uniform group drawing a sharp line of distinction between itself and 'the others'. Kuyper created this organic inner circle in order to consolidate the community of true believers into a monolithic *laager*, but his object was not withdrawal of ultra-orthodox Calvinists from a world which had fallen under the spell of liberalism and whose religious fibre was being corroded by secularism. The essence of his vision was that the inner kernel or core had a message for the whole of society and that the Calvinist world outlook could, and should, permeate the whole nation by working outwards in ever widening concentric circles.

In the case of the Broederbond, its relationship to the rest of society may be depicted in terms of three concentric circles. The inner circle consists of the Broederbond core: the supreme repository of Afrikanerdom's religious and national values. The middle circle consists of the Afrikaners: disunited, prey to secularisation and vulnerable to Anglicisation. The outer circle consists of the rest: English speakers, Catholics, Jews and 'non-whites'. Whereas in Holland the dividing lines were ideological (since the nation was culturally and linguistically homogenous), in South Africa the outer circle is divided from the other two by culture, language and colour. This means that the Broederbond's chief pressures are exerted on its own community: those who share its religion and culture, but are not conscious Nationalists. Its influence can only reach the others through control of the state machine, the educational system and the media. A further difference is that whereas the ideal of the Dutch inner circle was evangelistic and welcomed converts, the AB remains a tightly closed club and exclusive inner core. Conversion of the outer circle does not mean their integration into the Afrikaner camp, but merely that they should accept, within the fixed forms of their own cultures and customs, the tenets of the AB's creeds.

The similarity between the Kuyperian inner core and the AB is closest in the corporate organisation of every department of life within the Christian-National community. However, whereas Kuyper's 'society within a society' remains public, its Afrikaner counterpart has a secret council of elders at its core. The manner in which Afrikaner Calvinists have adapted Kuyper's system of separate confessional organisations to cater for the organic community of its followers may be seen in the attached diagrams. The Broederbond did not itself create all these bodies, but its prominent representation on their executive organs enables it to act as a central co-ordinating mechanism and to ensure that all manifest a common Christian-National spirit (see Figures 2.1 and 2.2).

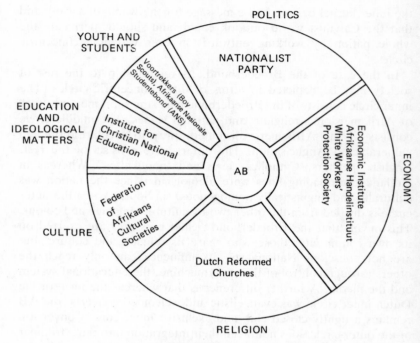

Figure 2.1   AB and Afrikanerdom, *c.* 1950

THE BROEDERBOND'S RELATIONSHIP WITH OTHER-BODIES

The Broederbond's strategy for gaining power is to penetrate organisations with a view to using their resources, facilities and machinery. This is accomplished by deliberately recruiting persons in leading or policy-making posts, or assisting brethren to gain election or promotion to such posts. As a result of systematic infiltration the Broederbond has won a considerable foothold in the premier organs in the public sphere. It is thereby able to exercise a significant sway over the course of the Nationalist movement and the decisions of South Africa's government. Within the Afrikaans community the Broederbond seeks to infiltrate every kind of organisation in every walk of life. Cells are formed, leaders recruited, potential leaders groomed. The object is to gain public mouthpieces or platforms, to transmit Broederbond policy to the rank and file, and to shape the totality of the policies of all Afrikaner bodies. The

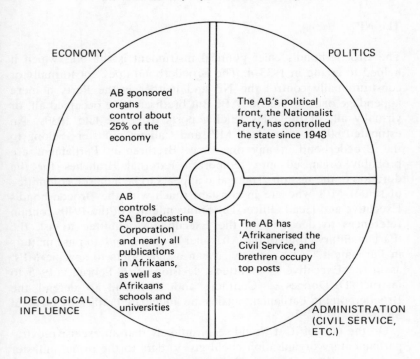

ECONOMY

AB sponsored
organs
control about
25% of the
economy

POLITICS

The AB's political
front, the Nationalist
Party, has controlled
the state since 1948

AB
controls
SA Broadcasting
Corporation
and nearly all
publications
in Afrikaans,
as well as
Afrikaans
schools and
universities

The AB has
'Afrikanerised the
Civil Service, and
brethren occupy
top posts

IDEOLOGICAL
INFLUENCE

ADMINISTRATION
(CIVIL SERVICE,
ETC.)

This illustrates the AB's impact
on the 'outer circle'

Figure 2.2   AB in state and society, *c.* 1950

institutional context within which the Broederbond works constitutes
an extensive network of unilingual, unicultural and unireligious
bodies which, numbering some 2 000 in the 1960s, effectively blanket
the whole of Afrikaner life.

Within the total arena of state and society, the AB champions
Afrikaner supremacy everywhere. Its aim is to achieve Broederbond
control over the Nationalist movement and to achieve Afrikaner
control over the Civil Service and the economy. Although the
Broederbond's activities can be divided between those confined to
the domestic affairs of Afrikanerdom, and those designed to alter
state and society generally, the line separating these spheres is a
vague one. This is because every Afrikaans body serves a double
function: to integrate Afrikaners internally, and to assert their power
externally. Consequently we shall not adopt a rigid classification of
the Broederbond's spheres of operation.

The NP

The Broederbond's chief political instrument is the NP, which it helped to create in 1933–4. The Broederbond does not formally or constitutionally control the NP and neither is the Party a mere appendage or front for the AB. But brethren have occupied all, or virtually all, of the NP's leading posts from the late 1930s. An estimated 80 per cent of all MPs and Cabinet ministers belong to the Broederbond at any one time. Brethren in Parliament are probably organised into temporary External Branches for the duration of the session. There also appears to be a liaison committee of senior MPs who are in constant touch with the Broederbond's Executive and Head Office. The Smuts minutes of the 1940s contain references to decisions of the Executive Committee to ask the 'Parliamentary group of the Afrikaner Broederbond' to raise matters in Parliament.[6] Alternatively, it can assign briefs to specific MPs, as in the Executive Committee's decision of 27 February 1945 to instruct Dr Dönges, J. Conradie and Dr Malan to defend the Broederbond in Parliament against an anticipated attack by General Smuts.

On the face of it, it would seem unlikely that an exclusive extra-parliamentary organisation could give orders to the prime minister and government. Certainly there is no question of the Broederbond attempting to advise the government on day-to-day tactics and strategy. But, in so far as prime ministers, Cabinet ministers and party leaders belong to the Broederbond and participate in the formulation of its policies (where their opinion carries considerable weight), they are obliged to execute Bond policy. Problems arose under the premiership of Malan when the Transvaal-dominated Broederbond apparently favoured more militant policies than Malan felt advisable, but on the whole brethren in the Party do not seem to have suffered from conflicts of loyalty. During the premierships of Mr Strydom and Dr Verwoerd the Broederbond enjoyed greater freedom and power within the Party than previously. This was partly because both men, particularly Verwoerd, were more devoted members of the Broederbond than Dr Malan had been.

Despite the close affinity between the two bodies there has none the less been tension in their relations. The most important cause is the fact that the Party, operating in the electoral arena, has to aim at winning popular support and winning votes in elections. This means that it must compromise to some extent with the prevailing mood and possibly with other interests. By contrast, the Broederbond does not need to defer to other groupings. It need not trim its sails to the passing winds of fashion or try to placate its opponents. Lacking a public organisation's accountability, it has the freedom to stand for absolute and uncompromising policies. As the supreme guardian of all Afrikanerdom's interests, the AB regards politics as merely one field among many, and refuses to subordinate its views to the Party's tactical needs. The Broederbond takes the view that the nation comes first and the Party second.

The first NP was formed in 1914 by General Hertzog. It came to power in 1924 under his leadership (in coalition with the Labour Party) and remained the party of government until 1933. During these years the Broederbond operated as a minority pro-Republican pressure group of Young Turks within the NP. The aftermath of the Great Depression caused a fundamental shake-up in South African politics. In an act known as 'fusion', Prime Minister Hertzog dissolved the NP in 1933–4 by amalgamating it with General Smuts' South African Party, which had been the official opposition since 1924. The new ruling party, with Hertzog as Prime Minister and Smuts as his deputy, became the United Party. With Hertzog's dissolution of the NP, the Broederbond emerged as the focal point of the counter-offensive in order to preserve an independent Nationalist voice in politics. In January 1934 the AB's Chairman, Professor J.C. van Rooy, reminded brethren that their objective was 'the Afrikanerisation of South Africa in all its aspects'. This was a clear repudiation of Hertzog's new policy of white integration and thus amounted to a call to resistance. A new 'Purified' Nationalist Party, composed of breakaway Nationalists and led by Dr Malan, was formed in June 1934. Later, van Rooy claimed that the Broederbond had engineered the formation of the Purified Nationalist Party as 'the best instrument to bring about a Republic'.

While the Broederbond exercised little influence in the NP under Hertzog, it became the major force in Malan's splinter grouping. All Nationalist prime ministers from 1948, up to and including President P.W. Botha, have been brethren. The same goes for the majority of NP leaders in Parliament and the provinces. With members of the Broederbond occupying the key posts in the Party, they have been able to secure the election or promotion of other members to positions of influence. At the same time, they have been able to secure the NP's endorsement of Broederbond policy. Among the Broederbond proposals adopted by the Party are

Christian-Nationalism as the movement's official ideology, the conversion of South Africa from a monarchy into an independent Republic outside the Commonwealth, rigid parallel development of the races, and the Afrikanerisation of other sections. Thus, because the Broederbond has furnished the NP leaders, and on account of its manifest influence over Party policy, it seems fair to describe the Broederbond as the most important single extra-parliamentary force in South African governments since 1948.

The DRC

The DRC is divided into three sections, the Nederduitse Gerefor-meerde Kerk (NGK), the Nederduitse Hervormde Kerk (NHK), and the Gereformeerde Kerk (GK). All subscribe to the same creed: the Canons of Dort, the Heidelberg Catechism and the Netherlands Confession. The vast majority of Afrikaners are members. The Afrikaans churches are the oldest and probably the most powerful of all Afrikaner institutions. They have enjoyed more power within Afrikanerdom than any other modern Protestant church in any existing state, and their creed forms the official philosophical basis of Afrikaner Nationalism in South Africa. The Broederbond is strongly sympathetic to the DRC, and works within it to promote inter-church unity and to strengthen its links with the population. But the Broederbond is more than a mere extra-ecclesiastical Calvinist pressure group. In line with Christian-Nationalist doctrine it propagates a version of Calvinism which insists on racial apartheid, glorifies nation, culture and race, and demands the DRC's commitment to the Nationalist struggle.

In 1962 the Broederbond publicly denied that it 'interfered with the internal affairs of the Afrikaans Churches'. However, this denial conflicts both with the general opinion of DRC members, the evidence of the 1962 Broederbond circulars and the information obtained by General Smuts' Military Intelligence investigators during the Second World War. A prominent DRC theologian told the author in the early 1960s that:

> for many years it was fairly common knowledge that there were
> very close links between the Broederbond and the Afrikaans
> Churches. This was never an official link, and hundreds of Dutch
> Reformed Church Ministers were not aware of it. Through the
> great number of Dutch Reformed Church Ministers who are
> members of the Broederbond, this organisation and its basic

philosophy permeated and often directed the decisions of the Church, especially on racial, social and cultural matters. Of the eight thousand plus members of the Broederbond, more than six hundred are Ministers of the three Afrikaans Churches. They serve as channels for Broederbond ideology in the Church.

The 1962 Broederbond circulars reveal how the organisation instructs DRC members to adopt certain positions on ecclesiastical matters and how it champions apartheid doctrine in the church. For instance, the Extraordinary Circular of 1 August 1962 refers to 'onslaughts against our continued existence as an independent Christian-National, Western Community in South Africa' and instructs members to oppose these in meetings, church journals and the public press. Circular letter 3/62/63 of 1 October 1962 includes an Informational Document which encourages the three Afrikaans churches to combine in the interests of the Republic's development and to combat hostile attacks. It stresses the churches' need to suppress dissident voices within their membership opposing apartheid policies. A circular numbered 5/62/63 of 1 December 1963 gives brethren guidance in dealing with an expected attempt to criticise the Broederbond within Church Councils as a result of the NGK's condemnation of freemasonry.

The indications are that the Broederbond began to entrench itself in the DRC at an early stage. Calvinist leaders like Professor J.D. du Toit, the Reverend Dr W. Nicol (NGK Moderator), the Reverend C.B. Brink (NGK Moderator), Dr T. Dreyer (NHK Moderator) and Professor J.C. van Rooy (GK) were all leading members of the Broederbond. It was through them that the secret organisation began to exercise influence in the DRC in the 1930s, an influence which grew as they rose to senior positions within the churches. Significantly, it was prominent leaders of the DRC who publicly suggested the AB's various 'Volks-Unity' plans during the Second World War and attached their names to all the AB-inspired Republican Front declarations.

In the course of investigations into its operations, the Department of Military Intelligence (DMI) discovered that the Broederbond had gained an extensive grip on the Afrikaans churches. A DMI report dated 29 March 1944 expressed alarm at the Broederbond's success in drawing the churches into its orbit. In the 25 years following this report the Broederbond's hold on all three churches was strengthened. Young ministers, recruited into the Broederbond at an early point in their careers, gradually rose to become Moderators. These included men like the Reverends Beyers Naudé, F.O'B. Geldenhuys and J. Snijders, all of whom became NGK Moderators. The Gereformeerde (Dopper) Church lost influence within the Broederbond but has remained a Broederbond stronghold. The NHK emerged after Sharpeville as the most rigid upholder of the Broederbond's colour policies and it may be regarded as the most thoroughly Broederbond-controlled of all the DRCs. It was the NHK which accused and condemned Professor Geyser of heresy in 1962.

Yet, the Broederbond's control of the DRC has not always gone unchallenged. In contrast to its sway within the NP, the secret society's operations have drawn sharp criticism from eminent theologians of the rank and file. The reason is that Calvinist principles do not always lend themselves to the needs of apartheid. The DRC belongs to a long supra-national Protestant tradition and has proved vulnerable to external and international criticism. The church is also the defender of a fixed doctrine which was not evolved by the Afrikaner masses, and exists independently of Nationalism. In the 1950s three prominent theologians, Professor B.B. Keet, doyen of the Stellenbosch theological school, Professor Ben Marais, author of *Colour: Unsolved Problem of the West*, and Professor Albert Geyser sharply attacked apartheid as un-Calvinist. In Calvinism they found principles which were antithetical to Nationalism, white domination and segregation, and adopted a firm stand against Christian-Nationalism. It is indeed striking that Afrikaner opposition to apartheid since 1960 has often taken a theological form. Thus Calvinism, traditionally the ideological foundation of Nationalism, has also been used to divorce the church from Nationalism.

In 1949 the DRC's highest organ, the Federal Council, was obliged to set up a Commission of Inquiry into widespread allegations that the Broederbond was un-Calvinist and that it subverted the church. Two years later, in 1951, it reported that the Broederbond was 'wholesome and healthy' and sought the best interests of Afrikanerdom 'both temporal and spiritual'. By implication, the report indicated that the Broederbond did not interfere in DRC affairs and that no incompatibility existed between membership of one and the other.[7] A new crisis developed in 1962 after the DRC's rejection of a more tolerant colour policy had led to suspicions that the Broederbond was behind this position. These misgivings were strengthened by a Broederbond-inspired campaign to prohibit church members from belonging to the freemasons. As a result, a move developed for prohibiting church members from belonging to the Broederbond. Though the attempt failed, it did disclose the existence of a strong pocket of minority opposition to Christian-Nationalism and its chief exponent, the Broederbond.

In March 1962 the Reverend Beyers Naudé, Moderator of the NGK Southern Transvaal Synod and a respected brother of 23 years' standing, resigned from the Broederbond in protest against its pressure on the DRC to stand by apartheid. He told the Broederbond's Executive Committee: 'The basic doctrines of the Broederbond, on grounds of which sweeping conclusions are drawn, are based on an interpretation of the Scriptures to which I decidedly do not subscribe.' Greatly embarrassed, the Broederbond denied Naudé's charges, but there is little doubt that they were well founded.

The Civil Service

The AB systematically infiltrates all key posts in the Civil Service, post office, railways, army and police. To gain control of all branches of the administration is an essential part of its strategy for obtaining power over the state. Dr Verwoerd, speaking on behalf of the AB Executive Committee, told its annual conference in 1943:

> It was the calculated policy of the A.B. to gain control of as many key-points as they could. Members of the A.B. should help each other to become members of school committees, village committees, town and city councils, in short, the A.B. must gain control of everything it could lay its hands on, in every walk of life in South Africa, and must not refrain from pushing its members into any key-point whatsoever.[8]

As a result of AB efforts, Afrikaners have come to control a monopoly of all leading posts in the administration, post office, police and army. Most of these men are said to be brethren. Originally, however, the Broederbond's motives were not to conquer the whole Civil Service, but merely to help Afrikaners – and particularly its own brethren – to gain promotion. This was probably because the Broederbond's founding members contained a high proportion of teachers, such as I.M. Lombard and J.H. Greybe, and railwaymen, such as H.J. Klopper and D.H.C. du Plessis. These men felt the need for Afrikaners in general, and brethren in particular, to stand together and help each other in a predominantly English preserve.

In 1918 the Broederbond's founders agreed that members 'should help each other to gain promotion in the Civil Service or in any other field of activity in which they worked'. Quoting from its secret handbook in 1935, General Hertzog charged the Broederbond with threatening the Civil Service's standards and integrity and acting against the best interests of the state. Hertzog alleged that brethren in the service were compelled to give Broederbond instructions precedence over the 'lawful instructions of the Civil Service'. Moreover, they were bound to give preferential support for each other. There was therefore 'nothing to prevent the Bond from being misused as an instrument for organised action in conflict with the best interests of the State and public service'.

One of the key fields of AB penetration was the teaching profession, where the secret society was carrying out a heavy recruitment of teachers in order to gain a hold over the minds of the young. 'About a third of the total members of the Broederbond are teachers', revealed General Hertzog. 'Should it be allowed', he asked, 'that teachers paid by the State to educate our children, should abuse their opportunities of contact with young minds thus given them, for the sake of propagating disruptive political propaganda?' Hertzog revealed that, out of a total of 100 delegates to the 1935 AB Congress, 21 had been teachers. But, despite sounding the alarm, Hertzog took no effective action to halt the Broederbond's infiltration of the Civil Service. Ten years later his successor as premier, General Smuts, was persuaded that the Broederbond's undercover infiltration presented a danger to the state by filling vital positions with a potentially disloyal and pro-Axis network of cadres. A confidential DMI report, issued in January 1944, provided detailed evidence of AB infiltration into the teaching profession and Civil Service. It concluded that the Broederbond would have to be 'destroyed' if peace and amity was to be maintained in South Africa. A further Military Intelligence memorandum commented in 1944:

> There are prominent positions throughout the Civil Service which are held by Broederbonders, and the fact that some of these are vitally connected with the war effort is a cause for the gravest concern, since a clever man can always obstruct in such a way

that he keeps his activities 'within the law'.[9]

This report attributed the Broederbond's 'tremendous influence' to the fact that:

its policy is based on two fundamental principles, namely, to control the minds of Afrikanerdom through control of its educational institutions, and to control its actions by gaining a tight grip on its purse-strings. In other words, the Afrikaner-Broederbond has, octopus-like, spread its tentacles into the economic, as well as the educational and cultural fields in South Africa. In addition it has representatives in key positions throughout the Civil Service.[10]

Particular stress was laid on the 'insidiously clever' nature of the Broederbond's strategies. The document concluded with the demand that the organisation's influence would have to be 'eradicated root and branch', failing which it would 'WITHIN A FEW YEARS DESTROY SOUTH AFRICA'.[11]

Acting on this report the Prime Minister, General Smuts, struck a heavy blow at the Broederbond's infiltration of the Civil Service.[12] On 15 December 1944 he proclaimed the Broederbond a subversive organisation under the National Security Regulations, and gave Broederbond public servants, railway employees and teachers 14 days within which to resign from the organisation. Faced with this pressure the Chairman of the Broederbond, J.C. van Rooy, persuaded his Executive Committee on 3 November 1944 to permit its civil servant and teacher members to resign temporarily. This recommendation prevailed and by March 1945 the Government had been notified of 500 resignations from the Broederbond. Only eight members refused to resign (though by June 1945 18 civil servants had been charged for failing to resign from the Bond).[13]

After Dr Malan's Nationalist government came to power in 1948, large numbers of AB personnel who had resigned after the Smuts 1944 banning order were reinstated and many Afrikaners were rapidly promoted, often over the heads of senior English-speaking civil servants. Complaints that the new men were brethren could not be proved without their co-operation. The author interviewed a number of non-Broederbond senior civil servants, and all expressed the conviction that the Bond was the motivating force behind their promotions. Indeed if the Broederbond, working in opposition to a hostile Smuts regime, had succeeded in infiltrating the Civil Service to such an extent that Smuts was forced to take drastic counter-measures, it is reasonable to suppose that the extent and pace of infiltration would have grown after 1948.

FAK

The AB's premier front organisation is the FAK which acts as a co-ordinating centre of the network of Afrikaans extra-parliamentary organisations. Rather than being monolithic it is a federation of autonomous parts, each with its own mass base and distinctive sphere of operations. At the same time, the FAK controls its own network of auxiliary pressure groups and subsidiary mass organisations in particular fields which execute its policies of consolidating Afrikaans culture internally, and promoting Afrikaner interests in society as a whole. Together with the NP and the DRC, the FAK has been the third point of the tripod on which Afrikaner life (and Broederbond power) is based. Although the FAK's function is primarily integrative and co-ordinatory, it is the major public force in preserving Afrikaner culture and communal cohesion, and waging the struggle for Afrikaner autonomy and predominance.

The FAK attempts to maintain Afrikaner unity on a Christian-National basis and to formulate Christian-National policies for application to race relations, economics, welfare, education and statecraft. It embraces the idea that the Afrikaner nation is a special creation of God, and that the Afrikaans language is one of the factors determining its unique character. FAK policy is carried out directly in every city and village by a local organisation called the Skakel Kommittee. Containing representatives from all Afrikaner bodies, it supervises and co-ordinates Afrikaner cultural effort in the area. An illustration of how freely the FAK interprets the notion of 'cultural struggle' is contained in the 1952 report of the Johannesburg Skakel Kommittee. This exhorts Afrikaners to 'fight Communism and help our own factory workers in their fight against it'. Afrikaners are also urged to buy Afrikaans products, support Afrikaner businesses, and to use the services of Afrikaans welfare organisations.

At its inception in 1929 the FAK was composed of 20 co-operating bodies. Its organisational membership rose to 150 in 1945 and reached 1 200 in 1955. By 1962 the number had fallen to 350 and it declined even more after the Johannesburg *Sunday Times*' disclosure in 1962 of its link with the Broederbond.[14] Despite these fluctuations, the FAK remains the Broederbond's premier cultural organ. Among the most important co-ordinating bodies are the Afrikaanse Studentebond (ASB), the Voortrekkers (Boy-Scouts), Handelsinstituut (Commerce Institute), Vrouefederasie (Women's Federation), Noodhulpliga (Red Cross), Onderwysersvereeniging (Teachers' Union), the three DRCS and a large number of Afrikaans religious bodies. Other affiliates include the railwaymen's Afrikaanse Taal en Kultuurvereeniging (ATKV), the postal employees' Afrikaanse Taal en Kultuurbond (ATKB), the policemen's Afrikaanse Kultuurvereniging van die Suid-Afrikaanse Polisie (AKPOL), the defence force's Afrikaanse Kultuurvereeniging vir Volk en Verdediging (AKVV), and the nurses' Afrikaanse Verpleegbond (AVB).

In 1936 the FAK set up the Afrikaanse Nasionale Kultuurraad (ANK: or Afrikaans National Cultural Council) as a broad executive organ representing 25 important Union and provincial organisations. This body, which included the FAK Executive Committee, determined the broad lines of FAK policy, and was a focal point for a common front of all Afrikaner institutions. The FAK also created, and holds a controlling vote in, the executives of the Economic Institute and the Institute for Christian-National Education, as it also did in the cases of three historically important but now defunct bodies, the Reddingsdaadsbond (or RDB: 1939–55),[15] the Instituut vir Volkswelstand (1938–41), and the Nasionale Instituut vir Opvoeding en Onderwys (1938–49), or the National Institute for Training and Teaching (NIOO).

In each the FAK sets up liaison committees whose function is to co-ordinate local Afrikaner activities. Serving on these would be prominent local Afrikaner churchmen, businessmen, and trade union, civil and educational leaders. Formally the FAK can only issue instructions to Skakel Kommittees and control its auxiliary bodies, but its central position in Afrikaner life means that its influence reaches into the fields of church, labour, business, education, universities, schools, youth and women's affairs, and the Civil Service. The FAK is therefore the Broederbond's chief auxiliary organisation and instrument for implementing its cultural, educational and economic policies. The secret society uses the FAK as its mouthpiece, a cloak for its public activities and a machine for transmitting Broederbond ideas into every Afrikaner organisation, local community and home. Through the local Skakel Kommittees and the auxiliary bodies the FAK has direct access to Afrikaners in every region and occupation.

I.M. Lombard, the AB's first Secretary, told the Bond's twenty-fifth anniversary conference that it was wholly responsible for establishing and fostering the FAK. In a press statement the following year he claimed that the FAK's creation was 'one of the finest examples of the way the Afrikaner Broederbond works'. Dr Verwoerd told a Broederbond Executive Meeting on 11 December 1944 that 'the connection between [the Bond] and the FAK should be revealed so as to arouse the public into realising how much it owed to the Afrikaner Broederbond'.

Important corroborative evidence for the Broederbond's paternity of the FAK comes from a secret report to a Broederbond conference in 1932, three years after the FAK's formation. The conference Chairman, L.J. du Plessis, told delegates that the secret society was 'gradually delegating its cultural work to its considerably bigger son, the FAK'. Moreover, the Smuts Minutes contain numerous references to Broederbond leaders calling the FAK a child of the secret organisation, which the Bond had 'brought into existence'. There is substantial evidence to suggest that the AB has maintained control of its 'child', and that it continues to use it as an instrument of policy. The Broederbond Executive frequently adopts decisions for the FAK – as the Smuts Minutes show – which are then carried out by the same individuals, acting as the FAK Executive, because of the overlap between both committees.

In 1944 I.M. Lombard denied Broederbond control over the FAK.[16] But the facts reveal that brethren were in charge of the FAK's Head Committee and Action Committee for that very year (1944–5). What Lombard probably meant to convey was that the Broederbond did not *directly* appoint the FAK's Executive. Nevertheless, its influence has always been sufficiently strong to ensure that the FAK Executive is, and always has been, controlled by brethren and that it provides an umbrella for the Broederbond's secretariat. The FAK has sponsored a large number of subsidiary organisations which are affiliated to it, and sometimes controlled by it. All are based on Christian-Nationalism, owe their origin to Broederbond initiative and depend to a lesser or greater degree on continued Broederbond support for their existence or influence. A number of these organisations have already been mentioned but the most important have a significance of their own and deserve further discussion.

1. The ATKV, or the Afrikaans Language and Culture Society, was formed in 1932 by a group of brethren, namely J.H. Klopper and D.H.C. du Plessis, the Broederbond's first Chairman and Secretary respectively. It was set up on 'a Christian-National basis' for Afrikaans-speaking employees of the railways. Although it is ostensibly a cultural body, it has been a major political force in capturing the allegiance of Afrikaans railwaymen for the Nationalist movement. The Broederbond-inspired Voortrekker Centenary Celebrations of 1938 were organised by the ATKV and the leader of the symbolic re-enactment of the Great Trek was its Chairman, Henning Klopper. This celebration constituted the turning point of modern Afrikaner Nationalism and produced an unprecedented wave of support for the movement, leading to the formation of the OB and the RDB. Among senior Nationalists who led the ATKV were Henning Klopper, M.C. Botha, J.H. Steyl, P.Z.J. van Vuuren and A.F. de Wit.

2. The Spoorbond (Rail Bond) was set up by H.J. Klopper in 1934 on Christian-Nationalist principles and claimed 16 000 members by 1937. It was a mass Afrikaner Nationalist body of all Afrikaner railwaymen, whatever their craft category or type of work. Because it is open to engine drivers, guards, platform and railway office workers (provided that they are Afrikaners), it is not strictly a trade union. While the ATKV tends to concentrate on cultural–political interests, the Spoorbond 'confines itself to the labour interests and the protection of the interests of the railwayman as an Afrikaner worker as its first goal'.

3. The ATKB, or Afrikaans Language and Cultural Bond, was formed in December 1953 for Afrikaners in the Department of Posts and Telegraphs. Its aims are similar to those of the ATKV. Sheila Patterson recorded in 1957 that its membership was nearly 10 000.'[17] Closely linked to both the AB Broederbond and the NP, the ATKB regularly mobilises Afrikaners in the Post Office to support nationalist culture and language campaigns. One of its aims, according to the Postmaster-General A.J. Botes (a member of the Bond), was to 'encourage the Afrikaner to patronise his own businesses and financial institutions in preference to those controlled by the other group'.

4. The Institute for Christian-Nationalist Education. In 1938 the FAK established, as one of its auxiliary bodies, the NIOO. It was governed by an Executive Committee in which FAK Executive

members formed a majority. Prominent in the NIOO were Professor C. Coetzee and Professor J.C. van Rooy, both of Potchefstroom University, and Advocate de Vos Hugo. The NIOO played a prominent part in arousing Afrikaner opposition to the bilingual school system. Ten years after its formation a detailed programme of principles for Christian-National Education (CNE) was issued. At the same time the FAK dissolved the NIOO and established, in 1949, a new body, the Institute for Christian-National Education. The dominant group were, again, brethren. These included the Director, J.G. de Vos Hugo, J.C. Conradie, MP, and J. Chris Coetzee. The extremism of the Institute's programme aroused violent opposition and became the focal point of English-speaking opposition to Dr Malan's government. Since then, Nationalist governments have tended to carry out its principles, but have shied away from the emotive term 'Christian-National'. Nevertheless, successive Nationalist regimes have gradually reformed the education system, bringing it under the control of the central government, and injecting Christian-National doctrines into the syllablus.

5. The Instituut vir Volkswelstand (or Institute for People's Welfare) was established in 1938 by the FAK to cater for the Afrikaner's moral and social well-being. Headed by Broederbond member, Professor G. Cronje, a sociologist from Pretoria University, its directorate was composed of a majority of brethren. The Institute issued a theoretical journal called *Volkswelstand* which was edited by P.J. Meyer, who was its Secretary, as well as being Assistant Secretary of the FAK. After a brief two-year career, during which time it helped to formulate various Christian-National approaches to the problems of urbanisation and poverty, the Institute was merged with the RDB in 1940.

6. The Economic Movement and the RDB, or Salvation Deed Bond. An important field of AB operations is the economy, where the Afrikaners have always occupied an inferior position *vis-à-vis* English speakers. The vast bulk of the white working class is Afrikaans-speaking, and the overwhelming majority of businessmen, industrialists and financiers – at least until recent times – have been English-speaking. Thus, within the white ruling group, lines of culture and language have coincided with the division of wealth and consequently of prestige and status. While Afrikaners have always (by virtue of their numerical superiority at the polls) been within grasp of political power, they have not controlled economic power to anything like the same extent.

Notably, it was this division of power in Kruger's Transvaal Republic (where the Boers controlled the state and administration, but the Uitlanders controlled all the wealth of the mines) that touched off the Anglo–Boer War of 1899–1902. In Afrikaner eyes, that war came to be understood as a Gold War, an attempt by wealthy English mining magnates to achieve, by military means, what they had failed to gain politically: namely, control over the Transvaal state. After the 1902 Treaty of Vereeniging, the English-speaking financial barons consolidated their stranglehold on the economy and gained a virtual monopoly over South Africa's wealth; on the other hand, the Afrikaners were impoverished by South Africa's industrial revolution. Forced off their ruined farms after the war, tens of thousands of Afrikaners trekked to the cities in search of work in the mines and factories of English speakers. Lacking capital, skills or commercial experience, they became manual workers, miners or civil servants. By 1930 one-third of Afrikanerdom was classified as being 'poor white', and almost two-thirds were in English-speaking employ.

For these reasons the AB turned its attention in the early 1930s to the problem of improving the Afrikaner's economic position. Control of wealth was the key to uplifting the Afrikaner's status and strengthening his political power. The Broederbond saw, with great clarity, that the Afrikaners could never be the effective political masters of South Africa unless they also became masters of its wealth. In accordance with its strategy of launching a simultaneous and co-ordinated struggle for Afrikaner power along a wide front, the Broederbond therefore started to work for Afrikaner economic power in 1934, at the same time as it accelerated its intervention in the political and cultural fields. Although the Broederbond fashioned specific institutions and techniques for the economic struggle, it has always linked this closely to its struggles in the political and cultural spheres.

In 1934 the AB decided to challenge the English-speaking monopoly in banking by establishing the first Afrikaner bank, the Volkskas (People's Treasury). The Broederbond's role in setting up Volkskas is mentioned in the minutes of the AB's conference of 13 December 1943, and in a public communiqué from I.M. Lombard in December 1944. The first Chairman of Volkskas was the Classics Professor from Potchefstroom University, Secretary of the Calvinist Bond and an immediate past Broederbond Chairman, Professor L.J. du Plessis. All the original directors were drawn from the

Broederbond Executive Council. Indeed, there are indications that the Broederbond continues to control Volkskas. One pointer in this direction is the decision taken at a 1944 Broederbond Executive Committee meeting 'to appoint Dr A. Stals M.P., to the Board of Directors of Volkskas'. Beginning as a minor institution, Volkskas is today one of South Africa's richest banks. Between 1942 and 1952 it increased its share of savings nine-fold. Its assets rose from £7 million to £50 million between 1944 and 1955.[18] Volkskas' spectacular growth was no accident; it was a by-product of a carefully organised campaign by the AB to mobilise Afrikaner economic Nationalism, and to persuade Afrikaners to patronise only their own economic institutions.

The disclosure by the 1934 Poor White Conference of the existence of nearly 300000 poor whites, most of them Afrikaners, caused considerable anger in the Nationalist movement. Four years later, at the Voortrekker Centenary celebrations, the Reverend J.D. Kestell, a Broederbonder, suggested that the best monument to the Voortrekkers would be a great savings deed (*reddingsdaad*) by Afrikanerdom to save their 'sunken brethren'. What Kestell apparently had in mind was a vast Afrikaner charitable and benevolent movement; but the Broederbond, which seized on Kestell's idea and on Afrikanerdom's wish for some economic action, proposed a different and more far-reaching solution to the problem of Afrikaner poverty: the establishment of Afrikaner capitalism. Only by capturing 'a share of the means of production and distribution' could the Afrikaners eliminate their economic backwardness. The answer to Afrikaner poverty was not charity, but the adoption of the weapon of capitalism to end English-speaking mastery over the commanding heights of the economy.

In 1938 the FAK's Economic Committee set up a ten-man Board of Trustees to administer the monies collected by Kestell's Reddingsdaadfonds (Rescue Act Fund), six of whom were probably brethren. The following year it called the Economic Volkskongres (People's Congress), which established the machinery for economic power. The chief organisations were the following:

1. The Economic Institute, a small 15-member body, composed of Afrikanerdom's best economists, financiers and businessmen, to supervise and plan the whole economic struggle. This was to be the brains trust or general staff of the movement and was affiliated to the FAK, to which it was responsible.

2. The RDB, a 'great volks-organisation on a broad Christian-Nationalist basis' to mobilise the Afrikaner masses to buy, save and invest in Afrikaner undertakings.
3. The Afrikaanse Handelsinstituut, an organisation of Afrikaner employers in commerce, industry and finance, formed in 1942 to provide help and advice to Afrikaans traders and businessmen.
4. An Afrikaans finance company, Federale Volksbeleggings (Federal Volks-Investments), to act as a financial power house for the establishment of future Afrikaner businesses.
5. The Reddingsdaadfonds, a fund with a target of £1 500 000 which would be used to aid Afrikaner businessmen.

This structure, which comprised a large part of the Afrikaner economic movement, was controlled ultimately by the AB acting anonymously through its chief public front organisation, the FAK. Leading brethren within the economic movement included: L.J. du Plessis (Chairman of the Economic Institute and a professor of Classics and Law); Diederichs (Hoofleier (Leader-in-Chief) of the RDB, a former professor of Politics); P.J. Meyer (Secretary of the Economic Institute); T.E. Dönges (a member of the Economic Institute and RDB Executive, a barrister and MP); C.G.W. Schumann (a member of the Economic Institute and professor of Economics); and Jac Conradie (Chairman of the RDB), a DRC Minister. Others included: W. Nicol (Church Moderator); H.F. Verwoerd (newspaper editor); I.M. Lombard (FAK Secretary); Albert Hertzog (barrister); and J.C. van Rooy (professor of Social Work). Nearly all became, in due course, directors of Broederbond-sponsored business ventures.

Since the RDB also set up the Blankewerkers se Beskermingsbond (White Workers' Protection Society) to 'make the Afrikaner worker part and parcel of the volks-life', many of these brethren who had translated themselves into businessmen for the purposes of the struggle also became worker leaders. Notable among these were P.J. Meyer and H.F. Verwoerd, who served simultaneously on Afrikaner worker bodies and the Afrikaner Handelsinstituut. From the Broederbond's point of view, this multiplicity of class functions was not anomalous. The RDB was supra-class, claiming to serve the economic interests of all Afrikaners, whether rich or poor and regardless of status. It recognised only the conflict between nations and tried to suppress any manifestation of class division among Afrikaners. The RDB's ideal was to create an autonomous Afrikaner economy or market in which Afrikaner businesses would sell Afrikaner manufactured goods to Afrikaner consumers.

The RDB played an important part in harnessing the Afrikaner working-class and middle-class aspirations to the Nationalist movement. It integrated the Afrikaner's class struggles into the mainstream of the Nationalist struggle, transforming an economic struggle into a *volks*-struggle. The RDB operated as a mass organisation until the early 1950s, by which time Afrikaner capitalism had gained its feet and no longer needed a mass 'Buy Afrikaans – Boycott English' organisation. Later, it was permitted to run down, and it ceased to function as a force in 1955.

CONCLUSION

The AB is a tightly-knit, highly disciplined, messianic, secret society dedicated to preserving Afrikanerdom's unity and national identity and to ensuring its predominance in all spheres of public life. Starting as a small cultural 'ginger group' it became, increasingly after 1930, the founder of the struggle for Afrikaner separatism, the spearhead of the Afrikaner Republican struggle and creator of the community's corporate apparatus.

The Broederbond's basic assumption is that it is the divinely-chosen instrument for leading the Afrikaner people to a fulfilment of their preordained mission in Southern Africa. To implement its policy the Broederbond has systematically sought – and achieved – influence over Afrikanerdom's domestic organs as well as those agencies (the executive, legislature, administration and judiciary) serving the whole community. This end has been attained by creating unilingual Afrikaans organisations (paralleling English bodies in the same fields) designed to promote and serve exclusivist Afrikaner interests, by recruiting Afrikaners from the top echelons of various fields, and by creating clandestine factions or lobby groups within independent organisations and institutions.

As a result, the Broederbond is powerfully entrenched in the upper hierarchy of major Afrikaans organisations such as the NP, the DRC, the FAK and the Afrikaans Chamber of Commerce and Industry. Within this closed framework the Broederbond acts as a liaison agency and co-ordinator, an initiator of policies, the promoter of harmonious relations between different Afrikaner classes, groups and organisations, and the guardian of Afrikaner social cohesion.

Parallel to its organisation of Afrikanerdom into a single organic national unit divorced from society in general it also seeks to influence the policy and practice of the government and administration. The Broederbond is therefore Afrikanerdom's secret general staff and is able, through its elitist membership and influential secret caucuses, to exercise substantial influence over state policy and public opinion.

The AB resembles a secret Christian-National political party, and displays strong affinities to the Dutch Christian-National confessional party, the ARP. Of course, the AB is not a conventional political party. Operating underground, it does not engage in electoral contests for power. It is not, therefore, bound by a mandate, nor is it accountable to anyone but its members. Similarly, the Broederbond is not a mass organisation. Its ranks are not unreservedly open to all who support its policies. Nobody can join by applying, since admission is only by way of co-option. Finally, unlike a conventional political party, it is interested in power in fields that do not directly affect the electoral process. Alongside political power, the AB seeks power in labour, business, religious, cultural, recreational, intellectual, youth and educational affairs. As the central Christian-National organisation in South Africa, the Broederbond operates in the political, cultural, religious and economic spheres, seeking the appropriate form of power in each field.

Despite these qualifications, the closest body to which it can be compared, and from which it has doubtless acquired many characteristics, is Abraham Kuyper's ARP. Both are Calvinist confessional, and open only to practising Calvinists. Both subscribe to the creed of the DRC and base their policies upon the Holy Scriptures. Both believe that the nation's Calvinist heritage must be strengthened. Both believe that Calvinists are divinely called to capture power in state and society in order to reform communal life on a Christian-National basis. Both regard the state as a divinely-created institution, which must exercise power in God's name.

The chief differences are that the ARP in the Netherlands operated publicly, as a conventional, mass, election-contesting political party, whereas the Broederbond works in secret, through sympathetic Afrikaner organisations. A further difference is that, although the Dutch Calvinists control an interlocked network of bodies in the political, trade union, sporting, recreational, cultural, educational and intellectual fields, they lack a formal central co-ordinating directorate. In South Africa, on the other hand, the AB is the organised, central mastermind of the entire Christian-National empire in all its manifestations. The final, and most important, difference, is that the Broederbond is the organ of a Nationalist movement as well as a confessional doctrine. While the Dutch neo-Calvinists are purely interested in an ideological battle for the nation's soul, the AB also spearheads a Nationalist movement for creating and cementing Afrikaner unity in every field, and for winning Afrikaner political hegemony over all other groups.

3 Birth and Early Years

The AB was born in the shadow of threatening civil war between English and Afrikaans-speaking South Africans in 1918. In the last year of the Great War – at a moment when a German victory suddenly seemed possible – a patriotic mob of Empire Loyalists clashed with an equally fervent group of Afrikaner Republicans in the centre of Johannesburg. The street fight followed a stormy Nationalist meeting in the Johannesburg City Hall on 13 April 1918. The main speaker was 34-year-old Dr D.F. Malan, who had recently abandoned the pulpit to assume the leadership of the Cape NP. Young Malan (who was also editor of *Die Burger*) had travelled the 1 000 miles from Cape Town to bring the gospel of Republicanism to the Rand, the traditional focus of industrial and political power in South Africa, and stronghold of the pro-Empire SAP.

Addressing a capacity 1 500-member audience, Malan called on Afrikaners to rally to the Republican banner, and for a concerted effort to abolish the Monarchy and convert the Union into an independent Republic outside the Empire. He hit out at British 'injustices' against the Boers and demanded the restoration of their 'violated rights'. Malan depicted the Union Jack as the 'symbol of race domination'. Finally, he criticised South Africa's participation in the Great War, complaining that she had been dragged by Britain into a European quarrel in which the Afrikaners had no real interest. Although the Great War was being fought 6 000 miles away, it split white South Africans into two antagonistic factions, one loyally pro-Allied and the other pro-German. Those factions coincided with the division between the SAP and the Nationalists and inflamed other differences between them. To the Nationalists Britain's war against Imperial German was not South Africa's direct concern. In October 1914, a coterie of ultra-Nationalist ex-Boer War generals, headed by the Chief of the Union's armed forces and supported by a dissident section of the army, launched an armed insurrection to restore the Republic. This rebellion, which had parallels with the Irish uprising of 1916 and the Scottish anti-war movement, was crushed and 10 000 Nationalists arrested. In a massive upsurge of Nationalist solidarity Afrikaners raised £160 000 in 1915 for the legal defence and rehabilitation of their martyrs. Hopes for a German victory flared up early in 1918 when German forces broke through

British lines at St Quentin, threatened Amiens and bombed Paris. In the tense atmosphere Dr Malan's bold call for a Republic and his attack on the Allies was a highly provocative line to take.

So high was feeling that Saturday night that a young Nationalist enthusiast in the audience, W.H. van der Merwe, dramatically pulled down the Union Jack above the platform and tore it to shreds. This flamboyant gesture angered a group of English-speaking patriots who gathered outside the hall and attacked the audience as it emerged. A vigorous fight ensued. Singing 'It's a long way to Tipperary', the song of the South African volunteers fighting in France, they then stormed the Nationalist club and burned the car of Dr A. Moll, a leading Nationalist.

The fracas touched off consequences which were ultimately to reshape South Africa. A group of angry young militants who had watched the riot from the Selbourne Hall balcony, including W.H. van der Merwe, H.J. Klopper and D.H.C. du Plessis, got together secretly afterwards to decide what could be done to promote the Nationalist cause.[1] A month later 14 of them formed a Nationalist society called Young South Africa, which shortly afterwards became the Afrikaner Broederbond. It is significant that the Broederbond was born after a vandalistic attack on the Union Jack: the flag which symbolised the Union's hated tie with Britain, and reminded them of the much-mourned conquest of 1902. The struggle to abolish that flag and to efface all traces of British influence was to engage the Broederbond's energies for the next 40 years.

In one sense the AB was an heir to the nineteenth-century Krugerist tradition of Afrikaner political autonomy and the vigorous resistance to the cultural and political consequences of defeat in the Boer War. It was the newest manifestation of the forces which created Christian-National schools in 1903, the various language movements for the recognition of Afrikaans, the demand for strict bilingualism in the Orange Free State (OFS), the SA Academy of Letters and Art in 1909, the NP in 1914, the Republican rebellion of 1914 and the Helpmekaar movement of 1915. Like all of these the Broederbond would be preoccupied with the maintenance of Afrikaner solidarity, the promotion of the nation's rights and status, and the survival of its tongue and culture. Like them it began as a cultural body, and from there moved logically into political action.

During its first decade the AB was a relatively unimportant cultural pressure group on the Witwatersrand, being merely one of a number of extra-parliamentary bodies which fought to unify

Afrikaners, maintain Afrikaner culture and promote the Afrikaans language. Gradually, however, the Broederbond carved out an independent role and evolved a distinctive persona. From 1926 it repudiated the mainstream of Prime Minister Hertzog's increasingly moderate Nationalism, and began to press aggressively for a Republic. It became the focal point for a rising generation of young ultra-Nationalists, who scorned friendship with the English speakers and who glorified their Afrikanerdom. The most important events of the Broederbond's early years were its decision to go underground in 1922 and to embrace the doctrine of Christian-Nationalism towards the end of the 1920s.

The rise of the AB, paralleling that of the Nationalist movement, is the epic story of a conspiracy that succeeded. Starting off as a small 17-member cultural ginger group, it developed into a powerful secret society. From the outer right-wing fringes of politics, it grew into the central high command, supreme general staff and co-ordinating core of the Afrikaner establishment. It dropped the shield of back-to-the-wall defender of Afrikaner identity to become the attacking vanguard corps and the elite shock troops for the Afrikanerisation of South Africa. It expanded from a group of obscure junior railwaymen into a society of prime ministers, governors-general, church moderators, university principals and Civil Service chiefs. Within a generation of its birth, the Broederbond resolved the conflict between English- and Afrikaans-speaking South Africans in favour of the latter.

As with much of its subsequent history the AB's birth is shrouded in mystery. At least five different dates have been given for its decision to go underground. The account of its formative years which follows is pieced together from a set of sources which seem to be the most reliable:

1. the memoirs of Louis J. du Plessis, a former railwayman who was one of the Broederbond's earliest secretaries;
2. an authoritative review of the Broederbond's first 25 years given in 1942 by its Secretary, I.M. Lombard, and based partly on the diary of W.H. van der Merwe;
3. the 1920 Constitution, an original copy of which came into the hands of the Johannesburg *Rand Daily Mail* (*RDM*).

There is no evidence that the formation of the AB in 1918 caused any ripple upon the waters. So far as we can ascertain, the event passed totally unnoticed, at least as far as the general Afrikaner public was concerned. No contemporary newspaper even recorded the occasion. Who were the early Broederbond leaders, later to become such important figures? W. Nicol was Moderator of the Transvaal DRC for 15 years and the first Nationalist Administrator of the Province; Klopper became leader of the Afrikaner railwaymen and Speaker of the House of Assembly; D.H.C. du Plessis became General Manager of the South African Railways and Harbours; and I.M. Lombard became General Secretary of the FAK. But at the end of the Great War they were newcomers – mostly in their early twenties – to the bustling, cosmopolitan industrial complex of the Witwatersrand. They were militant young Nationalists from the *platteland* (countryside), uprooted by the industrial revolution and plunged into Johannesburg's urban melting-pot where the dominant ethos was Anglo-Saxon and commercial. They were outsiders in a triple sense: most came from the homogenously Afrikaans OFS, they belonged to a defeated nation, and they were members of the poorer sections of the white group.

The idea of forming Young South Africa originated in the brain of a 24-year-old junior clerk in the railways, Henning J. Klopper. Born on the eve of the Anglo–Boer War, Klopper had grown up in a fiercely Republican OFS country town. In 1912 he became a founder member of General Hertzog's breakaway NP and in 1914 helped to establish various Afrikaner political and religious bodies in Johannesburg. A brilliant organiser and powerful speaker, his ideal was 'One Race, One Tongue, One Flag'. Immediately after the Selbourne Hall fracas Klopper began to discuss plans for a new organisation. These preliminary talks were held clandestinely in the veld, because it was risky 'to be overheard in a country where to think in Afrikaans was dangerous, let alone to speak it'.[2] Despite this claim, one feels that these extreme security measures were more a reflection of the subjective back-to-the-wall mood of the conspirators than a fair comment on prevailing conditions.

The security precautions may suggest that the conspirators discussed violence as a means to overthrowing the system. This was a course of action advocated in some militant Nationalist circles keen to set up secret commandos, like the much-admired Irish Sinn Fein. The semi-secret talks were attended by the du Plessis brothers, Danie and Louis, who were, like Klopper, railway clerks and had grown up with him in the OFS. Although both brothers were reared in a strongly Nationalist household, they parted ways in 1922: in that year Louis, who had become the Broederbond's Secretary, left in protest against its growing Anglophobia.[3] Danie remained, and became a prominent Afrikaner Nationalist figure. W.H. van der Merwe (who had started the riot by tearing down the flag) also attended the talks. He, too, was a Free Stater. The senior figure in the founding group was the Reverend J.F. Naudé, a member of a distinguished line of DRC ministers, who was descended from Cape Huguenot refugees. If Klopper supplied the extreme Nationalism, Naudé (who appears to have dropped out of the organisation), was the gentle, moderating influence.

After a month of preliminary meetings, 14 young men decided to set up the Young South Africa society. The inaugural meeting was held in Reverend Naudé's Roodepoort pastorage on 24 May 1918. The first official meeting took place on 4 June of that year, and Klopper was elected Chairman. The name 'Youth South Africa' suggests the influence of Europe's nineteenth-century patriotic societies – such as Young Ottoman, Young Ireland, Young Italy, Young Germany and Young Poland – all of whom fought for national unity, liberation from foreign or tyrannical rule, internal democracy and national independence. In any event, the term had been current in Nationalist circles since 1908 to denote the spirit of militancy among young post-war Afrikaners.[4] Implied in the term was the claim that Afrikaners, as descendants of the pioneer white settlers and the first conquerors of the country, were the only true South Africans (in contrast to English speakers, who were 'uitlanders' or 'foreigners').

Although it grew out of a violent street fight, Young South Africa was emphatically non-violent. Its cornerstone was the unity of all Afrikaners, and the struggle for their salvation. To this end, it pledged to foster a spirit of brotherhood and confidence in the Afrikaner cause. It would teach Afrikaners to develop faith in themselves. Campaigns would be launched for the recognition of the Afrikaans tongue in all spheres. Special attention would be paid to nurturing the Afrikaans culture, particularly among the vulnerable younger generation. Unity was the keynote and self-sacrifice the watchword. The society would stand aloof from the usual party-political disputes and be thoroughly South Africa. It also supported the colour bar.[5]

On 18 June 1918, the group changed its name to the Afrikaner Brotherhood, which conveyed, perhaps more graphically, their supreme objective: to weld all Afrikaners into a vast single brotherhood, based on shared ties of tradition, culture, language and religion. Reverend Naudé was elected President. Thus, two months after the Selbourne Hall riot, the nucleus of an organisation and an idea that was to transform Afrikanerdom had crystallised. But while the Broederbond ostensibly held aloof from party politics, its tendency was clearly Nationalist, and all its founders belonged to the NP. Nevertheless in 1918 many Nationalists still loyally supported generals Botha and Smuts, in the hope that they might yet return to the cause of pan-Afrikaner unity.

The AB'S non-political stance was intended purely in relation to the domestic party warfare among fellow Afrikaners. By its very standpoint the Broederbond was a sworn foe of all that General Botha's policy of 'conciliation' and open-hearted collaboration with the English speakers implied. Moreover, its chief 'cultural' objects could only be realised by political action and by effecting important political changes. For example, the total unification of Afrikanerdom required the dismantling of collaborationist institutions, from the SAP to integrated schools. Recognition of the Afrikaans tongue required the state to abolish Dutch as an official language, and to achieve Afrikaner cultural autonomy it would be necessary to forge new organisations which embodied the principle of self-determination. However, the infant AB saw itself as a primarily 'cultural' organisation.

In 1919 (regarded by some authorities as the date of the Broederbond's birth) the organisation's membership was enlarged by the recruitment of Ivan Makepeace Lombard, a schoolmaster recently graduated from the Heidelberg Teachers' Training College.[6] The influence of teachers and intellectuals was clearly manifested in the AB's first official constitution in 1920. This document, contained in a small handbook, signals the Broederbond's emergence as a stable and ordered organisation. It discloses the Broederbond's strong educational interests and didactic character, its aspiration to provide guidance, and wish to integrate the new urbanised Afrikaner into a coherent bloc. Consisting of six articles, the Constitution pledged the Broederbond to the following objects:

1. the fusion of Afrikaners; enabling Afrikaners throughout the country who long for the 'upliftment of our people' to work together to remove differences of opinions on issues; and to bring about a healthy and progressive unity;

2. the development of a real full-blooded democratic society and the education of the Afrikaner to the proper use thereof;

3. the stimulation of the self-assertiveness of the Afrikaner and inspiring in him love for his language, traditions, country and religion;
4. the advancement of original South African art and culture in all its fields;
5. the ennoblement of society on the basis of decent old customs and characteristics of 'our people';
6. taking care of the economic interests of the Afrikaners, and especially those of Brothers of the Lodge.

Among the committee members who signed this document were four new recruits: Dr William Nicol, an energetic NGK clergyman, Minister of Johannesburg's Irene Church and Transvaal Editor of *Die Kerkbode*, the official NGK journal; L.J. Erasmus, a teacher who became chairman of the powerful Transvaal Onderwysersunie (Transvaal Teachers' Union); L.J. Fourie; and H.J. Ueckermann. The Chairman was still Klopper, and Erasmus was Vice-Chairman.

Significantly, the 1920 Constitution does not cast the Broederbond in a messianic or God-given role, and neither does it pledge the organisation to the doctrine of Christian-Nationalism. Its objects imply that the Broederbond hoped to work in the extra-parliamentary field so as to build up the Afrikaner's self-confidence, cultural unity and economic position. However, within a relatively brief period, the AB had graduated from a small sect concerned largely with internal fraternity into an instrument to promote all Afrikaner interests (a function usually fulfilled by the NP). This shift is indicated by a resolution on 17 May 1921: to make direct and indirect propaganda 'for Afrikaans and for all Afrikaans ideals'.[7] The other important decision of 1921 (a year which also saw the formation of the first AB branch outside Johannesburg) was to launch a campaign for the establishment of Afrikaans-medium schools. By taking up the sword on this issue the Broederbond affirmed the preservation of Afrikaans through segregation, and made its first demand for a structural change in society.

THE BROEDERBOND GOES UNDERGROUND

The post-war years brought a new turbulence to the Union. Industrial unrest, caused by a sharpening struggle between the Rand's white miners and their employees, climaxed in the 1922 general strike. Matters came to a head when the strike erupted into an armed civil war, the second in a decade. Once again, General Smuts called out the army and air force and crushed the rebels. Bitterly, Hertzog denounced him as 'the man whose hands dripped with the blood of his own people'. The Rand Rebellion was a manifestation of class conflict in which the newly-urbanised Afrikaner proletariat joined forces with the established English-speaking working class. But, for the Afrikaner workers, this was not merely an economic struggle. It was also a national struggle against the power of foreign English-speaking capital, whose wish to control Kruger's Transvaal sparked off the Anglo–Boer War. This marked an early realisation that Nationalist and class interests coincided, and that the mining magnates embodied the forces of foreign British imperialism which were oppressing the Afrikaner.

Against this background the AB decided in 1922 to withdraw from public view. As Louis J. du Plessis recalled, 'The last meeting I attended was round about 1922 in the Carlton Hotel when it was decided, by a majority vote, to go underground. What happened since I can only surmise.'[8] Whether the atmosphere created by Smuts' martial law measures influenced this decision we do not know. Indeed, the Broederbond's precise motives are obscure, and later justifications shed little light on this critical step. Despite the melodramatic cloak-and-dagger environment which surrounded preparations for its birth, the Broederbond functioned as an open and public body between 1918 and 1922. Originally, members were expected to wear buttonhole lapel badges with the letters 'AB'.[9] The Broederbond held open meetings on questions of Afrikaner unity to which prominent leaders of the SAP were invited. These included J.H. Hofmeyr, Principal of the University of the Witwatersrand, who became administrator of the Transvaal in 1924. According to one source, an early Broederbond meeting was addressed by the Premier, General Smuts.

As the AB expanded, it gradually tightened up on security. The 1920 Constitution laid down that matters discussed at meetings were to be confidential. In August 1921, shortly after establishing its Krugersdorp branch (the first outside Johannesburg), security precautions were tightened. Members were instructed that 'secrecy must be rigorously observed' and to avoid using the post.[10] Exactly why the Broederbond felt threatened is not immediately clear since its stated aims were perfectly legal, as were all activities of which we have any record. There is no evidence of any official persecution of the society or its members.

W.H. Vatcher, in his work *White Laager*, claims that the AB was forced to go underground because 'after the 1914 rising had been crushed with the aid of two of their own generals, open opposition to the status quo by the Afrikaners was no longer feasible'.[11] This explanation must be rejected, however, on the grounds that the NP continued to challenge the status quo openly throughout the war years and even presented the 1919 Versailles Peace Conference with demands for the replacement of Union by a Republic. Moreover, there is no evidence that the Broederbond ever challenged the constitutional status quo. Its policies from 1918 to 1920 were solely directed at arousing cultural nationalism. A further explanation surmises that the Broederbond was set up as an Afrikaner version of the Sons of England or the freemasons.[12] Although there is some sense in this claim, it should be noted that each of the masonic-type elements in the AB's make-up can be traced to non-masonic roots. The Broederbond's degrees of membership are strictly operational, and not symbolic. Hand signs are for security reasons and there is a total absence of ritualism in its meetings. Moreover, it is highly unlikely that the Broederbond's DRC ministers, the Reverends Naudé and Nicol, would have held any truck with masonry, to which Calvinists are bitterly opposed.

In the absence of substantive evidence or a convincing hypothesis, we are obliged to speculate that the AB submerged simply because secrecy gave it greater freedom of manoeuvre. Three other general factors suggest themselves: the Broederbond's subjective sense of an external threat; the presumed danger to the careers of brethren in the Civil Service; and the mutual benefit functions that the organisation performed for its members. Mutual aid, it may be noted, is a standard response of minority ethnic groups in an alien culture. Further, secrecy may have been a form of self-defence in a hostile world. Nearly all the Broederbond founders were junior members in the Civil Service, whose senior positions were occupied by English speakers. The young members of the Broederbond were on the threshold of their careers and may have felt in danger of victimisation for being overtly connected with a Nationalist pressure group.

DISAFFECTION WITH HERTZOGISM

While the AB was submerging, the NP was riding the flood of electoral popularity. In 1924, a decade after his founding of the splinter NP, Hertzog became Prime Minister. An electoral alliance of the NP and Colonel Creswell's Labour Party won 81 seats against the SAP's 53. Thus General Smuts' SAP, which had ruled continuously since Union, was unseated. The new Pact Cabinet consisted of eight Nationalists and two English-speaking Labour Party members. On the face of it the alliance was a strange one. It joined a unilingual Afrikaans language party which was anti-Britain, anti-Royalist, Calvinist and pro-Republican, with a unilingual English language party, which was pro-Britain, pro-Empire and socialist. What linked these two disparate groups was the struggle against the common enemy, Smuts, who had emerged as both the 'handyman of the Empire' and 'defender of Capitalism'. Although Creswell's Labourites and Hertzog's Nationalists arrived at their conclusions by different paths, there was a point of intersection around which the Pact could crystallise.

In their overriding wish to unseat Smuts both sides made considerable programmatic concessions. Hertzog bound his party to take no step towards a Republic for the duration of the next Parliament, while retaining the right of individual Nationalists to make propaganda for secession and a Republic. Colonel Creswell, for his part, scrapped the Labour Party's blunt commitment to socialise the means of distribution and exchange, and replaced it by a wordy commitment to democratic and public ownership of wealth. Behind the Pact was an important, if subtle, change in the character of the NP. Heavy industrialisation had transformed Afrikanerdom from a rural into an urban people. The nation of Boers was emerging as a nation of proletarians, and the Boer party had now become a party of workers as well as farmers.

The often traumatic disruption caused by this rapid change had both helped and threatened the Nationalist Government. What it meant was that a growing and vocal section of Afrikanerdom was now engaged in a class as well as a national struggle. Fortunately, the propertied class was composed of the nation's perceived enemies, the 'foreign capitalists'. The correspondence of lines of wealth with those of culture obviated any conflict between Afrikaner economic and political aspirations. Sensitive to mood, the NP adopted the jargon of anti-capitalism in an attempt to win over the industrial workers, the majority of whom still supported the SAP. In 1919, for example, General Hertzog told an NP Congress that: 'Bolshevism is the will of the people to be free. Why do people want to oppress and kill Bolshevism? Because national freedom means death to capitalism and imperialism. Do not let us be afraid of Bolshevism. The idea in itself is excellent.'[13]

Despite the victory of the Pact, grave misgivings were caused among purist and extreme Afrikaner Nationalists. First, the very principle of ethnic co-operation with English speakers offended the narrowly Anglophobic sectors of Afrikanerdom. Second, it seemed scandalous to backveld Calvinists that their party, whose constitution explicitly recognised God's providential guidance, could be consorting with one tainted by atheistic Bolshevism. Third, the NP's price for coalition was the abandonment of its most cherished ideal, the Republican struggle. Hertzog's promise to take no steps towards a Republic for five years looked like a surrender of his cause, a grave compromise of principle. These misgivings deepened after the 1926 Balfour Imperial Conference with Hertzog's insistence that South Africa had been given, in effect, her sovereign independence, thereby making the Republican struggle irrelevant.

These misgivings caused grave dissension within the Broederbond in 1923 and 1924, whose three cardinal principles of Afrikaner unity, Afrikaner exclusivity and Afrikaner isolation had all been jeopardised by the Pact. The bitter disputes within the Broederbond – referred to by Lombard and the DMI reports – suggests the existence of a pro- and anti-Hertzog faction within the organisation. The latter would have been strengthened by the recruitment of die-hard Anglophobes like Nicol, Lombard and Erasmus, who shared a horror of assimilation and whose rigidity may have made it difficult for them to comprehend the tactical niceties of the NP leader. However, the controversy died down when it became clear that the new regime, particularly the Minister of the Interior, Dr D.F. Malan, was pursuing an aggressively Afrikaner policy.

The Broederbond's internal struggle is the first evidence of its swing to ultra-Nationalism, its mistrust of Hertzogism, and its profound objections to any form of fraternisation with the English. According to the Broederbond's first Secretary, Louis J. du Plessis, these tendencies were evident before the Pact's conception.[14] But there is little doubt that 1925 marks the parting of the ways between the Broederbond and Hertzog's Nationalists. The rifts deepened as Hertzog began to dampen down Republican fervour. After the 1926

Balfour Conference, which recognised South Africa's juridical autonomy, Hertzog declared that the Empire had been liquidated and South Africa was free. All that remained was 'a free alliance of seven dominion states which co-operate together as friends'.[15] In 1928, the OFS NP incorporated into its Constitution a statement that the Balfour Declaration was 'tantamount to our attainment of sovereign independence and of powers to exercise our functions as a State at our own discretion'. It was necessary only to defend the state's 'freedom and existing rights'. Republicanism had therefore become excess baggage to Hertzog. It was redundant since South Africa had attained independence. To the wrathful astonishment of his followers, Hertzog now claimed that the NP 'had never been a Republican party'.[16]

This view was not shared by all Nationalists. Among the new parliamentary backbenchers, chiefly from the rural constituencies, were men like N.J. van der Merwe, C.R. Swart, J.G. Strydom, E.H. Louw, K. Bremer, J.H. Conradie, A.J. Stals and S.P. le Roux, who frequently took advantage of the rule permitting individual propaganda for a Republic. As early as 1923, J.G. Strydom had been unhappy with the modification of Republicanism. He declared, 'I want to give timely warning to our leaders that we are republicans in marrow and bone and that if they impose something else, an "enhanced status" or a "sovereign independence", upon us, they will drive the ship of our party on the rocks of disunity.'[17] C.R. Swart, who stood for Parliament in 1923 as an avowed Republican, boldly told the Assembly five years later:

> I am convinced that republicanism is the best form of government. What is the use of disguising it? . . . I do not say that we should establish a party therefore or employ violence to that end, and that we should exercise it by force or agitate for it. But it is wrong to say that the feeling for the republican form of government is dead, and so I want to deny it. I am speaking for myself, but many share my view.[18]

THE BROEDERBOND EMBRACES CHRISTIAN-NATIONALISM

After 1925 the AB began to expand rapidly in terms of numbers, fields of activity and influence. In 1927 it decided to 'take an active part in the life of the community and that no avenue should be neglected'. Brethren organised pressure on Hertzog's government to maintain the pace and scope of Afrikanerisation. The Bond sponsored Afrikaans-medium schools and the use of Afrikaans on South African coins. Wider recruiting took place in the Civil Service, among teachers and at the universities. The Broederbond made contact with the militant Potchefstroom University for Higher Christian Education, an event which had profound results for both. It sent a message of support to the formation of the Kristelike Nasionale Bond. In 1929 it was decided to form branches in every town and village in the Transvaal. The same year saw the establishment of the FAK, an achievement of immediate and enduring significance. This project was the Broederbond's first known intervention in the public arena and yielded its first and most important front organisation. In 1930 the Broederbond formed its first branch in Cape Town, and began to build a Cape section. Taken together, this expansion reflected a widening range of Broederbond interests, which in turn extended the organisation's influence.

Although the AB was, from its birth in 1918, a Christian and a Nationalist body, the term 'Christian-Nationalism' does not occur in any of its (available) internal records pertaining to the first decade of its existence. There is a strong body of circumstantial evidence to show that the Broederbond was in touch with Potchefstroom, Kuyperian and *gereformeerde* circles from the early 1920s. Added to this is proof that the Broederbond positively supported the formation of the Kristelike Nasionale Bond van Kalviniste in 1929, and was therefore organisationally in contact with the rising Christian-Nationalist movement. Further evidence suggests that, by the early 1930s, the Broederbond was thoroughly transformed into a Christian-Nationalist organisation.

Strong affinities existed between Abraham Kuyper and the Afrikaner cause in the late nineteenth century, especially at the time of the first and second Boer Wars. These links were strengthened by the rise of the Calvinist Amsterdam Free University which served as a training ground for many postgraduate Afrikaner theologians who rose to prominence in the DRC. Also important was the establishment of the small Potchefstroom University in 1905 which was modelled on the Amsterdam Free University. Potchefstroom grew out of the splinter fundamentalist GK, set up in 1859 by a Dutch follower of Kuyper, Dirk Postma. Among the founders of this church was Paul Kruger, who later became President of the Transvaal Republic.

One of the most important Afrikaners to fall under Kuyper's spell was J.D. du Toit, son of S.J. du Toit, the great nineteenth-century Afrikaner intellectual and leader of the First Language Movement. Young du Toit, or Totius as he is more commonly known, completed his postgraduate theological studies at the Free University during the second Anglo–Boer War. While in Holland he became attracted to the idea of self-isolation as a means of preserving identity and of defending a threatened system of values. He saw the Voortrekkers, who trekked away from the British and into the interior, as a South African incarnation of the Kuyperian concept of retreat from an infected liberal society. Attracted by the concept of boundaries and isolation, Totius returned to South Africa in 1902 and preached that the *volk* could only attain salvation and greatness by deliberately segregating itself, not only from 'non-whites' but also from English influences.[19]

Du Toit conceived of Afrikaners as a holy community with a sacred mission, whose group identity was a gift from God, and should not be diluted by intermarriage. Following Kuyper, he held that Calvinists should play a leading part in the nation and, even more importantly, in the incipient post-war Nationalist movement. As a Calvinist, he insisted that Christianity should be the senior partner in the Nationalist movement. Du Toit is widely remembered as a patriotic poet, but he was probably also the greatest prophetic figure and most fertilising intellectual influence in twentieth-century Nationalism. He played a prominent part in launching the Christian-National school movement in 1904 which established a system of 200 private Afrikaner schools as a counter to Lord Milner's anglicisation programme. Writing under the pseudonym 'Totius', du Toit rapidly became a leader in the 1905 Second Language Movement, the aim of which was to replace Dutch with Afrikaans.

Du Toit's most important role was probably to help in the development of Potchefstroom University College for Higher Christian Education into a replica of Amsterdam's Free University. He was one of the three original professors when the institution opened in 1905. There he perfected the Christian-Nationalist creed, and gathered around him a group of students who were later to become energetic and influential exponents of the idea. Among those who fell under his spell were J.C. van Rooy, L.J. du Plessis, H.G. Stoker, D.W. Kruger, A.H. van der Walt and D.J. van Rooy.

All later became professors at the college. Taken as a group, they constituted the most virile and extreme exponents of Afrikaner Nationalism. During the 1930s and 1940s they were responsible for almost all the theoretical work on Christian-Nationalism. The majority of this group also became leaders in the AB, and doubtless played a leading role in its conversion into a Christian-Nationalist organ.

It was the son of the famous Abraham, Professor H.H. Kuyper, who first implanted the idea of a formal organisation of Christian-Nationalists in South Africa. During the course of a goodwill tour in 1926 (sponsored by the Netherlands' Reformed Churches), the young Kuyper urged the creation of a specific Christian-National organisation. He urged Calvinist-Nationalists to form themselves into a confessional-political body modelled on the ARP which his father had founded in Holland. As the bearer of the most revered name in Dutch theology Kuyper was royally received in DRC circles. He held talks with such graduates of the Free University as E.E. van Rooyen, Ben Keet, D.J. Keet, W. Nicol, D.F. Erasmus, P.S.Z. Coetzee and N.J. van der Merwe, all of whom were leaders in the NGK. He also addressed a special Synod of the Potchefstroom's small GK, a sister church to the one to which Kuyper belonged. Throughout, he hammered a single theme: the need for inter-church unity among the Afrikaners, and for Kuyperian-oriented Calvinists, irrespective of their ecclesiastical affiliations, to consolidate forces (through confessional bodies of the Dutch style) for the purpose of propagating the Calvinist world-outlook.

Professor Kuyper's bold invitation to form a Christian Party was treated cautiously because it demanded a formal split in Afrikaner nationalist ranks between Nationalists and Kuyperians. There seemed little prospect of support from rank-and-file nationalists for such a move. In Potchefstroom, however, Kuyper's call for a movement to 'Calvinise' the Afrikaner nation's thought and life (just as Kuyperians were working to Christianise the Dutch nation) was warmly received. Accordingly, in 1927, the KU was established at Potchefstroom with the aim of propagating the Calvinist *weltan-schauung* among intellectuals, teachers and scientists. This represented a pioneer attempt to publicise Kuyperian Calvinism in an organised fashion. The Chairman of the KU was the venerable Professor G. du Plessis, and the Secretary was L.J. du Plessis, both of Potchefstroom University College. The latter, then aged 30, was already a rising star in the Nationalist movement.

In line with the strategy used in Holland, the KU began to set out the Calvinist position on philosophical, scientific, anthropological and biological questions. By 1927 it had issued nine booklets, all written by Potchefstroom professors. Among the titles were 'The Evolution Theory and Modern Biology' by H. Stoker; 'The Holy Scriptures and Evolution Theory' by J.D. du Toit; 'Natural Law and Miracles', also by J.D. du Toit; 'The Bible and Astronomy' by van Wageningen and Postma; and 'The Holy Scriptures as Norm' by C.J.H. de Wet. In 1928 Potchefstroom launched a theoretical journal, *Wagtoring* (*Watchtower*), edited by C.J.H. de Wet, 'to propagate in various fields of life, the principles of the Holy Scriptures, according to Calvinism'.

At the same time Potchefstroom University began to lay the groundwork for a more ambitious and extensive Christian-National intervention into the political arena. In 1928 the KU issued the first twentieth-century exposition of the Christian-National viewpoint on Afrikaner history, the nature and justification for Nationalism, the role of the nation, and race relations. This was contained in a modest booklet called *Dingaan's Day: A Guide to its Celebrations*. Ostensibly, the booklet was merely a handbook of themes for public speakers at Dingaan's Day meetings. However, in attempting to bring out the inner significance of the anniversary of the 1838 Boer victory over the Zulu nation at Blood River, the anonymous authors formulated a comprehensive, popular and authoritative Christian-National account of Afrikaner custom, stressing God's guidance and the key role of Calvinism. Many of its ideas had already been expressed (mostly in piecemeal fashion) particularly in church sermons, and notably in Dr S. du Toit's pioneer *History of the Afrikaners*, published in 1868. But this was the first attempt by organised Christian-Nationalists to crystallise and codify the concept of the 'chosen people'. The booklet signalled the KU's decision to step out of the narrow confines of specialist philosophical and scientific discussions and to present their own standpoint on the colour bar, the 'black peril', and the aims of Nationalism. The concepts in the publication formed the kernel of the Christian-Nationalist doctrine which captured the imagination of the Afrikaner intelligentsia and masses in the 1930s and 1940s. Indeed, it foreshadows the principles of Verwoerd's policy of separate territorial development which became state policy 20 years later.

The 1928 Dingaan's Day booklet was the prelude to launching a Christian-National offensive on much wider front: the creation of

South Africa's first Christian-National organisation. In June 1928 a conference (sponsored by the KU) duly set up the 'Kristelike-Nasionale Bond van Kalviniste in Suide Afrika'. This new organisation pledged to act on the 'basis of the Word of God as interpreted in the Calvinist world-outlook *in accordance with our Christian-National volks traditions*'; it sought, further, to apply and realise the demands of the eternal word of God *'for the various fields of our modern volks-life'*. Convened by the KU, the two-day founding Conference was attended by an impressive number of leaders, including Nationalist MPs from various parts of the country and walks of life. A striking fact is that it was dominated by Calvinists who were already, or who later became, members of the AB. These included the organisation's Chairman, Dr N.J. van der Merwe, MP, and its Secretary, L.J. du Plessis. The main speakers were also already, or destined soon to become, Broederbonders. In addition to N.J. van der Merwe, these brethren included J.D. du Toit, who gave the keynote address on 'Calvinism in South Africa as an Historical Phenomenon', and Dr H. Roussouw, a NGK theologian from Stellenbosch, who spoke on 'Deviations from the Calvinist Path in our National Life'. Significantly, the Broederbond (in a unique breach of its rigid secrecy) disclosed its existence by sending a message of support to the conference in the name of its Secretary, whose identity was not, however, mentioned.

What hand the AB had in calling and shaping the conference we do not know. Since the Broederbond was still a Johannesburg-based, Transvaal organisation, it is unlikely that it conceived and organised the meeting. But the presence of so many brethren or future brethren certainly raises the possibility of an undercover link. The conference's significance was three-fold. First, it established contact between leading pro-Nationalist Calvinist clergymen in the DRC, and created a framework for them to pool ideas and energies for promoting Calvinist ideas in the intellectual, social, economic and cultural fields. The hard core of this group were Kuyperians and graduates of Amsterdam's Free University. Second, the conference formulated a programme for concerted Christian-National action which diverged from General Hertzog's policies in several important respects, particularly in its implacable Republicanism and uncompromising assertion of Afrikaner autonomy. Third, it produced an extensive and authoritative elaboration of the tenets of Christian-Nationalism which enhanced the respectability and precision of the term.

A striking aspect of the 1928 conference was the attack on aspects of the NP, which rejected it as a suitable vehicle for the realisation of the Christian-National vision. Dr van der Merwe, a Nationalist MP, said that a 'God-forsaking' and 'heathenish' spirit was strongly manifest in all political parties. While the NP had formally recognised God's guidance in the destiny of peoples, he could not deny that it contained the 'spirit of the French Revolution'. Dr S.H. Roussouw also made an oblique attack on the quality of Nationalist MPs: 'regarding the type of man who is often chosen by Parliament, there is *among us* a deplorable departure [from Calvin's standard of God-fearing rulers]. All too often rascals and enemies of God are chosen, and not truth-loving, avarice-hating and God-fearing men.'

Professor du Toit found the NP's acknowledgement of the guidance and providence of God in its Constitution to be inadequate. He objected to the use of the 'colourless' word 'Providence' in place of 'God'. All delegates agreed that there was a crying need, in various fields, for independent action based on a Calvinist world outlook. It was this consensus of thought which led to the momentous decision to create the Kristelike-Nasionale Bond van Kalviniste. The subsequent history of the organisation, which became known as the Calvinist Bond, is unimportant for our history. Failing to attract the broad mass of Christian Afrikaners, the Bond gradually contracted into a narrow Calvinist pressure group composed almost entirely of Potchefstroom professors, which struggled without notable success for inter-church unity. It foundered because ingrained inter-church rivalries raised suspicions that the Bond was really an attempt by Potchefstroom professors to establish their leadership on theological matters. Moreover, it was perceived as a clerical intrusion into politics and, as such, a potential rival to the NP. As a result of this hostility its conferences became smaller and smaller. However, the Calvinist Bond's gradual disappearance from the public stage did not mean the disappearance of its ideas, the confessional tendency, or the ties forged amongst Calvinists and Republicans at the 1928 conference.

There is a striking similarity between the Kristelike-Nasionale Bond and the AB in terms of their confessional basis, extra-parliamentary methods of work, insistence on Afrikaner autonomy and misgivings about Hertzog's retreat from Republicanism. Indeed, the Broederbond emerged from the late 1920s as the chief carrier and embodiment of all the Kristelike-Nasionale Bond's aims and characteristics, especially its Republicanism and its commitment to

Christian-Nationalism. It was as if the Broederbond swallowed the Kristelike-Nasionale Bond, becoming its reincarnation beneath the surface of politics. This remarkable process was of crucial significance to the Broederbond's future.

One key explanation must lie in the incursion of Potchefstroom elements into the AB. There is a strong probability that a substantial bloc of Christian-Nationalists were recruited into the Broederbond around the time of the 1928 conference. This inference can be drawn from the fact that L.J. du Plessis (Secretary of the KU and the Kristelike-Nasionale Bond) was elected Chairman of the AB in 1930 or 1931, and was succeeded by another Potchefstroom professor, J.C. van Rooy. Since a Broederbonder had to be a member of at least two years' standing before qualifying for election to the executive, this implies that du Plessis must have, at the very least, been a brother in 1929. It seems likely that having failed to mount a successful Christian-National organisation in public, or to capture the imagination of the Afrikaner masses, the Potchefstroom group decided that the Broederbond was a more effective instrument for achieving their aims. Direct methods appeared doomed to failure, and the alternative, a secret society, therefore seemed both proper and practical.

The available evidence strongly suggests that the Broederbond was transformed into a Christian-National Republican body between the years 1929 and 1932. By precisely what means and how this transformation took place, we do not know. The change was probably gradual, since there is evidence to show the existence of a Free University, Kuyperian and GK influence within the Broederbond from its earliest years. Of decisive importance, however, was the rise of an independent Christian-Nationalist voice in Afrikaner politics after the 1925 visit to South Africa of Professor H. Kuyper, the establishment of the Kristelike-Nasionale Bond, and the recruitment of key ideologues of Christian-Nationalism into the AB, such as J.C. van Rooy, L.J. du Plessis, N. Diederichs, H. Verwoerd, P.J. Meyer and N.J. van der Merwe. It is also of great significance that the first AB front organisation, the FAK, was set up in 1929 as a Christian-National body. However, leaving aside the precise date at which the Broederbond circle established close links with Potchefstroom's personnel and ideas, it is worth pointing out that the two bodies would, sooner or later, have gravitated naturally into each other's orbit on account of what they shared in common.

A second factor in the Broederbond's emergence as a Christian-National Republican organisation was General Hertzog's dissolution of the NP in 1934. The NP entered the 1930s having achieved glittering success in the Afrikaner cause. Since attaining power in 1924, Afrikaans had become an official language of the Union, the 'civilised labour policy' had been introduced to protect Afrikaner urban workers from cheap black competition, the Union Jack had been abolished as South Africa's sole flag, and South Africa had become an autonomous dominion within the Empire. Indeed, it seemed that by 1929 Hertzog had exhausted the arsenal of Afrikaner Nationalist grievances. His central slogan for the election of that year was the 'black peril', which shifted the focal point of political debate from Boer–Briton discord to the maintenance of white rule. Power had mellowed Hertzog, according to his friends; corrupted him, said his foes. Certainly, South Africa's gain of dominion status had weakened his Republican resolve. Increasingly he began to use the SAP's vocabulary of 'white unity', and put forward the old Botha–Smuts ideal of a 'consolidated South African nation' based on an accord between the two fraternal white groups.

Events in the early 1930s hastened this process. The severe world economic depression led to a considerable weakening to the South African economy and resulted in calls for a government of national unity. In February 1933 a Coalition Cabinet, headed by Hertzog and containing six Hertzogites and six followers of Smuts, was sworn in. In May of that year the Coalition won a resounding electoral vote of confidence, winning 138 of Parliament's 150 seats. In October 1933 the two parties agreed on a merger, and in June 1934 they amalgamated in an act known as 'fusion' to form the new United South African National Party, subsequently known as the United Party. Twenty years after its formation the NP had gone into voluntary liquidation: Hertzog had dissolved the party he founded, and evaded the drawn-out political extension of the Anglo–Boer War. The unity he achieved was, however, of political and limited economic interests rather than a marriage of hearts; and the same intransigent forces which had resisted the Union settlement in 1910 now began to mobilise for the overthrow of the 1934 accord. Hertzog had destroyed the NP, but the grassroots of Nationalism remained.

Although a big majority of Afrikaners faithfully followed Hertzog into fusion, the disappearance of the NP caused widespread bewilderment. By drawing Nationalism into an alliance with its traditional foe, Hertzog suddenly blurred the old familiar dividing lines between 'in' and 'out' groups, even between good and evil. Crucially, fusion left a vacuum on the ultra-Nationalist right, thereby depriving Republicans, Calvinists and cultural autonomists of their political organ. These three groupings shared a common concern, the preservation of Afrikanerdom's separate identity: a goal which appeared to be threatened by Hertzog's policy of collaboration. It was the Broederbond, together with Malan's Nationalists, which filled the breach and became the focal point of resistance to fusion. The organisation's reconstruction of the Nationalist movement on a totally new basis – that of doctrinaire Christian-Nationalism – is a central theme of the history of Afrikanerdom in the 1930s.

4 The Afrikaner Broederbond's Christian-Nationalist Counter-Offensive

INTRODUCTION

The counter-offensive to fusion was led by the AB. It was already playing an important part in cultural nationalism through its 'bigger son', the FAK, of which I.M. Lombard was Secretary;[1] and in religious nationalism through the Calvinist Bond, of which L.J. du Plessis was Secretary. Now it began to build up its political arm, the Purified (Gesuiwerde) National Party (GNP). With the fortunes of exclusivist Nationalism at their lowest point of the century, the AB rallied all the elements with an interest in preserving Afrikanerdom's separateness. It recruited extensively from activists in all areas. Nationalist counter-offensives were launched on every front. The newly-formed United Party represented the institutionalisation of political co-operation between Englishman and Afrikaner; this, it was claimed, would inevitably strengthen integration in other fields: schools, trade unions, welfare bodies, sporting clubs, professional organisations, students, and so on. To counteract these integrationist pressures the Broederbond began to extend its operations into all fields where there were pressures for *samesmelting* (amalgamation) or *verbroedering* (fraternisation). Its strategy was to form Afrikaners into separate unilingual blocs, each of which would then be integrated as a separate corporate unit into a monolithic Afrikaner *laager*.

The counter-offensive was mounted with particular energy in the cultural, educational, ideological, political and economic fields, with simultaneous and centrally co-ordinated campaigns. In each, the objects were a mixture of defence and aggression. A central aim was to maintain Afrikanerdom's cultural isolation and national unity against the potential threat of engulfment by English speakers. In this respect the operation was designed to rescue Afrikaners from the jaws of assimilation and to protect their identity. It was a

backward-looking movement, summoning up the memory of the
Voortrekker heroes, the nineteenth-century rock-like figure of Paul
Kruger, and demanding absolute fidelity to the 'old ways of our
forefathers'. 'Hou Koers' – Keep Faith – was the motto. 'Our volk
is in the throes of a crisis, a confusion of the spirit . . . [and must]
. . . throw up a dam against the foreign currents which are suffocating
us', wrote two Nationalist professors.[2] Once again, as in 1838, 1902
and 1913, the *volk* had to form a protective *laager*, or else disappear.

A further aim of the Broederbond was to demolish the foundations
of the new integrated order based on an English–Afrikaner
partnership being built by Hertzog and Smuts, and finally to replace
it with an exclusively Afrikaner-dominated political and economic
system. In this respect the movement was revolutionary: by aiming
to restore a Republic, it sought to overthrow the constitutional ties
which pre-dated fusion. Certainly there was a strong dash of
Afrikaner imperialism (reminiscent of Kruger's cry of 'Africa for
the Afrikaners – from the Zambesi to Table Bay') to the
Broederbond's new call to battle. Perhaps the Broederbond overre-
acted; alternatively, it may merely have brought aspirations to the
surface which Hertzog had kept under tight reign for the past eight
years; in any event the advent of fusion released an aggressive
Afrikaner messianism that had not been seen since 1881.

The new situation was seen to threaten the survival of Afrikanerdom in its totality: Hertzog had dismantled the barriers against
'foreigners', and had opened the gates to 'alien influences' which
threatened to melt the Afrikaners into a new, amorphous,
Anglo–Afrikaner white nation. It was true that Afrikaans culture
was stronger than in 1902 and had made enormous strides towards
full equality since 1913; but, said the purists, there was a fatal flaw
in Hertzog's argument that the realisation of Afrikanerdom's legal
demands had brought victory: the nation was not a static entity. It
therefore had to go forward, or it would sink. Fusion, it was feared,
imposed a paralysing moratorium on the Nationalist struggle, an
armistice during which the *volk*'s inner bonds would gradually
weaken, leading to its eventual disintegration.

The Broederbond's counter-attack was a defensive strategy with
aggressive tactics. It involved the consolidation of the Nationalist
hard-core and the inclusion of Afrikaners in a vast homogenous
laager, with the creation of sub-*laagers* in every sphere of activity.
It also meant the mobilisation of Afrikaner forces in every possible
field, in order to achieve dominance and to capture control of

governing organs. This plan of action bears remarkable similarities to Abraham Kuyper's 'retreatism' of the late nineteenth century, when he withdrew orthodox Calvinists from an infected society into a tight inner circle with its own governing, political, cultural, recreational and economic organs. The parallel is no coincidence, for the Broederbond's motive force during this period was provided by the Republican Calvinists of Potchefstroom who subscribed to Kuyper's doctrine of 'sovereignty in own sphere'.

THE POLITICAL OFFENSIVE

As an ostensibly non-political body the Broederbond contained followers of both Hertzog and Malan. It was therefore plunged into a momentary crisis by fusion. Its members were affected by the sense of confusion among Nationalists during the coalition talks between Hertzog and Smuts, and by the fact that the bulk of the NP MPs, especially in the Transvaal and OFS, were supporting Hertzog. In August 1932 L.J. du Plessis, the Broederbond Chairman, made it clear (in defiance of the NP's new direction) that the organisation would faithfully propagate Republicanism. He told the Bond's annual secret conference:

> National culture and national welfare cannot unfold fully if the people of South Africa do not also constitutionally sever all foreign ties. After the cultural and economic needs, the Afrikaner Broederbond will have to devote all its attention to the constitutional needs of our people. Added to that the objective must be an entirely independent, genuine Afrikaans form of government for South Africa . . . a form of government which . . . through its embodiment in our own personal head of State, bone of our bone and flesh of our flesh . . . will inspire us to irresistible unity and strength.

In effect, Du Plessis' speech totally rejected the prevailing spirit of *toenadering* (rapprochement) within the NP. It served notice that whatever the party leader, General Hertzog, and the docile rank and file might do, the Bond would faithfully pursue its objectives of a Boer-dominated South Africa. Moreover, it specifically rejected Hertzog's contention that independence had been won, and that no further obstacles lay in the way of the reunification of Afrikaners and in the Nationalist and the SAP parties.

Meanwhile, the parliamentary *toenadering* movement rapidly gathered force. In January 1933 Hertzog and Smuts met secretly and agreed, in principle, on coalition; in February the leaderships of both parties quickly agreed on a programme of principles, and on the last day of that month a coalition ministry of six Hertzogites and six Smutsites was formed. From the start Dr Malan and Dr N.J. van der Merwe, supported by about 30 other Nationalist MPs, baulked at coalition, fearing that it would endanger the Afrikaans language and culture. According to Oswald Pirow, who was intimately involved, behind them were the party's 'die-hard Republicans . . . [whose] ideal was a Kruger Republic which would place the Afrikaner on top for all time . . . [and] a section which saw the only hope for the survival of the Afrikaner in complete isolation.'[3]

The dissidents began to crystallise their positions after August 1933, when Hertzog indicated that coalition would inevitably mature into an amalgamation of the two parties. W. Visser, MP, warned Hertzog of the danger of an open breach. In September 1933, Dr N.J. van der Merwe led a deputation from the OFS Head Committee to ask Hertzog for an assurance that members of the proposed new party would retain the right to propagate Republicanism. In October 1933 the NP's Federal Council approved of fusion by 13 votes to 7, revealing the beginnings of a split among Nationalists. Leader of the opponents was Dr Malan, who categorically stated that the Cape Nationalists refused to dissolve in order to join any fusion, and objected to continued NP/SAP negotiations.

This resistance was welcomed by the Broederbond, whose members played an important role in stiffening the morale of the Nationalist dissenters. At its 1933 Conference the Broederbond reaffirmed its devotion to the *'everlasting existence of the Afrikaner nation'* and, more significantly, to the fight for *'the Afrikanerisation of South Africa in all aspects of its life'*. Coupled with its Republicanism, this suggested that the Broederbond's vision was of a totalitarian, exclusively Afrikaner-controlled Republic, divorced from Britain, and excluding English speakers from the levers of power. A 1934 New Year communiqué from Professor J.C. van Rooy (who succeeded L.J. du Plessis as Chairman in 1932) and the Secretary, I.M. Lombard, signals the Broederbond's emergence as the chief challenger to Hertzogism. Curiously retaining the formal fiction that it was aloof from party politics, the message nevertheless clearly instructed members to take the lead in fashioning new political instruments to fight fusion:

> Brothers, your Executive Council cannot tell you to promote party political fusion or union, or to fight it . . . but we can appeal to every brother to choose in the party political sphere that which is most profitable for the Bond's objects and ideals, as outlined above, and as is well-known to us.

The communiqué reminded brethren that the 'test for brotherhood and Afrikanership does not lie in a party political direction but . . . in aspiring after the ideal of a separate Afrikaner nation, with its own culture'. All Broederbond energies should henceforth be single-mindedly directed at one overriding goal. 'Let us focus attention on the fact that the primary consideration is: whether Afrikanerdom will reach its destiny of mastery in South Africa.' To achieve this the Broederbond had to gain a controlling say in government: 'Brothers, our solution for South Africa's ailments is not that one party or another shall obtain the whip hand, but that the Afrikaner Broederbond shall govern South Africa.'

This was more than an ill-disguised call to support the Malan–van der Merwe faction; it was more than a declaration of war on fusion; it was more than a command to man the barricades on the cultural front; the significance of the directive, as subsequent events show, was even more far-reaching. It finally marks the AB's transformation from a 'cultural' and 'non-political' pressure group into the spearhead of a revival of Republicanism and an all-out offensive for total Afrikaner domination over the English speakers. Henceforth, the Broederbond was an autonomous force in the political process, aspiring to control the organs of government.

An article by Professor L.J. du Plessis in 1933 provides what may be an important clue to the hidden meaning in the striking phrase, 'the Broederbond shall govern South Africa'. The article states that the principal line of division within Nationalism was Republicanism: an issue 'of immediate practical and overwhelming importance in our politics'. Du Plessis goes on to make the first of many public calls for a new political party dedicated to a Republic which would *progress unswervingly in a straight line to ultimate mastery*'. He anticipated a difficult task ahead of constitutional reform before attaining the 'final goal'.[4]

Writing at the moment at which the NP's leadership had decided to dissolve their party and amalgamate with their foes, du Plessis asserted that 'confidence in parliamentary democracy has been greatly weakened', and he referred scornfully to 'the political wire-pulling of parliament'. He called for the abolition of political parties and their replacement by a 'volks council' backed by a syndicalist-style network of 'sectional representative councils'. Whether this advocacy of an authoritarian–corporate and party-less state as an alternative was official Broederbond policy, or merely showed du Plessis' own preference for aspects of the Nazi–Fascist systems, is hard to answer. In my opinion du Plessis' particular scheme could only have been supported by a small number of those brethren who were disenchanted with party politics.

The AB's chosen political front was the GNP, led by Dr Malan, and established during the second half of 1934. Professor van Rooy, the Broederbond Chairman immediately before, during and after the GNP's formation, reportedly claimed that the Broederbond 'had engineered the formation of the National Party as the best instrument to bring about a Republic'. How this was accomplished we do not know. However, from 1927 onwards, the Broederbond gave financial and other assistance to 'approved' candidates standing for election to Parliament or to the provincial council.[5] Moreover, it is likely that the Broederbond backed all the anti-fusion Nationalists who stood in the May 1933 General Election. A key link between brethren and the rebel MPs was Dr N.J. van der Merwe, whom Pirow describes as the 'leader of the Republicans' in Parliament.[6] He was Chairman of both the FAK and the Calvinist Bond and as such was obviously a vital contact between parliamentary Republicans, Christian-Nationalists and cultural nationalists. Many other brethren, including prominent university professors and churchmen, had their own links with anti-Hertzog MPs as well.

In a series of articles published in *Koers* during 1934, Professor L.J. du Plessis outlined various possibilities for the establishment of a one-party system based on strict Christian-National lines. He urged the new party to stress Republicanism, economic reorganisation favouring farmers and workers, colour segregation, bilingualism in the public service and the introduction of Christian-National education. Clearly the Broederbond (or at least the section for whom du Plessis spoke) desired the new party to be more than a straightforward replica of its predecessor. The Broederbond was trying to shape a radically Nationalist party based on the working and farming masses, strictly confessional, and irrevocably bound to the Republican ideal. The GNP was a radical right-wing reconstruction on the lines envisaged by du Plessis, rather than a continuation of its dissolved predecessor. It mirrored the Broederbond's outlook to a remarkable degree, and du Plessis – whose writings had undoubtedly helped to shape its character – was chosen as its Deputy Leader in the Transvaal.

To all intents and purposes the GNP was the parliamentary incarnation of all that the Broederbond stood for. Like the Broederbond, it declared itself to be a 'Christian-National' confessional party. Hertzog's NP had also used the words 'Christian National' in its constitution (though without a hyphen) but the term was infrequently used and denoted little more than a polite recognition of the powerful place of the DRC in Afrikaans life. Doctrinaire confessional Calvinism, as expressed in the hyphenated 'Christian-Nationalism', played no part in its thought and practice. The GNP formally wrote a Republican clause into its Constitution, thus indicating that it equated 'sovereign independence' with the abolition of the monarchy and secession from Empire.

During 1934–5 the AB recruited nearly all the prominent dissident Nationalist MPs. In this way a link was forged between the Malanites, the FAK and the Kristelike-Nasionale Bond, thereby transforming the Broederbond into the focal point of the new Nationalist resurgence. It also gave the Broederbond the power to intervene directly in the political field. The most important of the new recruits was Dr Malan himself, whose appearance at the Johannesburg City Hall in 1918 triggered off the events that led to the Broederbond's formation. Malan, Cape Leader of the NP since 1916, founder of *Die Burger* and an influential Cabinet minister, was a powerful figure. Now 50 years of age, he was the obvious rallying point for the ultra-Nationalist dissidents in Parliament. Unlike the Broederbond's Young Turks, Malan belonged to the Nationalist Old Guard and had already carved a respectable niche for himself in the history of twentieth-century Afrikanerdom.

A contemporary of Totius, Malan belonged to the generation of post-Boer War militants who helped to mount the cultural counter-offensive in the bleak days after the 1902 collapse. His brand of nationalism contained an almost mystic religious fervour. When a group of 1914 Afrikaner rebel prisoners smuggled out a request that he accept editorship of *Die Burger*, the first Nationalist daily, he abandoned the pulpit for politics. Bidding farewell to his congregation, Malan explained that a call from the nation was like a call from God: in serving the first, he would continue to serve the second. The idea that service to one's nation was tantamount to service to God, and that the *volk* was a holy entity, imparted an absoluteness to his nationalism. As Minister of Health, Education and the Interior in Hertzog's 1924 Pact Government, Malan was responsible for inserting a clause into the Constitution acknowledging God's guidance in the destinies of countries. Malan abolished Dutch and made Afrikaans an official language of the Union. He also replaced the Union Jack as South Africa's sole official flag and introduced a new Union Flag, whose design incorporated the emblems of the two defeated Boer Republics.

The two former Boer generals, Hertzog and Smuts, both clever barristers and adroit politicians, had little difficulty in drawing up a new contractual alliance based on mutual compromises. But Malan, like Totius and J.D. Kestell, had the stiff-necked, principled intransigence of a Calvinist theologian. The nation was a holy and absolute object, and its rights could not be bargained with. Since Malan's chief power base was in the Cape he was a valuable catch for the Transvaal-based AB. Together with him a number of other rebel Nationalist MPs joined the Broederbond. These included two OFS MPs, Dr N.J. van der Merwe, Chairman of the FAK and the Calvinist Bond, and C.R. Swart, a young barrister who had joined the rebels in 1914 and first entered Parliament in 1923. Among Cape Nationalists, S.P. le Roux, Dr Karl Bremer and Dr Stals joined the Broederbond. All were to become Cabinet ministers in the future. The only Transvaal Nationalist MP to oppose fusion was J.G. Strydom, a barrister known as the 'Lion of the North'. He was also recruited by the Broederbond and eventually succeeded Dr Malan as Prime Minister in 1954.

The extent of the Broederbond's control over the GNP is a matter for inference and speculation. So far as can be determined, all the founder-leaders of the GNP, its three provincial leaders and an influential secton of its 19 breakaway MPs were brethren. The degree of control must therefore have been considerable, if only because of the Broederbond's energetic hand in establishing the party and the weight of its representation among the highest echelons. But it seems doubtful whether the Broederbond controlled the GNP as absolutely as it ran the FAK. Certainly the Broederbond Executive, if Professor du Plessis' writings are any guide, kept a watchful and slightly critical eye on Nationalism's political wing.

Two factors suggest that the word 'control' should, however, be used with caution. First, the AB was not Malan's only power base.

He needed its support but owed it nothing. The Transvaal and OFS, where the Broederbond's power lay, did not furnish the majority of his 19 MPs. On the contrary, his Cape party was the dominant regional factor in the GNP. Moreover the Transvaal, with Strydom as its sole MP, was 1 000 miles away, creating a problem in communications. As a brother, whose chief lieutenants were brethren too, Malan faithfully followed Broederbond policy. But his prestige also gave him enormous influence within the Bond. There is evidence of tensions between the ultra-Republican rural and extra-parliamentary Calvinists of Potchefstroom, and Dr Malan's more sophisticated Cape Nationalists who had been schooled in the old Cape parliamentary tradition. These seemed chiefly to be confined to personalities, but also had roots in the differing relationships of the Broederbond and NP to the *volksbeweging* (people's movement). In sum it seems that, while the Broederbond was the driving force and most important single influence in Nationalism throughout the 1930s, it did not run the Party as an obedient disciplined satellite, but was rather its senior partner.

The AB also looked outside Parliament, particularly in the professions and universities, for recruits. In 1937 it enrolled Professor H.F. Verwoerd of Stellenbosch University, an organiser of the 1934 Poor White Conference and founder-editor of the *Transvaler*, the first Transvaal Nationalist daily newspaper.[7] Dr E.G. Jansen, a barrister, who attended the founding conference of the KU and was now active in FAK affairs, may also have joined at this time. Two further barristers were recruited from the Cape: J.C. Conradie, who later entered Parliament as a Nationalist front-bencher, and Dr T.E. Dönges, formerly assistant editor of *Die Burger* and a law lecturer at Stellenbosch University. Dönges joined the Cabinet in 1948, succeeded Malan as leader of the Cape Nationalists and, after a distinguished career, was chosen State President-Elect on the eve of his death in 1967.

From the University College of the OFS the Broederbond recruited Dr N. Diederichs, recently returned with pro-Nazi leanings from studies in Germany, and founder-leader of the militant students' union, the Afrikaanse Nasionale Studentebond (ANS). Diederichs became leader of the RDB and Minister of Economic Affairs in 1958. Another talented young intellectual, P.J. Meyer, who became the FAK's Assistant Secretary in 1935, also probably joined at this point as did S.H. Pellisier, a future Director of Education in the OFS, and Dr A.J.R. van Rhijn, Editor of *Die Volksblad* (the daily nationalist newspaper) and a future Cabinet minister. Finally, the Broederbond recruited the son of General Hertzog, Dr Albert Hertzog, an Oxford-educated Pretoria barrister who was making his mark as leader of the Christian-National movements to 'reform' the trade unions. Hertzog, a future Cabinet minister, was to leave the NP in 1969 on the grounds that it was becoming too liberal.

These young barristers, teachers, journalists and professors who were part of the 1934–5 Broederbond intake were already outstanding champions of an Afrikaner revival in their particular fields. In bringing them together the Broederbond welded them into a tightly-knit elite corps which set the pace for the next 30 years and eventually assumed control of the Party when the Malan generation finally left the scene. The personal loyalties forged in underground struggle between Verwoerd, Meyer, Diederichs, Dönges, Hertzog, van Rhijn, Swart and Strydom goes some way to explain their later predominance over the NP.

THE EXTRA-PARLIAMENTARY OFFENSIVE

Attention has been focused in the preceding pages on the Broederbond's intervention into the party political arena; but this was only one of the many fields in which it now began to operate. The 'Calvinist world outlook' called for activity in every field; and the flame of Nationalism had to be kept alive in areas outside Parliament, particularly in universities and the church. It was through the Broederbond's network of extra-parliamentary bodies like the FAK, the Calvinist Bond, the Voortrekkers and the ANS, rather than the GNP itself, that the impressive Nationalist upsurge of the 1930s was mobilised. The NP eventually reaped the electoral rewards, but it was the extra-parliamentary struggle which proved decisive in the long run, and it was the Broederbond that planted and cultivated the seedlings.

Characteristically, the first moves were made in the field of youth and education. In 1934 a Congress on Christian National Education was held, the first major gathering on Afrikaans education since 1918. The Congress praised the old banner of CNE by demanding the 'group principle', which gave Protestant Calvinist parents 'the first say over who teaches their children and what they teach' rather than the state. Bearing in mind that Afrikaners were a 'baptised nation', it argued that the 'spirit and direction' of all education should be Christian-National. Afrikaans parents were urged to form local CNE associations to act as watchdogs over schools.[8] Professor J.A. du Plessis, of Potchefstroom, was elected Chairman of the campaign committee. Other members were J. du Toit, a member of the 1902 CNE movement, J. Chris Coetzee and F. Postma, all of Potchefstroom.[9]

Despite the Committee's zeal the movement developed slowly, possibly because of an excessive emphasis on religious dogma, which smacked perhaps of heavy-handed clericalism at the expense of Nationalism. In any event, the campaign for religiously-oriented schools was quickly merged into the movement for single-medium Afrikaans Nationalist schools which became a popular rallying cry. Nevertheless, CNE remained a strong issue in the *platteland* and the CNE movement steadily gained strength, culminating in the formation of the FAK-sponsored Institute for Education and Training in 1939.

Two important youth organisations were established under Broederbond auspices. The first was the students' organisation, the Afrikaanse Nasionale Studentebond. In April 1933 a conference of student militants from the universities of Pretoria, Potchefstroom and the OFS decided to break away from the integrationist National Union of South African Students (NUSAS) which had been founded in 1924. The split paralleled the growing split between Nationalist die-hards and fusionists in politics; it was not only a rejection of the 'liberalism' of NUSAS, but also of Hertzog's concept of co-operation between the two white groups at all levels. Meeting at Potchefstroom, the 200 delegates decided to form a new all-Afrikaans student movement. The leading figure within this project was Dr N. Diederichs of the University College of the OFS, and a future Chairman of the AB. The full extent of Broederbond involvement is revealed in the list of conference speakers which included J.C. van Rooy, L.J. du Plessis, C.J.H. de Wet and G. Cronje, a sociology lecturer at Pretoria University, who represented the pro-Nazi Dietse Studentbond. Other brethren or future brethren who attended included J.D. du Toit, G. Dekker, D.F. Malherbe and Theo Wassenaar.

In October 1933 a further preliminary conference was held in Bloemfontein where representatives of the northern universities persuaded the more tolerant Stellenbosch University in the Cape to complete the exodus from NUSAS. The chairman of this meeting was P.J. Meyer, a dynamic young OFS Nationalist leader who became Deputy Secretary of the FAK in 1935 and a leading figure in the Broederbond. The chief speaker was Dr D.F. Malan, who delivered an address on 'Nationalism as Life Outlook'.

Under Dr Diederich's chairmanship, the founding conference of the ANS adopted a constitution in April 1934. It asserted that: 'The Bond rests on a Protestant-Christian and cultural nationalism basis and acknowledges the leadership of God in the sphere of culture as in every other sphere of life concerning the Afrikaans peoples' traditions as embodied in history.'[10] Like all the other Broederbond satellites the ANS, under the guidance of Diederichs and Meyer, duly affiliated to the FAK. The ANS quickly developed into a powerful youth base for Republicanism, sometimes outdoing the NP in militancy.

At the same time the Broederbond's theologians helped to launch the Federation of Calvinist Student Associations (FCSV) in August 1933. Formed at the Volks-Festival to celebrate the Bible's translation into Afrikaans, the FCSV linked Potchefstroom's 'Korps Veritas Vincet' and Stellenbosch's Calvinist Student Society into the core of a prospective country-wide network of student bodies. This was based on the Three Formulae of Unity (the Canons of Dort, Netherlands Confession and Heidelberg Catechism) and sought to 'defend Calvinist principles in science, in the greater student community and society'. They also planned to issue popular scientific works by DRC theologians, and sponsored *Koers in Die Krisis* (*Faith in the Crisis*), an important anthology of Christian-National essays published in 1934. The Reverend J.D. Vorster, brother of the future Prime Minister, was joint editor of this work together with H. Stoker.

A major step forward on the education front was Potchefstroom's attainment of full university status in 1933 with the right to impose a restrictive confessional test on students and staff. The victory for confessionalism was dwarfed by a spectacular Christian-Nationalist breakthrough, the publication of the Bible in Afrikaans, 60 years after the idea was first mooted by Pannevis, the pioneer Cape cultural nationalist. It was issued, somewhat ironically, under the aegis of the British and Overseas Bible Society which, 60 years earlier, had refused to translate the Scriptures into a 'dialect'. This dialect had, however, not only survived the hazard of Anglicisation; it was now an official tongue. The publication of an Afrikaans Bible was almost as important a stimulus for Afrikaner Nationalism as the appearance of vernacular bibles had been for the nascent European nationalisms whose rise coincided with the Reformation.[11]

In 1944 I.M. Lombard claimed that the AB had been 'instrumental in having the Bible translated into Afrikaans'.[12] The board of translators included J.D. du Toit and J.D. Kestell, while its secretary was L.J. du Plessis. Van der Merwe also played a prominent role. A stalwart of the Calvinist Bond, J.A. du Plessis of Potchefstroom University, hailed the translation as a 'milestone in the struggle for the rights and the use of our tongue in Church and household worship, and a sign of victory in the yet uncompleted struggle for these rights and their public use'.[13] It was both a striking cultural victory and the fulfilment of a deep need within the *volk*.

In 1932 the Broederbond initiated the first of a series of all-Afrikaans 'cultural' bodies amongst different sectors of the Civil Service. The function of these bodies was to organise Afrikaans civil servants into a separate bloc at the point of employment. A group of founder brethren, led by H.J. Klopper and including D.H.C. du Plessis and J.E. Reeler, established the ATKV, the Afrikaans Language and Cultural Association. This Union-wide association of railway officials was 'cultural' in the same broad sense as the FAK to which it was affiliated. Objectives included the maintenance of the Afrikaans language and the cultural enrichment of members. There was also a study loan and death fund. But the orientation was 'Christian-National', and its allegiance was to the Broederbond line of purified Nationalism.[14] H.J. Klopper was elected Chairman in 1933 and was instrumental in getting the ATKV to sponsor the climactic Nationalist manifestations of the 1930s: the Voortrekker celebrations of 1938.

The Broederbond now began to mobilise an assault on the economic front and to rectify 'the backwardness of the Afrikaner in the economic field'.[15] Brethren – or brethren-to-be – played a leading part in the 1934 Poor White Congress which was called on the DRC's initiative to deal with the shattering revelation that there were 300000 whites living in poverty. W. Nicol, Broederbond founder, was Chairman, Malan delivered a keynote address, and Verwoerd was Chairman of the committee dealing with the sociological aspects of poor whiteism. Later, Verwoerd recalled that his efforts to implement the conference decisions 'led me to one conclusion: the plight of my people cannot be remedied except by political machinery'.[16]

However, the AB was not preoccupied with poverty as such; the 300000 poor whites were viewed as a further manifestation of the same forces which thwarted the rising bourgeoisie: that is, the relative poverty of Afrikaners compared to English speakers. Not surprisingly, much of the Broederbond's thinking revolved around possibilities of a radical redistribution of wealth between the whites, using the techniques of nationalisation and socialisation of the means of production and distribution. It is highly significant that Dr Malan blamed the poor white problem on 'world capitalism which produced the paradox of over-production and poverty and unemployment'. Was it not significant that Russia, which had 'broken with the capitalist system' was the only country free from unemployment the world's economic depression? Malan attacked capitalism because 'it is based upon self-interst and the right of the strongest'. It was a doomed system.[17]

Verwoerd, too, admitted that 'radical changes such as nationalis-ation of the mining industry or the reorganisation of South Africa as a socialist state' were possible solutions.[18] However, the tragic sufferings of poor whites demanded practical first aid measures which could be carried out at once. Another indication of the drift of Broederbond economic thinking was du Plessis' sharp attack on the system of 'economic individualism'. The plague of Afrikaner poverty would not be exorcised by doctoring South Africa's economy. Drastic political and economic changes were necessary: 'The reason [for Afrikaner poverty] is the fact that our constitutional and economic authorities are British oriented so that they have an actual or apparent interest in Afrikaner helplessness in economic respects, and partly that our national and scientific tradition is that of economic individualism.'[19]

The Broederbond's response was that 'something should be done to cultivate a little place for Afrikanerdom in the business and industrial world': in other words, to develop an indigenous Afrikaner capitalism. In fact, this amounted to a decision to strengthen the rich rather than to lighten the lot of the poor. As a result, Volkskas, the first-ever Afrikaans bank, was set up by a 'small group' of brethren in April 1934. According to Lombard in 1944, 'Volkskas was established purely under AB auspices and the AB still hold control of Volkskas today.'[20] Among its founders were L.J. du Plessis, Chairman of the Board of Directors, and J.J. Bosman, a Transvaal businessman, its Manager-in-Chief. Bosman described Volkskas as 'the first pure Afrikaans bank – grown out of our own soil [bodem]' and contrasted its *volks*-basis with that of the English banks 'which are merely out for profits'.[21] Designed to break the monopoly of the two great English banks, Barclays and Standard,

Volkskas developed into a cornerstone of the new Afrikaans financial structure and one of the major South African banks.

THE IDEOLOGICAL COUNTER-OFFENSIVE

Since the arrival of Jan Van Riebeeck at the Cape in 1652, Calvinism has permeated Afrikaner culture and thought patterns: it has always provided the four walls within which other conceptual systems have evolved; it was the cradle in which Nationalism was born; it provided the lens through which Afrikaners saw their own awakened race-consciousness. The Afrikaners are a Christian nation in a more profound sense than the nineteenth- or twentieth-century Hollanders, and more so than any other twentieth-century Protestant people. Irreligion, atheism, liberalism and humanism were virtually non-existent. In Kruger's South African Republic secular political struggles for power were often fought out in religious terms, as in seventeenth-century Holland. In the twentieth century, the DRC was able to mount a powerful counter-attack against the forces of urban secularisation and the new secular religions. Potchefstroom was the spearhead, but it is important to remember that all the constituent churches in the DRC also engaged in the fight to maintain the Afrikaner's religious heritage. This explains why NGK leaders outside Potchefstroom, like Dr Kestell and Dr van der Merwe, were so active in the Kristelike-Nasionale Bond. It also accounts for the Broederbond's religious-confessional character: as the protector of a threatened Afrikaner culture, the AB also automatically defended the Afrikaner's religious heritage.

The doctrine of Christian-Nationalism crystallised an unwritten folk or popular ideology, an informal and unsystematised network of orientations and sentiments. Christian-Nationalist ideologists isolated and coupled together similar elements in both Calvinism and Nationalism, welding them into a unified system. To Calvinism's aristocratic and elitist elements, expressed in the notion of election, they married the Afrikaners' sense of racial superiority, their consciousness of being superior biological–ethnic beings, and their claim to constitute a *Herrenvolk*; to Calvinism's strict divisions between believers and heathen, elect and damned, they attached the Afrikaner's rigid insistence upon the colour bar; to Calvin's teachings of predeterminism and vocation they linked the nation's sense of mission and destiny.

This formal marriage of Afrikanerdom's twin folk traditions integrated the two most dynamic strains within Afrikaner life and resolved the points of tension between them. It reconciled Calvinism's universalism with Nationalism's particularism, Calvinism's all-inclusive evangelicism as against Nationalism's exclusivism. More importantly, the new doctrine wove these strains into a single, coherent and optimistic world outlook. It presented Afrikaners with an overall world view which cast them in a significant role in the scheme of things, gave them self-respect in the present, pride in their past and faith in their future. By depicting the *volk* as having been planted in South Africa as a special instrument in the divine master-plan it became meaningful, and indeed a privilege and honour, to belong to a nation with a mandate to transform Southern Africa. Christian-Nationalism brought a high degree of integration to Afrikaner behaviour. Acts of religious piety became political acts; the political struggle became a religious cause; national salvation, in a Republic, was equated with religious salvation. Finally, Christian-Nationalism freed Afrikaners of doubt over their destiny and, by calling on them in God's name to realise a Republic, released a flood of Afrikaner energy and justified their national existence in religious, ethical and historical terms.

The new doctrine captured the imagination of the Afrikaner masses by giving them meaning, community, status, hope and self-respect. It responded to the yearnings of a confused, disoriented, fragmented and uprooted Afrikaner nation then in the midst of the difficult economic, social and psychological transition from *platteland* to city. Not only did it link them spiritually with the Voortrekker rural ethos, but it also evoked a spirit of Afrikaner community and camaraderie in the cosmopolitan and anonymous cities. In the ideological struggle against the politics of compromise, racial tolerance and liberalism, Christian-Nationalism gave an emphatic Calvinist answer, and also asserted a credible and uniquely Afrikaner counter-position to the new twentieth-century doctrines of socialism and Fascism. It gave the Afrikaner intelligentsia a compass point and frame of reference for finding their bearings in a sea of conflicting ideologies. Christian-Nationalism forged a shield against the assault of new ideas. Now Afrikaner intellectuals could confront liberalism with a powerful counter-ideology which was rooted in God and in Afrikaner history, but also linked, by natural affinity and specific concepts, with the challenging totalitarian and authoritarian Fascist movements that were sweeping liberal ideas and structures from the face of Europe.

In the final resort Christian-Nationalism's authority rested on the fact that its principles and philosophy were embodied in the giant institutional network of which the Broederbond was the nerve centre. The Broederbond injected Christian-Nationalist ideas into the arteries of Nationalism. This ideological diffusion was carried out not only by individual brethren, but also by the organisations sponsored or controlled by the Broederbond.

The first shots in the Christian-Nationalist onslaught came – as might be expected – from Potchefstroom, where a group, including two Broederbond Executive members, launched the journal *Koers* as a theoretical forum for expounding the Christian-National position on all questions, from politics to agriculture. Despite Potchefstroom provenance, *Koers* could be regarded as the most important theoretical journal for the development and propagation of Christian-Nationalism, and it sheds important light on this strand of Broederbond activity for the next 20 years. Contributors were not confined to Potchefstroom professors but included individuals outside the GK, such as N.J. van der Merwe, P.J. Meyer, H. Verwoerd, H. Strauss and D.J. Vorster, most of whom are known to be Broederbond members, *Koers* was not, however, the only mouthpiece for Christian-Nationalist ideas: these were expounded in books and speeches by brethren who, within the framework of Christian-Nationalism, often displayed differences of opinion in the practical application of the doctrines. While the Broederbond ensured a broad unanimity on fundamental tenets, goals and strategy, it seems to have permitted, within defined limits, a variety of interpretations which endowed the doctrine with suppleness and flexibility in the rapidly changing climate of the 1930s.

Just as Calvinism kept an open mind towards new ideas, boldly incorporating 'moments of truth which belonged to God' from other systems, so, too, was Christian-Nationalism highly receptive to new concepts generated by the rise of totalitarian movements. Indeed, one of the chief tensions within Christian-Nationalism was the pull of past versus present, and the struggle of activists – like du Plessis, Meyer, Vorster and Diederichs – to inject new contemporary concepts into the system, originating in seventeenth-century Holland and embodied in the practice of Kruger's nineteenth-century Republic. On the one hand, there were narrow traditionalists like J.A. du Plessis, whose Calvinism was completely rooted in the sixteenth and seventeenth centuries, whose model was the Voortrekkers, and who insisted on upholding the 'ways of our fathers'. Into this group fell figures like Kestell, who pleaded for faithfulness to the creed in its frozen ancestral form. On the other hand, there were younger men, inspired by the highly aware, self-critical, flexible dynamism of Kuyper, who saw that Calvinism could only influence the contemporary world by boldly challenging all new ideas. This involved exposure, struggle and, sometimes, adaptation.

Deeply sympathetic to the new conservative radicalisms, the latter group opened up the gates of the 'Nationalist' part of Christian-Nationalism, to admit new doctrines of *volk*, nation, culture, state, government and society. This, however, led to more divisions of views within the Christian-Nationalist camp over the extent to which Nazi-Fascist ideas – which deified Nation and State – could be reconciled with Calvinism's cardinal insistence on a single divine absolute. The debate over Nazi-Fascism reflected a deeper and permanent paradox inherent in Christian-Nationalism, arising out of its worship of both the nation and God. By designating the nation as God's instrument, the Calvinists only disguised the conflict. Worship of God and worship of nation were equated; but in practice, the result was a glorification, an idolisation, of nation.

As nation-worshippers, the Christian-Nationalists were intuitively and ideologically drawn to Nazi-Fascism. But the totalitarian nationalisms were not, like Afrikaner nationalism, founded on a religious base: their inspiration was essentially secular, Mussolini being a socialist and Hitler a National Socialist. Consequently the Nazi-Fascist deification of nation and state was stark, absolute and uncompromising, asserting the subordination of church to state, a feature which became more pronounced as time went on. Towards the late 1930s this began to pose problems for Christian-Nationalism, dividing those who leaned more towards estatist–totalitarian–racist nationalism from those who leaned towards Calvinism. It brought the doctrine's inherent schizophrenia to the surface. Even the pro-Nazi Calvinists, like du Plessis and Stoker, were divided over the limits of Calvinism's alliance with Nazism; to the former, who took the broadest possible view of Calvinism, there seemed no contradictions, but Stoker, though interned during the war for pro-Nazi activities, stated firmly that Calvinists could not accept that part of Nazi-Fascism which set up rival idols. These differences, although theoretically profound, did not weaken the unity of Christian-Nationalists on practical questions. Nevertheless it is important to bear in mind that the doctrine was by no means monolithic.

Coinciding with the reconstruction of the NP and the foundation of an extra-parliamentary corporate-style network was an intense ideological offensive against fusion. The chief impetus came from Potchefstroom University, where the spirits of Kruger's Republic and Kuyper's Christian-National idea flourished. It was from their work that the Broederbond drew the Christian-Nationalist concepts which gave status and significance to 'Purified' Nationalism. We turn now to an examination of Potchefstroom's contributions to the development of the Broederbond's creed.

The journal *Koers* was founded in June 1933 and it soon became the most authoritative theoretical organ of Christian-Nationalism. Its founders were the Broederbond Chairman J.C. van Rooy; J. Chris Coetzee, the most influential protagonist of CNE; A.H. van der Walt, Potchefstroom's Professor of History; and D.J. van Rooy. This group, most of whom probably belonged to the AB, were later joined by L.J. du Plessis. *Koers* replaced the more narrowly Calvinist *Wagtoring*, a quarterly devoted to 'propagating in the various fields of life, the principles of the Holy Scriptures according to Calvinism', which was edited by C.J.H. de Wet. The new editorial board promised that *Koers* would remain faithful to the basis of its predecessor, namely the 'Holy Scriptures'. It would appear more frequently and cover a greater variety of topics.[22] The new name (which translates as Faith, Spirit or Direction) better expressed their aim than the defensive-sounding *Wagtoring*. Although de Wet claimed that the change was merely organisational, in fact the new journal was more aggressive and far-reaching in tone and object. In its first statement of policy *Koers* declared: 'We live in a time of disturbing confusion [*onsettende verwarring*] and lack of direction [*koersloosheid*]'. And it stated the editors' wish to attempt, 'to the best of their abilities and with all due modesty [*beskeidenheid*] to provide direction in the various fields of our nation's life, in the light of the principles of God's Holy Revelation, as well as in the light of our own Christian volks-past'.[23]

Koers attempted to formulate the Christian-Nationalist position on 'all questions and events of the day'. Articles dealt with philosophy, economics, literature, social questions, education theology, agriculture and race relations. For many years L.J. du Plessis contributed a Christian-Nationalist analysis of domestic and international politics. Although the bulk of the contributors were either Potchefstroom professors or belonged to the GK, it was not a narrow denominational organ. Members of both the NGK and the

NHK, such as D.F. Erasmus, J.D. Vorster, P.J. Meyer, H.J. Strauss, J. van Wyk de Vries and D. Dekker, wrote for it as proponents of Christian-Nationalism.

The first major attempt to present a wall-to-wall exposition of Christian-Nationalist policy was *Koers in die Krisis*, a collection of essays edited by H. Stoker of Potchefstroom University and F.J.M. Potgieter of Stellenbosch University. It was published in 1935 by the FCSV.[24] This theoretical work was virtually an encyclopaedia of Christian-Nationalist ideas and revealed the Christian-Nationalist determination to apply 'the Calvinist world and life outlook' to all spheres of life. The book was divided into eight sections: Calvinism, the Bible, the Church, Theology, Culture, Education, Society, and World Views and Theories. The contributors included many distinguished Afrikaner theologians and politicians as well as Dutch writers such as A.A. van Schelven, a Fascist in 1940, and V. Hepp, a Nazi sympathiser throughout the war.

Introducing the book, Dr J.D. Kestell wrote: 'The aim . . . is . . . to honour and uphold the great spiritual orientation which we inherited from our fathers. The danger exists of our volk being detached from the precious heritage bequeathed by our ancestors.' But the aim was not purely to conserve the Afrikaner's religious heritage, *Koers in die Krisis* sought to provide a compass point in the confusions generated by the 1930s' economic depression, urbanisation, secularisation and fusion.

The editors warned that:

Afrikanerdom . . . being overwhelmed by un-Biblical cultural streams and hypnotised by alien cultural products [was] beginning to be unfaithful to the creed of our forefathers: Geus, Huguenot and Voortrekker. Our volk is in the throes of a crisis, in a confusion of spirit, and is suffocated by the streams of unbelief – particularly due to ignorance. This collected work will help throw up a dam against the foreign currents which suffocate us, by indicating the direction revealed by God's Word. Organised action is necessary to deliver our volk, through knowledge, from the banishment of modernism, liberalism, humanism, evolutionism and other foreign tyrannies.[25]

To this the editors add that the book's chief aim was 'to conquer a place [for God] in the volk's heart and to help unite all Calvinists in our country, whatever their church, province or profession, for common Calvinist action'. The time was ripe for a Calvinist revival, based on a development and reapplication of Calvinism's sixteenth-century principles to contemporary conditions. Calvinism could not remain stationary because it was 'a dynamic and developing life force'. The editors therefore called for 'a struggle as never before against the foes of the Christian faith in South Africa, in all circles, for the glory of God'. This struggle would also be fought in the political life but would not identify itself with party politics.

The editors of *Koers* paid special tribute to H. Kuyper and Amsterdam's Free University and expressed gratitude for the work which its teachers and graduates had done for South Africa. Professor Kuyper sent a message on behalf of Holland's Calvinists expressing pleasure at the growth of new ties 'not only of language and blood, but also of common religious convictions which bind us so closely to our brother-volk in South Africa'. He welcomed the book as a clear-cut expression of the application of Reformed principles to all terrains of life, and an important contribution to world Calvinism.[26]

Underlying Holland's support for the Afrikaner's ideological offensive Colijn, the Prime Minister of the Netherlands and leader of the ARP, gave his official blessing to the book. In a special foreword he stressed that 'universality' was one of Calvinism's most prominent characteristics. It knew no territorial limits and was not confined to a particular sphere of life. The whole of national life had to be brought under the dominion of its fundamental concepts.[27] Another token of Dutch support which, *inter alia*, reassured the Afrikaners that racial discrimination was compatible with Calvinism, came from G. Besselaar. Pointing out that variety was the defining characteristic of God's work, he said that Calvinism had inevitably developed differing national types. Nations differed but did not lose their identity on turning to God any more than individuals did. The Reformed creed was everywhere the same in basis and principle, but there were differences in its appearance according to the differing national problems confronting different nations. Thus the policy of segregation was a Calvinist answer to a problem with which other nations did not have to cope.[28]

Although *Koers* appeared at a critical moment in the birth of a new type of Afrikaner Nationalism, it was also linked with an international Calvinist revival directed from Amsterdam. This partly explains world-wide messages of support from ultra-Calvinist movements elsewhere and also the fierce, if somewhat irrelevant, attacks on theological phenomena (Pantheism, Methodism, Humanism), which were real threats to Holland's Reformed Churches but which had little, if any, influence within the ultra-conservative climate of the three South African DRCs. The Kuyperian tone of the book is set by J.D. du Toit in the opening article, entitled 'Some of the Basic Principles of Calvinism'. Here du Toit argues that all Calvinists have a fixed calling to keep their creed powerful in every field, that the Calvinist world view is superior to all others – whether in the ecclesiastical or the secular fields – and that in politics Calvinists had a special duty to ensure that 'the Word of God must light the way ahead'. In effect, du Toit is asking here for confessional-type politics as formulated by Kuyper, who is quoted extensively throughout.

The scope of the writings in *Koers* is extremely broad and there is not the space here to give an adequate account of them. A theme which recurs constantly is the need to anchor Afrikaner politics on a confessional foundation as were the nineteenth-century politics of the Voortrekkers. But Calvinism is also seen as a dynamic, modern force, a system capable of being developed to confront the twentieth-century ideologies of Nazism, Fascism, liberalism and communism. While all the authors hold to a common set of Kuyperian-Calvinist beliefs, there are early signs of a division of opinion over the challenging right-wing totalitarians in Europe. Professor van der Walt and J.D. Vorster clearly regard Nazism (race worship), Fascism (state worship) and the dictator principle (man worship) as idolatry. On the other hand, L.J. du Plessis proposes that the future Afrikaner dominated Christian-National Republic should be authoritarian and, in its early stages at least, a dictatorship. He finds in Calvinism's rejection of the 'dogma of the will of the people' fertile soil for cultivating an anti-democratic system. Yet we shall see that despite these differences all three joined the pro-Nazi OB in the 1940s.

5 General Hertzog's Attack on the Afrikaner Broederbond

In 1933 a crisis arose in the AB as a result of the fusion between General Hertzog and Smuts. In 1935 an even greater crisis arose when General Hertzog openly attacked the AB.

(I.M. Lombard, Chief Secretary of the AB, 1943)

The South African public first learned of the Broederbond's existence when the Prime Minister, General Hertzog, tore aside its mask in a sensational and vehement exposé on 7 November 1935. His attack ranks as one of the most sensational speeches in South African political history, and shook both the Broederbond and the infant GNP to their foundations. But it could not have been totally unexpected: echoes of the upheaval caused by fusion in Broederbond ranks had inevitably reached Hertzog's ears. Like future crises in the Broederbond, news of this one filtered through to the external world, and the secret organisation was to learn that internal purges, small though they might be, tended to weaken security and discipline. Moreover, Hertzog had betrayed anxiety over the Broederbond's growing power in a passing reference to it at the OFS United Party Congress a month or two earlier. He warned delegates that the Broederbond had outgrown its original role and that it had become an 'important political instrument in the hands of purified politicians'.[1] In spite of its beaver-like activity in nearly every OFS town and village few of the United Party's rank and file knew anything about the secret society. Indeed, only an extremely small group of people even knew of its existence.

Encouraged by his right-hand man, Nikolaas Havenga (the Minister of Finance), Hertzog decided to make public the contents of explosive confidential documents disclosing a secret connection between the AB and the GNP. They included the organisation's Constitution, rules, the 1934 New Year Circular and a conference report, and were generously amplified by a wealth of background material such as the identity of brethren. The source was probably a pro-fusionist dissident within the Broederbond and possibly an

MP. None of the facts in this material were questioned by the Broederbond or the GNP, although the disclosures were grievously damaging and provoked a grave crisis within the organisation.

Hertzog began by attacking Malan, van der Merwe and their 'schismatic followers' for causing a breach which was 'tearing the Afrikaner people right to the depths'.[2] Malan, he said, was motivated by a feeling of ill-will and racial prejudice towards the English speakers, over whom the dissidents wished to 'rule and to domineer' instead of co-operating on a basis of equality. Hertzog went on to explain why Malan had 'changed so suddenly from a supporter to an opponent of Afrikaner national unity'. His recruitment by the Broederbond since Coalition meant that he was now obliged 'to discard the policy of national unity with the inclusion of the English-speaking Afrikaner' and 'to enter the road of national disunity and disagreement'.

Hertzog levelled three principal charges against the Broederbond. First, he drew attention to the 'close relation' between the GNP and the Broederbond. 'The leaders and the leading spirits of the one are the leaders and leading spirits of the other', he said, and went on to name many of the national and provincial leaders of the GNP. 'There is no doubt that the secret Broederbond is nothing else but the purified Nationalist Party, secretly busy underground, and that the purified Nationalist Party is, as the secret Afrikaner Broederbond, carrying on its activities above ground.' In a perceptive reference to the Broederbond's Christian-Nationalist Republican character, Hertzog exclaimed: 'Between the two, the unity of Afrikanerdom is exchanged for a Republican–Calvinistic Bond!'

Second, Hertzog alleged that whereas the Broederbond originated in 1918 as a purely cultural and non-political society 'with the praiseworthy object of caring for and watching over the cultural needs of Dutch-speaking Afrikanerdom', it had entered the political arena and embraced the cause of Afrikaner domination. He quoted statements from 'the two Potchefstroom teachers' in the Broederbond's leadership, L.J. du Plessis and J.C. van Rooy, to show that the organisation's target was political power. He noted that the Bond had recruited heavily since 1932 within the GNP leadership, though not a single prominent United Party member had been admitted. As a direct result the Broederbond 'has been misused for purposes and objects for which it was never intended', and was driving non-Nationalists into protest. Attacking Afrikaner Jingo self-glorification and the 'mad, fatal idea' that some 'are the chosen of the gods to rule over others', Hertzog said that neither the English speakers nor the Afrikaans speakers would ever succeed in dominating the other. Again, he singled out 'Potchefstroom fanaticism' for reviving issues which split Afrikanerdom and could lead to its downfall.

Third, Hertzog claimed that teachers within the Broederbond – who comprised a third of the society's membership – were misusing their positions to indoctrinate schoolchildren against the English speakers. Worse, brethren were probably misusing secrecy to further each other's interests in appointments and promotions in the Civil Service to the detriment of non-brethren. As an example of its deceit, Hertzog accused the Broederbond of having secretly arranged for telegrams to be showered on practically all MPs from their constituencies in order to pressurise Parliament into a specific course of action. This amounted to a falsification of public opinion and constituted a further abuse of secrecy for political advantages.

Thus, from the materials at his disposal, Hertzog sketched a pen-portrait of the secret society which conforms in essentials to later disclosures about the Broederbond, particularly in 1944 and 1963.[3] The picture he painted was of a small, exceptionally active, stringently secretive, fanatical and exclusive elite, aiming at a Republic and Afrikaner domination, with cells in most towns and villages, and tirelessly pursuing a vendetta against fusion. He claimed that the Bond and the GNP were 'one and the same body, functioning in two different compartments – the one above, the other under the ground'. He revealed that the Broederbond was composed of a large number of intellectuals, especially teachers, that it was inspired by 'Potchefstroom fanaticism' and by the ideal of a Calvinist Republic. It had acquired control of the GNP and a network of important organisations in the cultural, youth, and religious fields.

According to I.M. Lombard's 1943 account, Hertzog's attack precipitated a crisis within the AB. A special congress was called to consider the Prime Minister's charges. The Broederbond could afford to take its time, but Dr Malan and the NP, embroiled in party politics, were obliged to respond immediately to this shattering attempt to discredit them. At Victoria West on 15 November Malan admitted that he had recently joined the 2000 members of the organisation. He asserted that the Broederbond was nothing more than a non-political Afrikaans association which sought 'to uplift the Afrikaners, just as do numbers of other organisations, each in its own sphere'. The Bond had performed very good work during its 17 years of existence. Moreover, he claimed that it was 'utterly untrue that only Nationalists have joined the Broederbond since coalition'.

Malan argued that Hertzog's 'tirade' was directed not at the Broederbond but against himself. He rejected Hertzog's charge of race hatred, saying, 'We have not yet called the Union Jack, as he has done, a stinking rag, or named Afrikaans-speakers [in the United Party] as traitors and people without soul.' Malan drew attention to his earlier insistence that the coming Republic would assure equal rights for both languages, despite the objections of 'a small section of Afrikanerdom' to such a guarantee. He suggested that Hertzog's deeper motive was to pave the way for the Dominion Party's affiliation to the fusionists in order to unite all English speakers against Afrikaners.

On the same day the Transvaal leader of the NP, J.G. Strydom, also replied to Hertzog's accusations. He defended the AB and denied that it was a political body. Neither was it politically partisan, he continued, since many followers of Hertzog could be counted among the ranks of brethren. While Strydom neither admitted nor denied his membership, the gist of his remarks (particularly in regard to the Broederbond's nature and composition) conveyed the impression that he belonged to the society.

Such was the dramatic impact of Hertzog's onslaught that even the AB's Executive fleetingly lowered its secrecy. For the first time in the organisation's history a Broederbond Chairman issued a press statement. This took the form of a curt five-line disclaimer by J.C. van Rooy to the Johannesburg *Star* in which he denied that the Broederbond was anti-British or anti-English, let alone political. Hertzog's attack, he claimed, had been motivated by ulterior party political ends.

It is significant that while Malan, Strydom and van Rooy disputed Hertzog's interpretation of Broederbond policy, none challenged the authenticity of his documents or description of the Broederbond's constitution and neither did any of the 13 politicians named by Hertzog deny their membership. The AB's special congress did not issue any public statement, but instead sent the Chairman, J.C. van Rooy, to see Hertzog privately. At a meeting between the two in March 1936, van Rooy attempted to persuade the angry Premier that the Broederbond was merely continuing the work which he himself had started and that its activities were in no way harmful.[4]

Van Rooy mollified Hertzog by reporting that the Broederbond had agreed to two substantial concessions: first, that it would abandon its 'secret character', and second, that future Executive Committees would be constituted from members of both the United and the Purified Parties.[5]

On the strength of these gratifying assurances Hertzog promised not to listen to further anti-Broederbond allegations. In a letter to van Rooy on 10 June 1936, referring to the promise that the Bond's secret character had been abandoned and other proposed changes, the General stated that his grounds for complaint had now fallen away and he wished the Broederbond well for the future. Hertzog said he was completely convinced that the Bond had shed its secrecy.[6] This letter was subsequently used by defenders of the Broederbond to prove that Hertzog changed his view of the Bond, ignoring the fact that he wrote it under a total misapprehension.

Whether van Rooy deliberately misled the Premier, or whether the Broederbond decided to surface but later changed its mind, is not known. There is, however, no evidence by the Broederbond of any attempt either to shed its secrecy or to water down its extreme Nationalism. On the contrary, the period between 1936 and 1942 was one of redoubled and extensive clandestine activity. It resulted in the emergence of a powerful Nationalist movement which finally smashed the United Party and drove Hertzog into the political wilderness.

EXPANSION AND CONSOLIDATION, 1936-7

How much damage Hertzog's attack wrought one cannot tell. According to Vatcher 'a number of his followers resigned from the AB'.[7] Whatever the effects, the steady progress in building a monolithic Christian-National empire continued. The year 1937 was a year of expansion and consolidation. It saw a further diversification of Broederbond interests, the appearance of more brethren in key positions and a proliferation of the activities of Broederbond-controlled bodies such as the FAK (to which more than 300 organisations were now affiliated).[8] The year 1937 also saw new efforts to consolidate *volk* and Bible; important steps were taken to 'Afrikanerise' worship, and the DRC called on Afrikanerdom to celebrate 'Bible Year'. Dr Verwoerd, the former Stellenbosch professor, emerged as a leading personality with his appointment as first editor of *Die Transvaler*.

During this period the FAK moved to the centre of the extra-parliamentary stage by significantly broadening its executive to incorporate representatives of the DRC. It also established effective machinery for top-level co-ordination of an accelerated Nationalist effort in the cultural, religious and economic spheres. The administrative secretariat was enlarged to include Dr P.J. Meyer, a young OFS intellectual, who became Assistant Secretary to Lombard. In 1936 the FAK set up an extended Executive Committee, the ANK, as a broad executive organ representing 25 important Union-wide and provincial organisations. This was headed by the FAK Chairman, Dr N.J. van der Merwe, and incorporated the existing FAK Executive. The council included representatives from the three DRCs, the ATKV, the various provincial Vrouevereenigings (women's organisations), teacher organisations, the three Helpmekaar organisations and the Voortrekkers. The formation of the ANK marked the greatest measure of formal co-ordination of cultural, religious, trade and economic bodies in Afrikanerdom's history. It was a practical expression of the AB's preoccupation with unity and organisational coherence.

Addressing the 1937 FAK Congress, Dr van der Merwe said: 'The Federation is out to unite all Afrikaners of all political parties in the cultural struggle.'[9] The Congress reportedly resolved to support united Afrikaner fronts in every sphere (such as agriculture, public service and industry) and to encourage the formation of separate Afrikaner bodies in all fields. The word 'cultural' was interpreted in a very broad sense, implying that members of the FAK had a duty to carry their cultural struggle into the political arena. It was decided to give active support to the Afrikaner Bond of Mineworkers in its struggle against the Mine Workers' Union, and its blessing to Dr Albert Hertzog's organisation for the creation of Christian-National trade unions. Delegates pledged the FAK to fight all manifestations of communism. The Broederbond-sponsored campaign to make 'Die Stem van Suid Afrika' the official national anthem was also approved. Van der Merwe said that an interpretation of C.J. Langenhoven's words would be prepared 'so that persons who do not understand Afrikaans but want to identify themselves with us will at least understand what we are singing'.

Commenting on the 1937 Congress, a report in the *RDM* said that the FAK had 'ceased to be a cultural body and has set itself the larger task of creating an Afrikaner bloc in the public life of the country . . . Its aim is to create a separate Afrikaans organisation for every activity in which Afrikaans-speaking people are engaged. It will not be satisfied until it has established a United Front of Afrikaners'. The report concluded: 'A year ago, General Hertzog foreshadowed this development. It has now come to pass, and a new era of bitterness has dawned upon South Africa.'[10]

Not content with establishing a network of exclusively Afrikaner businesses, brethren now launched a powerful campaign to draw Afrikaner workers into ethnic Christian-Nationalist trade unions. The key figure was the barrister son of the Prime Minister, Dr Albert Hertzog, who abandoned his legal practice to spread Nationalism among the Witwatersrand's industrial workers. In this he was supported by T.E. Dönges, the Cape barrister, and L.J. du Plessis, the newly-appointed Chairman of the two-year-old Volkskas. In October 1936 a National Council of Trustees was formed 'to rescue the Afrikaner miners from the evil materialistic influences of the Witwatersrand', and Dr Hertzog was appointed Chairman. An energetic drive was launched to draw Afrikaners 'into Christian-National workers' organisations' (on the lines of the Spoorbond) especially in the mining and textile industries.

Dr Hertzog's first venture was the Afrikaner Bond of Mine Workers, which was launched in April 1937. It was a confessional cultural/class body which intended incorporating Afrikaner workers 'into the life of the volk and encouraging its members to remain faithful to the Afrikaner's cultural and religious traditions'. According to Dr Dönges, communism was trying to 'capture the Afrikaner worker' and to awaken a class struggle. Although communism was ostensibly hostile to capitalism it had, from the Afrikaner Nationalist point of view, joined hands with capitalism 'to root out the Afrikaner's soul and to detach the Afrikaner worker from his people and religion'.[11] All Afrikaners, regardless of party, had to close ranks to fight the threat made to their unity by trade unions and communism. One of the chief objects of the new worker's movement, therefore, was to free Afrikaners from the corrosive effects of trade unions with their internationalist outlook, either by creating exclusively *Nationalist* unions or by capturing control from within and reforming their policies along Nationalist lines.

An excellent summary of what may be taken as the AB's reasons for launching a Christian-National attack on trade unions is given by L.J. du Plessis in *Koers* of 1937.[12] Implicit in this attack is a total rejection of international socialism, with its blurring of national, linguistic, colour, race and cultural lines, and its insistence that class (rather than nation) is the primary human grouping. Yet the Christian-Nationalists did not wholly reject socialism; rather, they nationalised it, producing a doctrine of Afrikaner national socialism which envisaged a redistribution of control and ownership of the means of production and distribution, in which all wealth was vested in the hands of Afrikaners whose organs and leaders would exercise it for the good of the *volk* as a whole rather than in the pursuit of private profits.

An important ideological intervention of this period was the publication of Diederichs' book, *Nationalism as Life Outlook and its Relationship to Internationalism*, in 1936.[13] This work was one of the most important pioneer attempts to express the Christian-National doctrine. Its most striking characteristics are the adoption of the Nazi concepts of 'Volks-staat' and 'Totales-volk', but the rejection of blood and race as the chief criteria of the nation. Born in Ladybrand in 1903, Diederichs was educated at Grey College where he was influenced by Malherbe and Kestell. Later he studied in Berlin, Munich and Keulen in Germany, and at the Rijks University in Leiden, where he gained his doctorate in 1929.

In *Nationalism as Life Outlook* Diederichs begins by arguing that people are spiritual beings whose task is to create culture and ideal values. Only by transcending their lower, animal nature do people really become people and realise their true calling. This personal calling can only be fulfilled within the context of the nation. Although he does not use the term 'organic', Diederichs seems to regard humankind's relation to nation in biological as well as spiritual terms. Nevertheless, he does not adopt the Nazi view that race is the essence of nation, which he sees principally as a spiritual–cultural entity. Like the Nazis, on the other hand, he holds the nation to be the pinnacle of social life and most total of human units. 'Of all groupings of people, the nation is the highest, the most all-embracing, the most total group. In this human world, there is nothing higher than the nation.'[14]

Diederichs specifically rejects the proposition that a blood relationship or common ethnic descent was the essential ingredient of a nation. Such a test of nationality betrays the spirit to the flesh, it makes the nation into a biological group 'and reduces it to the level of the bestial'.[15] For, if descent was the highest yardstick, then other animals would qualify as nations too. As in Nazi theory,

Diederichs subscribes to the concept of the 'Volk-State'. The state, and indeed the government, are servants (*dienskneg*) of the nation. He rejects, by implication, the Fascist view that the state is primary and unlimited in its scope. For Diederichs, the state is merely a juridical organisation to create conditions for the nation to realise its spiritual ends.[16]

Here Diederichs parts company with Nazi theory, especially as it developed in the latter part of the 1930s, by firmly insisting on the religious basis of Nationalism and the idea that the nation is an institution of God himself.

> God willed that there should be nations, thereby to raise the richness and beauty of his creation. Just as He decided that no deadly uniformity should rule nature, but that it should display a richness and variety of plants and animals, sounds and colours, forms and figures, just so has he willed the existence in the human sphere of a diversity of nations, languages and cultures. And just as the plenitude [*veelheid*] of sounds enhances a melody's beauty and the plenitude of colours enhances a painting's beauty, so too the heterogenous [*bont*] pluriformity of nations, languages and cultures enhances the wonderfulness and richness of His creation.[17]

Of all the characteristics of Nationalism, the most important is its religious anchorage. Nationalism, says Diederichs, is necessarily religious because it regards every nation as the product of the Highest Creator, and 'destined to fulfil a calling and contribute a portion to the realisation of the Divinely-determined purpose of universe'. Stripped of this purpose, the nation's existence would be without sense or meaning.[18] Nowhere in this book does the term 'Christian-National' appear, but it was none the less a major contribution to the developing doctrine. Perhaps its greatest importance lay in its appearance outside the Transvaal, reflecting the rapid spread of Christian-National ideas throughout Afrikanerdom. Although Diederichs was not a direct product of the Transvaal's neo-Calvinists, he came into contact with Potchefstroom ideas in 1933 while helping to establish the Broederbond-sponsored Afrikaans Studentebond.

In October 1937 the GNP launched a new daily newspaper in the Transvaal, the power centre of South African politics. Whereas the Broederbond was at its strongest in this region, the NP was weak, having only one MP, J.G. Strydom, at the time of its formation.

With control of *Die Burger* in the Cape Province and *Die Volksblad* in the OFS, the Nationalists were obviously making a bid to capture the important remaining sector of the Afrikaans-reading public. Two years earlier, on the initiative of Cape Nationalists, a country-wide fund was launched for the establishment of a daily newspaper in the north. This resulted in the setting up of a company, the Voortrekker Pers, to publish and print *Die Transvaler*. According to its articles of association, the newspaper would 'help interpret and fulfil the general principles of the National Party . . . to plead for the establishment of a free republic on Christian-National foundations'.[19] Dr Verwoerd was appointed Editor of *Die Transvaler* in 1936 and resigned his Stellenbosch professorship in sociology.

Die Transvaler added significantly to the AB and Christian-Nationalist control over the Afrikaans media. The original board contained at least three brethren – Malan, van der Merwe and Strydom – and the contents of the first issue followed Christian-National patterns of interest. L.J. du Plessis wrote on 'The Asiatic Flood in South Africa', Strydom's contribution dealt with 'The Maintenance of White Civilisation', Verwoerd wrote on 'The Jewish Question', and from a Potchefstroom lecturer came a piece headed 'Liberalism carries Germs of Future Disaster – Leads only to a levelling of natural differences – Creates dangerous friction regarding Jewish Questions'.[20] Through its editors the Broederbond now controlled at least two of the three existing Nationalist daily newspapers.

THE VOORTREKKER CELEBRATIONS OF 1938

As the centenary of the Great Trek approached, a number of important works appeared from the pens of Afrikaner historians of the Voortrekkers, with particular reference to their colour policies.[21] These represented an attempt to rewrite history from an Afrikaner viewpoint, and to give Afrikaners pride in their past. They not only corrected the anti-Afrikaner bias in British histories, but also delineated the Trekkers as heroes. Finally, they also sought to show that the Voortrekker standpoint demanded the strictest segregation.

The conception and organisation of the Voortrekker centenary celebrations was one of the Broederbond's greatest successes. By linking contemporary Christian-Nationalism with the heroic

Voortrekker ethos, Broederbond activists gave a historical legitimacy to the new doctrine and helped to entrench it as a popular mass basis of reawakened purified Nationalism. The celebrations, in which all sections of Afrikanerdom joined, were an exercise in self-identification; the Afrikaners rediscovered their past and were led to discover that the Trek, which had formed the nation, was an archetypal Christian-National experience. To understand why it is necessary to examine briefly the elements of that historical event.

The so-called Great Trek was an emigration of some 12 000 frontiersmen, largely in protest against the British colonial regime's attempts to implement a policy of extending certain civic rights and liberties to non-whites. This policy, which was rooted in the thought-streams released by the French Revolution and encouraged by philanthropic missionaries, brushed aside the colour bar as an absolute guiding principle in legal, religious and, to some extent, in political matters. Frontier anger had been aroused by the decisions to grant legal rights to 'Hottentots' in 1828, and to free slaves in 1834, which were backed by a special court known disparagingly as the 'Black Circuit'. This court helped to enforce the new pattern of colour, political, labour and property relations, and invited complaints from aggrieved black servants against their white masters.

The Trek was therefore a response to the assault on the traditional principle of a white monopoly of political power, property and prestige, access to all of which was reserved exclusively for whites. In certain respects the British regime had placed blacks on a footing of equality with whites. This threatened to undermine the foundations of white privilege and superiority. White hegemony rested in the ultimate resort on superior technology and fire-power, but its generally accepted principle was the legislative colour bar which followed the lines of black and white, conquerors and conquered, and also paralleled the lines of class and property. Nevertheless the forces that produced the Trek were not new, having been latent in the eighteenth century and the twilight years of Dutch colonial rule. These included: a desire for self-rule and constitutional independence from European metropolitan powers; land hunger and the drift into the interior; insistence on white Christian privilege (coupled with a conviction that white hegemony was divinely blessed); as well as opposition to any extension of political and economic rights to blacks and the evangelistic activities of missionaries.

In ideological terms the Trek was the first shot of a lengthy conflict between two world views, one originating in the French

Revolution (and held largely by English speakers, particularly missionaries), the other based on seventeenth-century Dutch Colonial Calvinism (and epitomised in the Boer claim to Christian hegemony). The Trek's enduring significance lay in creating conditions for the birth of Afrikaners as a separate entity, divorced from Europe both in its British and Dutch colonial incarnations. It was a deliberate act of auto-emancipation: out of the Trek flowered separate institutions which embodied the Boer identity, outlook and way of life, consolidated an autonomous Afrikaner nationality, and led to the nineteenth-century awakening of Afrikaner Nationalism.

In an attempt to justify their departure to the hostile Cape DRC and those Afrikaners who remained under colonial rule, the Boers dovetailed two of the chief elements of their culture (ethnocentrist racialism and Calvinism) into an expression of scriptural or confessionally-based Nationalism. This found its highest expression in their claim to be a 'chosen people'.[22] There is weighty evidence to show that, since the time of Van Riebeeck, Dutch settlers viewed their society, the universe and their relation with blacks through scriptural lenses. By an act of self-separation they isolated themselves, and also their doctrine, from the colonial Cape. In the process they turned to Calvinism, their only ideological code, to furnish moral authority and a conceptual explanation for their actions.

Viewing themselves in biblical metaphors, the Trekkers drew a parallel between themselves and Israel's flight from Egyptian servitude to the freedom of the Promised Land. Their analogy was false and pretentious. Frontiersmen had not been opposed by a British pharoah, but were emigrating in protest against the partial liberation of non-whites from white oppression and enslavement, whereas the genuine Hebrews were fugitives from actual slavery. The important point is, however, that the Boers drew on the Bible for their concepts, norms and analogies. Testifying to the extreme extent to which they believed their myth were place-names like Bethlehem, Nylstroom, Land of Goshen and Golgotha.

If one were to choose the moment when the idea that the Afrikaners were a chosen or covenanted people took place, one could pinpoint the Battle of Blood River in 1838 which was the central event of the Trek. As recounted earlier, the Boers entered into a symbolic contract with God to remain eternally faithful and to observe the battle day as a sabbath for eternity, if they were granted victory. The triumph of their arms over the Zulu impis convinced the Trekkers that God had intervened on their behalf, thereby signifying His acceptance of their contract. Henceforth, the Afrikaners saw themselves as a covenanted and blessed people, an instrument in God's hand. This theocratic tendency was formally embodied in the constitutions of the Boer Republics, which obliged the state to observe the creeds of the DRC and to acknowledge the DRC as the national church. This theocratic tendency persisted through to the end of the Boer Republics when, just prior to the Boer capitulation at Vereeniging in 1902, we read of guerrilla generals debating in their tents the answer God required them to give to Lord Kitchener's peace terms. Thus the Voortrekkers represented, and the nineteenth century embodied, the basic elements of what later came to be known as Christian-Nationalism.

The concept of a vast Voortrekker commemoration culminating in the unveiling of the Voortrekker monument in Pretoria probably originated with the Broederbond. It was conceived by the FAK and executed by its subsidiary, the ATKV. In 1931 the FAK's central executive decided to establish a permanent Voortrekker memorial in Pretoria to coincide with the projected celebrations in Pretoria in 1938. Two bodies, both established by the Broederbond, were set up to deal with the monument's erection and celebrations: namely, the National Volksmonument Committee and the Central Centenary Festival Committee. E.G. Jansen was Chairman of both.[23] The idea of ceremoniously re-enacting the whole trek originated in the fertile brain of Henning Klopper, Chairman of the ATKV, who had begun to collect materials for the project as early as 1926. In 1933 he proposed that the ATKV should organise a symbolic trek, following the original route from the Cape to Pretoria. He was made chairman of the appointments committee.

In July 1938 stinkwood replicas of the old covered wagons left Mossell Bay on their laborious five-month journey to Pretoria. Dressed in Voortrekker garb Klopper, as ATKV Chairman, was leader of this trek. As they slowly wound their way northwards the wagons attracted great attention. At every step the symbolic Trekkers were greeted by a mounted guard of men in Voortrekker beards and costume, and members of the Voortrekker (boy scout) movement. Meetings would be held recounting Trekker exploits in that area and stressing the significance of the historical event. An estimated 10 000–12 000 people gathered nightly at hundreds of meetings throughout the country.[24]

The Hertzog government contributed to the cost of the monument and gave a cautious semi-official blessing to the symbolic Trek.

Oswald Pirow, Minister of Railways, and J.H. Conradie, the Cape Administrator, attended the departure ceremony in Cape Town. But, in an obvious snub, Hertzog was not invited to the monument, the platforms being monopolised by Nationalists (one of whom was the opposition leader, D.F. Malan). Of the 37 major contributions and addresses listed in the official record of the Trek, at least 16 were brethren. Speakers at local celebrations also included a high percentage of Broederbonders.

Nearly all the speakers dealt with the same themes. Most of the speeches ran to a set pattern: they stressed the Voortrekkers' religious and God-fearing outlook; their heroism and daring; their colour consciousness, pride in blood purity and refusal to intermarry; their Republicanism and their pioneering efforts to open up South Africa for white civilisation. From the speeches emerged a new hero – the Voortrekker – as a romantic figure filling the centre of the historical stage: man of God, conqueror of the heathen, trailblazer for civilisation. Curiously, the festivities were held not in 1936, but in 1938, and were thus linked to the Battle of Blood River, with its undertones of Afrikanerdom's special covenant with God and the confrontation of colour. Often they drew parallels between 1838 and the challenges facing Afrikanerdom in 1938.

A fairly typical address was that delivered by Dr H.F. Verwoerd at the local celebration in Middelburg, Transvaal. He said that the ox-wagon stood for the 'heroic period of the Afrikaner's history' and 'created the opportunity for the manifestation of national consciousness, fatherhood-love, honouring of heroes'. The Trek threw up heroic figures like Piet Retief, Andries Pretorius, Hendrik Potgieter and Sarel Cilliers, who imprinted themselves on the *volk*'s memory and whose example roused energy for service to the nation.[25] Verwoerd claimed that the message from the ox-wagon of the past was religion, unity, freedom, constitutional independence and white trusteeship. Like other speakers, he translated these concerns into a contemporary idiom, pointing to the existence of 300 000 poor whites, constituting nearly one-quarter of the Afrikaner *volk*:

> Is the message not that we must take possession of the heritage [*erwe*] of our forefathers? Afrikanerise the cities, and take a legitimate place in commerce and industry. This task must not be undertaken in pursuit of profits, which is the conventional goal, but to bring our compatriots to independence in the new [urban] circles of life.[26]

Thus Verwoerd stressed that the Voortrekker spirit had to be translated into deeds. It should mean the total upliftment of the impoverished part of Afrikanerdom by the Trek's acceptance of the city and the business world: the trek to economic independence of the volk.[27]

As the above quotation suggests, the celebrations were not just an orgy of nostalgia or a return to the past and a turning away from the future. Indeed contemporary challenges, particularly that of poverty, dominated most speeches. Nearly all speakers placed the commemoration in the context of a Second Great Trek into the cities. 'The Trek', said J.H. Conradie, the Cape Administrator, 'is no longer over our borders but within them – from the platteland to the cities'.[28] Likewise, L.J. du Plessis said that the wagons were a symbol of the Second Great Trek. The Afrikaners controlled the veld; now the cities, dominated by foreigners, had also to be made Afrikaans. The Afrikaners had to become employers rather than employees.[29]

Just as the 1836 Great Trek marked a turning point in the first awakening of Afrikaner Nationalism, so did its commemoration in 1938 mark the start of an upswing of the fortunes of purified Nationalism. Whereas the year 1838 validated the viability of a distinct Afrikaner nationality in the interior, so the year 1938 saw the revival of Afrikaner self-consciousness in an urban context. The celebrations were a brilliant success, lifting the Nationalist struggle to an entirely new plane and marking the start of the Broederbond's real ascendance over the Afrikaner masses. They released an upsurge of Nationalist feeling, a sense of solidarity, a yearning for unity, pride in a heroic Afrikaner past and hope for the future, based on a renewed belief in the *volk*'s divinely-willed destiny. They boosted Nationalist sentiment to a new militant level and generated a spectacular country-wide resurgence which swept Dr Malan's NP to power a decade later. Held against the background of the Broederbond's preoccupation with the Afrikaner's economic backlog and Afrikaner disunity, the celebrations yielded two important positive developments: the formation of the economic-Nationalist RDB movement and the OB, a mass extra-parliamentary movement designed to keep alive Voortrekker ideals and to consolidate the unity manifested at the 1838 celebrations.

THE RDB

One of the highlights of the 1938 celebrations was a dramatic plea from the Reverend J.D. Kestell for aid for the Afrikaner 'poor whites'. He urged the celebrants to translate their new-found sense of fellowship into concrete acts of solidarity and to honour the Voortrekkers by uplifting their descendants who had sunk into poverty. Like Totius, the octogenerian Kestell was a *volksvader* – a patriarchal father of his people – and one of the best-loved figures in Afrikanerdom. During the Anglo–Boer War he was chaplain to the Republican forces and had distinguished himself by tending wounded Boers under heavy gunfire. On account of his exceptional bravery a town was named after him in 1905. A prolific writer of plays, historical books and pamphlets, Kestell was the moving spirit in having the Bible translated into Afrikaans and was, until his death, a member of the Translation Board. Like Totius, he was a spiritual figure in a prophetic cast, deeply respected by Afrikaners of all parties.

Kestell was the father of the RDB movement which, literally translated, means 'savings deed'. The essence of this concept was that, rather than having poor Afrikaners dependent on state aid, their more prosperous compatriots should be responsible for their salvation, thereby saving the *volk* as a whole. Welcoming the wagons when they passed Bloemfontein in October 1938, Kestell repeated his call for a vast nation-wide fund for the poor based on the principle of mutual help, co-operation and unity. As a result of his dramatic initiative, *reddingsdaad* committees spread up throughout the country with a target of £500 000. Support for the charitable movement spread like wildfire: it had become the tangible expression of the *volk*'s concern for its poor, of solidarity between prosperous and impoverished.

The immediate success of Kestell's call was related to the growing anxiety of Afrikaners over the impoverishment of a large section of the *volk*. Afrikaners were the poorer of the two white groups. Control of the means of production and distribution lay almost entirely in the hands of English speakers, who dominated mining, finance, industry and commerce. As a nation of farmers, the Boers had not participated in the opening, exploitation and development of diamonds and gold, although they controlled the political machinery of the two Boer Republics. President Kruger's attempts to exclude the economically-dominant *uitlanders* (foreigners) from political power had generated an internal struggle which crystallised in the Anglo–Boer War of 1899–1902. Britain's victory confirmed British control of the economic resources of the OFS and the Transvaal and gave them the political power denied by Kruger.

Afrikaner poverty predated the war: bad methods of farming and the traditional sub-division of farms had produced a class of poor *bywoners* (squatters or share-croppers) and a landless proletariat. Rural and urban impoverishment was already a growing problem in the closing years of Kruger's Republic. Defeat emphasised Afrikaner poverty. Lacking industrial or clerical skills, the Boer peasants experienced great difficulty in adapting to industrial society in the face of competition from cheaper black wage labour and qualified English-speaking immigrants. During the first and second decades of the twentieth century the NP had courted the votes of these elements, demanding a curb on subsidised foreign immigration, more aid for the poor and a strict industrial colour bar. The grave extent of poor whiteism was dramatically revealed in 1932 when the Carnegie Commission estimated their numbers at 300 000. Poverty threatened the cohesion of the nation. Kestell's warning that no nation could survive with so many lost souls in its midst was a reference to the loss of cultural and spiritual identity among poor whites.

In 1934 Afrikanerdom's religious and cultural leaders called a Poor White Conference. The Chairman was Dr W. Nicol, and among the 400 delegates Dr Malan and Dr Verwoerd were especially prominent. Malan argued that the poor white problem was partly rooted in world capitalism which had produced the paradox of overproduction, poverty and unemployment. He found it significant that Russia was the only country without unemployment during the recent world depression, whereas suffering and unemployment had reached unparalleled heights in the USA where capitalism 'reached its highest perfection'. Malan predicted that the capitalist system was doomed. In a hint to Afrikaners to consider the possibilities of a socialist system, he warned that South Africa would have to formulate 'a correct and new adaptation' to the new developments.[30]

In 1937 the FAK set up a special commission 'to investigate the Afrikaner's economic conditions which formed the background to his cultural development' and to formulate plans for the Afrikaner 'to achieve his rights in this field'. As an ostensibly cultural body the FAK justified its interest in economic matters by arguing that Afrikanerdom's cultural life could not grow if the people's energies were drained by the economic struggle against poverty. In 1938 (shortly after Kestell's dramatic appeal) the FAK's National Cultural Council approved plans to launch an economic struggle and to hold an economic Volkskongres. Kestell's *Reddingsdaad* movement was now taken over by the FAK and a national Board of Trustees (of whom at least four out of ten were Broederbond members) was set up to administer the funds. The FAK indicated that these monies should be held in trust pending the Volkskongres decisions. Meanwhile, a 22-man preparatory committee was set up to organise the congress. Again, known brethren were prominent and formed a majority. Held in October 1939 under the patronage of Father Kestell, the Volkskongres was completely dominated by Nationalists and may therefore be considered to have been virtually an AB achievement.[31]

Of the 19 addresses at least eight came from brethren. Dr Nicol delivered the Chairman's address; Dr J. Van Rensburg (the Administrator of the OFS) and Dr N.J. van der Merwe made the opening speeches. L.J. du Plessis spoke on 'The Aim of our Economic Struggle'; Dr Dönges dealt with 'The Mobilisation of the Capital and Savings Power of the Afrikaner'; Dirk Mostert outlined the principles of savings organisations; Dr Verwoerd dealt with consumer societies; Dr Hertzog spoke on labour organisation; C.G.W. Schumann analysed the Afrikaner's 'capital power'; G.E.N. Ross traced the role of Afrikaners in the factory system; and J.J. Bosman explained the principles of the co-operative shop. Other speakers covered every aspect of the economic struggle from People's Banks to agricultural co-operatives.

All the speakers presented detailed draft proposals which were incorporated into conference decisions. In sum, they constituted a battle plan for an all-out Afrikaner assault on the 'foreign elements' who controlled wealth with the object of gaining control of the means of production, distribution and exchange. In essence, the Volkskongres established the machinery for the Afrikaner's total mobilisation in the economic field. Through a series of interlocking executives the FAK controlled this machinery. M.S. Louw later described the relationship of this network as a family one: the FAK was the grandmother, the Economic Institute was the mother, and the RDB the daughter.

As a direct result of the 1939 Volkskongres an Economic Institute was established in order to implement the conference decisions. This Institute became the general staff of the whole economic movement, co-ordinating and initiating a vast field of operations, while also acting as the link between its subsidiary economic organisations and the FAK. One of the first tasks of the Economic Institute was to reorganise the Reddingsdaadfonds. Whereas Kestell had envisaged a straightforward charitable relief fund, it now assumed a totally new role as a treasury for developing the tools of capitalism. The Institute drew up a new constitution for the Reddingsdaadfonds and appointed trustees. It launched a fresh country-wide campaign to raise capital. Donations, subscriptions and voluntary taxes were collected from rich and poor: even Afrikaans schools were asked to contribute a monthly sixpence per child. The fund grew rapidly at first. After the first year a sum of £20000 had been raised, with outstanding promises of £100000, but in the end the fund fell far short of its £500000 target. Its object were abstract and removed from immediate bread-and-butter concerns; the emotional and practical rewards of giving were meagre.[32]

The 1939 Congress had decided to establish 'one great volksorganisation, Christian-National in its basis' as an all-embracing body to carry out the functions of savings, leisure-time and consumer organisations. Thus, in February 1940, the RDB was set up by the Economic Institute. Its role was to mobilise the Afrikaner masses and to implement the decisions of the Economic Institute. The Executive Committee consisted of a full-time organisation leader, Dr N. Diederichs, three members nominated by the FAK, three nominated by the Broederbond's annual congress, and two specially co-opted members. The Bond's activities were sub-divided into cultural, economic, farmers', women's, thrift, and labour sections. Of its profits, 50 per cent went to the Reddingsdaadfonds, 25 per cent to the FAK and 25 per cent to national causes as decided by the Executive Committee. By the end of the first year the RDB had established 130 branches.[33]

The 1939 Volkskongres had decided to organise the Afrikaner labour force in such a way that it could be purposefully incorporated into the life of the *volk* and could inject Christian-National principles into the worker organisations. In 1937 the membership of white trade unions was 223537. Of these, an estimated 80 per cent were Afrikaners (namely, 186830), although the leadership was largely English speaking. Of those Afrikaners who had risen to leading positions in the movement, some – like Joanna Cornelius, Hester Cornelius, L.J. Scheepers, Piet Erasmus and Piet Huyser – had renounced Nationalism in favour of a class analysis of society. It was in order to rescue Afrikaner workers from the clutches of a new anti-Nationalist ideology and movement that leading brethren, including company directors, turned their attention to the reorganisation of workers on Nationalist lines.

Addressing the Volkskongres Dr Albert Hertzog called for the mobilisation of Afrikaner workers to smash the death grip of the foreign capitalists over Afrikanerdom. He saw the struggle in terms of an Afrikaner proletariat against a combination of an English proletariat and capitalism. Hertzog alleged that the vast majority of trade union secretaries were 'bitterly hostile to Afrikanerdom' and 'prevented the Afrikaner from coming into his own'. He claimed that the 'overseas capitalist' had a tacit agreement with the 'overseas trade union secretary' to keep the workers quiet and to thwart unreasonable demands.

The 1939 Volkskongres laid stress on the need to develop Afrikaner mutual aid and thrift organisations. A Consumers' Division of the RDB was established which worked in close collaboration with a Traders' Society, consisting of storekeepers approved of by the RDB. All branches of the Consumer Societies were encouraged to trade with Afrikaners and 'favourably disposed' undertakings. Congress also called for 'the organisation of the savings power of the Afrikaner and the use of his capital to the strengthening of his share in commerce and industry in South Africa'. The Economic Institute authorised the publication of an Afrikaans Buyers' Guide (in whose preparation Dr Verwoerd had played a prominent part). Containing the names and addresses of more than 1 000 RDB-approved businesses, it was sent free to 100 000 specially selected Afrikaans families.[34]

Perhaps the most remarkable decision of the 1939 Congress was the establishment of a finance company, as proposed by M.S. Louw. The delegates described this as the 'most effective plan for the use of Afrikaner capital to advance the Afrikaners' positions in our country's commerce and industry'.[35] Louw suggested that the new company be called Sentrale Volksbeleggings Beperk, but its name was changed to the Federale Volksbeleggings Beperk (Federal Volks Investments). The immediate aim was to persuade Afrikaners (who between them had some £80–100 million invested in 'un-Afrikaans institutions' such as banks, insurance companies, building societies and trust companies) to transfer their funds to the new company. Launched with a share capital of £300 000, Federale Volksbeleggings offered 100 000 cumulative preference shares at £1 each. Two

Afrikaans companies, SANLAM and SASBANK (both of which were already lnked to the Nationalist movement) underwrote 55 000 cumulative preference shares; 25 000 were retained by the Reddingsdaadfonds, and various private bodies applied for the rest.[36]

In an illuminating policy statement on 5 September 1940, SANLAM publicly pledged support for the economic movement.

> Twenty two years ago SANLAM came into being as a practical expression of that long felt desire for an Afrikaans business venture – for enterprises run by Afrikaners for Afrikaners to help themselves. Through its successful growth SANLAM has proved that this development is a sound one – the Afrikaner can help himself! That success has given the Afrikaner new courage and inspiration for the task that lies ahead. Thankful for the opportunity it has had in the past 22 years of acting as a preliminary reddingsdaad movement, SANLAM now directs its best wishes to those who have tackled this great national question with renewed vigour.[37]

Dr P.J. Meyer depicted Federale Volksbeleggings as an instrument which, unlike other banks, would not enrich a handful of directors but would shower benefits on all facets of Afrikanerdom, including the workers. The large profits accruing from the venture would flow back to Afrikanerdom; by creating new businesses, it would make the Afrikaner the employer of his fellow Afrikaner; the future atmosphere in which the Afrikaners would work would be an atmosphere created and directed by fellow Afrikaners.[38]

In 1941 the Economic Institute decided to establish a body 'to protect the whole Afrikaans business community' and 'to act on behalf of the Afrikaner in commerce and industry'. At a conference of businessmen in August 1942 in Bloemfontein the Afrikaanse Handelsinstituut (Afrikaans Chamber of Commerce) was set up to encourage and direct the development of Afrikaner business undertakings. Its constitution provided for the 'closest possible cooperation with the Reddingsdaadbond', which nominated four of the eleven executive members. The Handelsinstituut's official organ was a monthly journal, *Die Volkshandel*, with J.G. van der Merwe as Managing Director and Piet Meyer as Editorial Secretary. An idea of the subjects treated can be formed from the following titles of articles: 'Establishment of Industries on the Platteland'; 'Continuation of the Economic National Conference'; 'The Afrikaner

Cause – First'; 'Co-operative Movement and the National Struggle'; 'Solution of the Poor White Question'; 'Afrikaner Business Progress at Bethel'; and 'Consumers' Division of the Reddingsdaadbond'.

An offshoot of the RDB movement was the Kopersbond wholesale company which set out to be a central supplier for Afrikaner commercial enterprises, especially the smaller ones. Sponsored by the Economic Institute and set up with a capital of £100 000, its business motto was 'Food for the little ones' and the trade mark depicted an eagle sitting over a frightened looking rabbit. Advertisements recalled how the Rochdale pioneers established the co-operative movement in Great Britain, from which Afrikaners should learn the lesson that 'one channel' purchasing was essential as a way of giving small businesses control over wholesale businesses.

The launching of the RDB completed the trilogy of Broederbond-sponsored or front organisations (the other two being the FAK and the GNP). Brethren now held the reins on the cultural, political and economic battle-fronts. The economic movement was an attempt to weld all Afrikaners, regardless of class, into a single economic unit devoted to increasing Afrikaner wealth. embracing industrial workers, small shopkeepers, farmer co-operatives and rich capitalists, the RDB was a supra-class organisation. Significantly, its leaders were largely Nationalist intellectuals who recognised the necessity of winning economic power in order to promote the wider goal of Afrikaner power.

A curious feature of the movement was its anti-capitalism, expressed forcefully by L.J. du Plessis and Dr Hertzog at the 1939 Volkskongres. This, it is important to note, was a critique of 'foreign British-Jewish capitalism' rather than a fundamental rejection of the system itself. No conference speaker advocated socialism or nationalisation. Indeed M.S. Louw, the outstanding financial brain of Afrikanerdom, bluntly stated the need to 'use the technique of capitalism . . . [to] spearhead the struggle which lies ahead to assure the Afrikaner of his just share in the commerce and industry of our land'.[39] Underlying the RDB was the notion of a 'people's capitalism' or Nationalist capitalism. The stress on mass participation in the creation of Afrikaner business, the accent on co-operative movement techniques, the pledge that all Afrikaner businesses would serve the *volk* and the denunciation of selfish profit seeking were all attempts to distinguish the movement from conventional British capitalism.

In practice, the RDB movement gave a powerful boost to the creation of an Afrikaner capitalism. Indeed, it was directly responsible for the establishment of a great number of important and highly successful institutions whose growth rate was accelerated by mass support generated by RDB members. Its businesses did not differ outwardly from their English-speaking counterparts except in their open appeals to Nationalist sentiment and their backing by a movement which urged people to 'buy Afrikaans' as a holy duty. One distinguishing feature was the fact that most of the directors of new businesses were Broederbond politicians or intellectuals, who entered the field of capitalism just as they had entered the fields of culture and politics in order to engage an enemy, but not because they were intuitively drawn by their natural vocations into these areas.

Later, however, a class of genuine Afrikaner entrepreneurs arose, and the pseudo-capitalists disappeared from the scene to devote their energies to the political Republican struggle. But to them, and the Broederbond in particular, credit must go for launching the movement. When Dr Kestell died in 1941 his original Reddingsdaad idea had been transformed out of all recognition. He had urged a poor relief fund: instead there had developed a movement to enrich the emergent bourgeoisie and to launch Afrikaner capitalism. He had urged a movement above politics: instead, the Reddingsdaad had become the economic wing of the NP. He had blamed the Afrikaners themselves for their poverty; instead the Reddingsdaad accused 'British-Jewish capitalism' and 'foreign exploiters' for villainously victimising the *volk*. By diverting attention from dead-end charity and articulating the powerful, if latent, class interests of the Afrikaner capitalist, shopkeeper and worker, and conscripting these in the cause of Nationalism, the AB had raised Nationalism to a new level of awareness.

6 Christian-Nationalist Colour Policy in the 1930s and the Impact of Totalitarian Thought

Dr Verwoerd's introduction of the policy of separate territorial development in 1959 represented a revolutionary departure from the traditional principle of horizontal apartheid. The switch to vertical apartheid (with its promise of black self-government) was certainly an innovation as far as the NP was concerned; but the concept of separate Bantu homelands was neither new nor was it Dr Verwoerd's own brainchild. As we noted earlier, its outlines were first sketched in the 1928 Dingaan's Day pamphlet and subsequently developed during the 1930s as part of the Broederbond's ideological counter-offensive to fusion. The concept of separate development was shaped by four major Christian-Nationalist ideas:

1. God creates all national, cultural, linguistic and ethnic groups and desires them to retain their peculiar characteristics;
2. variety is the hallmark of creation;
3. black Africans have a special role in God's master-plan;
4. the Afrikaner's task was not to 'Europeanise' Africans and so rob them of their ancestral culture, but to 'Christian-Nationalise' the inner norms and values of that culture.

The idea of developing separate homelands was designed to stem the flow of African labour into the cities where they competed with poor white; but it also asserted the right of Africans to cultural autonomy, and to that extent regarded them as a fellow nation in God's sense. Christian-Nationalist colour policy therefore accorded Africans a divine origin with the proviso that they were chosen to serve, not to rule. The doctrine showed little 'Christian' concern for the suffering imposed by the system of apartheid, and magnified the gap between Africans and whites both horizontally and vertically. It was evolved against the background of rapid African urbanisation, the rise of liberalism (centred on Witwatersrand University) and parliamentary controversy over a consistent and just 'solution to the Native problem'.

In October 1933 L.J. du Plessis wrote in *Koers* that race differences were often dismissed as merely differences of skin-colour and hair. He maintained that a disturbing movement in favour of equality was developing which claimed that the salient differences between people were due to civilisation, not race. This 'un-South African' view held that all races were amenable to civilisation and that people should be treated equally regardless of race. Liberals even went so far as to assert that there was 'a Christian duty to make them [Africans] equal by education, upliftment and so forth'. For du Plessis the 'typically' Afrikaner position was that racial group differences had to be honoured and that 'natives' should 'fill a lower position than the whites because, as a group, they are in no sense fitted for equality'. Admitting that black people were human beings who could become civilised and Christian, nevertheless 'the kaffir . . . always remains a kaffir, that is to say, different from the White man and obviously inferior to the White man'. For du Plessis, the idea of Christian unity was 'compatible with the sharpest differences and inequalities (as for example between master and slave)' because it represented an invisible union of faith in Christ and did not demand the abolition of practical differences.[1]

This essay by du Plessis plainly finds horizontal apartheid and an unequal distribution of power and rights to be compatible with religion. It amounts, in effect, to a scriptural justification of the status quo in its most negative form: namely, the permanent servitude and inferiority of black people. Subsequent Christian-National writers on race, particularly those involved in missionary work, evolved a more positive formulation of segregation; a system which would encourage African development within a segregationist framework. Characteristic of this line of thought was the recognition that Africans were a separate, divinely-created nationality in their own right, and that Bantu ethnic units should be transformed into Christian-National entities based on the same confessional-national principles underlying Afrikaner life. In time these ideas came to form the chief justification for the government's Bantustan policy.

A 1934 essay by P.J.S. de Klerk maintained that the 'peculiarities of native life must not be destroyed but sanctified by the Gospel', and that the principle of missionary education was to foster among Africans a sense of their own national worth and consciousness.[2] In de Klerk's plea to strengthen race barriers, freeze cultural differences and thereby prevent the African's acquisition of European skills and technology we can detect the germs of the theory of autonomous development. It represents the first stage of a Christian-National racial policy: namely, that Africans possessed a worthwhile culture of their own.

This line of thought was greatly expanded by the Reverend H. du Plessis in 1935, who asserted that African racial and cultural characteristics had a divine origin and that whites dare not tamper with the Lord's handiwork. The distinctive features of the Bantu people were therefore no accident, but a manifestation of the endless variety created by God. The object of missionary work was to convert nations, not individuals. Racial diversity was divinely ordained and this obliged Christians to preserve Bantu identity, while consecrating it. Indeed, Christianity had to be a bulwark against assimilation, denationalisation and Europeanisation: 'Just as our own Churches preserve us from disintegration, so will the Church of Christ among the Bantu, as maintainer of God's ordinances for the volk's life, be a bulwark against all national dissolution.'[3]

The chief significance of this essay is that it represents an advance on L.J. du Plessis' negative insistence on African inferiority. His namesake, a prominent missionary theologian and also of the GK, bluntly asserts that although Africans are destined to have their own cultural life, wholly different from that of Europeans, nevertheless 'we cannot call them an inferior race'. This notion of separate but equal introduces the second proposition of Christian-National race policy: the creation of autonomous Bantu territorial units. Further contributions to the evolution of a Christian-Nationalist race policy appeared in the first volume of *Koers in die Krisis*, which appeared in January 1935. These writers stressed that God created the black people and gave them a task and calling of their own. Subject to the proviso of white dominance, black people were entitled to all other rights of nationality.

Writing in June 1935, H. du Plessis was the first to propose total segregation as the ultimate Christian-National solution. In a pioneer expression of territorial apartheid, he argued that no middle way existed between the stark alternatives of assimilation or rigid apartheid.[4] His arguments are in line with the 1928 Dingaan's Day pamphlet, and similar to those used by Nationalists from 1959 onwards. Du Plessis starts by reaffirming the Calvinist standpoint that 'the variety of races is biologically and historically determined by God. All peoples are certainly 'of one blood', but God determined everyone's dwelling from the start. We must acknowledge the unity in diversity and attempt to maintain it.' Challenging this view were the 'neo-liberals', who had launched a growing campaign to 'detribalise' Africans, 'to maintain the rights of the individual regardless of the group to which he belongs' and to convert Africans to the ideals of Western civilisation. But the past showed that 'political and economical equality leads inevitably to social equality and to the bastardisation of Whites who sink to the level of the kaffir'. There was a danger that assimilation would lead to black domination. The only Afrikaner-Calvinist alternative was total segregation, and this involved the surrender of white-owned territory for the establishment of separate African homelands.

> We must base ourselves again on proven Calvinist principles and make sacrifices for them . . . there is sufficient ground; all that is necessary is that our volk sacrifice sufficient ground so that [Natives] can be segregated very gradually and in the most practical way . . . Within their own areas, they must develop under White guardianship until, ultimately, after 100, 1,000, or 2,000 years, they can be independent without presenting a danger to us Whites.[5]

L.J. du Plessis struck a balance between radical Christian-Nationalism and the more conventional point of view in 1936 when he defined the object of race policy as being to 'guarantee White domination, and thereby our Afrikaans-Christian civilisation'.[6] Opposing Hertzog's modified Native Bills, which provided for white 'native representatives' in Parliament (as a quid pro quo for the abolition of the Cape African franchise), he said that white mastership necessitated the total elimination of 'native-backed' participation in the Assembly. Coupled with this, however, should be the 'gradual development of native volks-representation as a basis for their self-government under White trusteeship'.

In 1935 the Afrikanerbond vir Rassestudie (Afrikaner Bond for Racial Studies) was founded to carry out scientific research into urgent colour questions and to propose policies. Its Secretary was M.D.C. de Wet Nel, a Transvaal NP organiser, and later Dr Verwoerd's Minister of Bantu Administration and Development. The Chairman was Dr P.J.S. de Klerk of Potchefstroom, and committee members were J.A. Engelbrecht, Professor of Anthropology at Pretoria University, J. van Wyk de Vries and C.W. Prinsloo, then of Pretoria University's Department of Bantu

Languages and later Chief Commissioner for Bantu Affairs. It is likely that most or all of the above were members of the Broederbond.

The programme of the Afrikanerbond vir Rassestudie revealed a preoccupation with urban and industrial issues, listing a series of first aid measures to halt racial integration in the cities. These were entirely negative and discriminatory, paying no attention to African claims for political and economic rights. The development of African culture was urged purely as an antidote to Europeanisation and to maintain maximum social distance. Through its journal, *Rassebakens*, the Bond demanded absolute and consistent segregation. For example, it condemned the DRC member churches for their decision to send delegates to the World Sunday Schools Association's international convention in Durban in 1940 on the grounds that 'Indians, Kaffir and Negroes, etc., etc.' were also present. In South Africa, 'such intimate association can only lead to a blunting of colour feeling', said *Rassebakens*.[7]

In 1941 Dominee J.G. Strydom submitted a plea for a policy of vertical segregation based on the principle that 'the coloured races must obtain their legitimate rights and privileges *apart from the white-man*'. He declared (in an early use of the term) that such a policy could 'best be understood by calling it apartheid'.[8] Thus Strydom rejected two popular current notions: absolute segregation and a 'horizontal dividing line' (a euphemism for naked white domination). The first, he said, was impractical; the second 'unfair and un-Christian', because it permitted the Coloureds to develop only to a certain level. Strydom proposed instead a Christian-National alternative: 'The policy of apartheid as championed by the Afrikanervolk [which] seeks to draw a vertical dividing line so that every race can develop on its own as far as it wishes.' He developed this idea in a strongly Calvinist idiom, asserting that 'everyone is called to preserve his own identity and to develop it. And every volk is obliged to respect and value its uniqueness [*eierdomlike*] and peculiarities [*besondere*].'[9]

Strydom's Christian-National policy of positive apartheid was designed to meet the Afrikaner's religious-ethical norms by promoting a form of national pride among non-whites and giving them opportunities for separate parallel development. Nevertheless, this formulation conceals the presupposition of continued white dominance and exclusive access to power and privilege. While it would be a mistake to underestimate the force of ethical-Calvinist concepts behind his formula, or not to concede that it marks a theoretical advance on horizontal apartheid, the objective is still recognisably the maintenance of white supremacy.

THE POLITICAL IMPACT OF GERMAN NATIONALISM

As the decade of the 1930s drew to a close, the rise of Nazism and Fascism attracted widespread Afrikaner sympathy, especially towards German Nationalism. Close ties with Germany – a parent country of the Afrikaners – went back for 300 years. Names of prominent Nationalists, like Dönges, Pirow, Hertzog, Diederichs and Meyer, betrayed elements of this ancestry. Germany too was a Protestant country, a cradle of the Reformation standing in the same broad religious tradition as Mother Holland. Fraternal political bonds with Germany extended back to Republican times when the Kaiser gave moral support to Kruger's Transvaal and Krupps helped to supply the Staatsartillerie. The fact that imperial Germany had been a rival of the British Empire since the end of the nineteenth century strengthened this sense of kinship. During the Great War an upsurge of pro-German feeling swept sections of Afrikanerdom. This reached a climax with the 1914 Afrikaner rebellion, which was a direct result of the Botha government's decision to invade German South West Africa on behalf of the British Empire. Germany's defeat in 1918 was mourned by many Afrikaners, who saw her as a fellow victim of British imperialism. The crippling Versailles settlement was opposed by all Afrikaners, and even General Smuts, that loyal supporter of Britain, asked the Allies to be lenient to its defeated foe.

The rise of Hitler was fully reported in the Nationalist press, and his accession to power in 1933 aroused the enthusiasm of young Afrikaner intellectuals. When Germany rose phoenix-like from the dust and ashes of defeat to challenge her conquerors, Afrikaner Nationalists began to detect a glimmering possibility of their own liberation from the imposed monarchy. Even the fusionist Premier, General Hertzog, echoed the general Afrikaner mood of sympathy for the struggle of a resurgent Germany. His own support for the Reich probably sprung from his wish to assert, as a matter of principle, South Africa's right to an independent foreign policy; and, also, his equation (in common with many Boer War veterans) of the Treaties of Vereeniging and Versailles. The fact that Hertzog was of German ancestry might also have played a part in shaping his outlook.

Among the Afrikaner Nationalist working class, rank-and-file identification with Nazism showed itself in the formation of the Blackshirts and Greyshirts, both of which were notable for their anti-Semitism. Recognising a potential ally in the Afrikaner Nationalists, in the 1930s the German Foreign Officers established cultural links with the Afrikaners, and began to organise cultural–academic exchanges. A Nazi youth movement expert, Hans Gerlach, helped to start the ANS in 1934 and there made contact with Nico Diederichs and P.J. Meyer, the organisation's Chairman and Secretary respectively.

Young Afrikaner postgraduates generally avoided Britain in favour of Holland. Now many (like Verwoerd and Diederichs) began to take courses in Germany in spite of the language barrier. Promising young Nationalists were invited to attend the Berlin anti-Comintern school. Among them – according to a Military Intelligence report – were T.E. Dönges and P.J. Meyer. Robey Leibbrandt, the champion Springbok boxer, decided to remain in Germany after the 1936 Olympic Games, joined the Wehrmacht and was smuggled into South Africa in a German submarine as a war-time Nazi agent in June 1941. Perhaps the most important convert to Nazism was a rising star in Afrikaner politics, Hans van Rensburg. A protégé of Pirow, former Secretary of Justice and the OFS Administrator, van Rensburg fell strongly under the Nazi spell in the mid-1930s. On an official visit to Germany he observed Wehrmacht manoeuvres with great admiration. A brief meeting with Hitler moved him to compare the Führer's emergence to the 'miracle of Joan of Arc'.

The habit of fishing in European thought currents for new justificatory ideas was an old one. Although South Africa was 6 000 miles away from the European heartland, both its white populations were expatriate sub-groups of European nations and strongly oriented towards their mother civilisations. European ideological and national military struggles invariably tended to be fought out (sometimes in caricature) at Africa's southern tip. In striking contrast to the undoctrinaire pragmatism of the British settler, the Dutch colonists displayed a high degree of ideological consciousness. This had its roots in the theological character of their culture and their need, as Calvinists, to square their conduct with their all-encompassing ideological and theological norms.

In 1706, the Cape Dutch businessmen who rebelled against the

Dutch East India Company's restrictive policies drew heavily on the civil rights slogans and ideals of Holland's patriot movement. In 1789, they adopted French Revolutionary slogans to justify the overthrow of Company rule and the establishment of independent, secessionist Republics on the frontier. In both cases the borrowings were highly selective, and it could indeed be argued that this betrayed a contempt for ideology. Nevertheless, the compulsive need to borrow demonstrates the high value attached to ideological justifications for social and political behaviour.

As a biblical people, the Boers were keenly aware of the need to justify and conceptualise their conduct in terms of their overarching Calvinist belief system. From it they continually selected the notions which suited their conditions and material interests, and they discarded those elements which were in conflict with their aspirations. Thus the Afrikaners magnified certain aspects in the Calvinist world-outlook – such as elitism, aristocracy and authoritarianism – in the pattern of their relations with blacks. Conversely, they minimised or ignored Calvinist tendencies whose consequences implied the sharing of rights with blacks – such as egalitarianism, individualism and democracy – although these remained highly prized qualities within the exclusive white community.

The same patterns governed the incorporation of Nazi–Fascist concepts into modern Afrikaner Nationalism. It was perhaps a coincidence that the right-wing Nationalist revival of 1932 crystallised at the same time as the rise of right-wing, ultra-Nationalist movements in Germany and Italy. However, for those Christian-Nationalists struggling against the overwhelming tide of Hertzog's accommodationism, the emergence of powerful totalitarian forces elsewhere was like manna from heaven. In South Africa concepts like the glorification of *volk*, race and culture were held only by a minority at the time of fusion. But the ideologists of Nazism and Fascism gave them the imprimatur of respectability. Some critics, like Brian Bunting, have equated Afrikaner Nationalism with Nazism.[10] The truth is more subtle and complex: distinctions should be drawn between support for Germany and total absorption of Nazi ideas; between those who adopted some Nazi concepts but rejected others; and between the Nazi concepts which expressed traditional Afrikaner thinking on race, and those which injected completely new ideas into Afrikaner ideology.

It is impossible within the scope of this work to examine all the permutations of the Nazi–Christian-Nationalist relationship.

Nevertheless, the topic cannot be avoided if we are to understand the development of Christian-Nationalism between 1935 and 1945. It is therefore proposed to outline the principal tenets of Nazi–Fascism, in particular the notion of the super-organism, glorification of race and nation and the totalitarian state. We also propose to touch on Nazi Christianity, whose un-Calvinist characteristics explain why the bulk of Christian-Nationalists were unable to identify themselves unreservedly with the Nazi doctrine and could not accept the relationship between the Party and the church under Hitler.

The concept of a collective super-mind or organism, to which all individual members are subordinate and outside which they have no reality, is a central idea in both creeds. In Nazism this is the *Totales Volk*; and in Fascism, the totalitarian state. In both, individual liberty is subordinated to the collective super-personality which replaces the former society based on individual freedoms. This mind, or organism, is politically sovereign, morally absolute and biologically self-sufficient, encompassing every facet of the individual and collective existence. It is therefore the implacable enemy of liberalism, whose stress is on individual rights.

Both Nazism and Fascism glorify the nation – its history, noble characteristics and destiny – and reject international brotherhood or cosmopolitanism. German Nationalism regards the *volk* as a biological–racial organic entity, bound by shared blood, in which resides the racial soul. Race, rather than the usual mixture of shared customs, history, language and culture, is the defining factor in nationality. It is the original force which determines the essence of the nation and character of its culture, psychology and outlook. The nation is total and absolute, and its spirit influences all facets of life. Conversely, the state is subordinate to the nation; it is a machine or instrument to achieve the racial nation's ends.

According to Nazi ideology races are divided into original and imitative, pure and mongrels, master and servant. Superior races are pure, original and produce culture; degeneration occurs through mixture of blood. Thus the superior races must avoid intermarriage, or else they will decay. Of all races, the Nordics or Aryans are the most developed. Jews are the epitome of an inferior, degenerate race. The *herrenvolk* principle also applied in relations between Germans and black people. A statement issued in 1939 by Gunther Hecht, in anticipation of the recovery of former German colonies, sets out the principles by which those will be ruled 'when they return to the Reich'.[11] Instead of detaching the natives from their traditional racial systems and robbing them of their tribal identity, the Nazis would pursue a policy based on inequality and absolute segregation.

In both Nazism and Fascism the state is all-embracing, totalitarian and hierarchical, headed by a single dictatorial leader. The chief difference between the two doctrines is that Fascism views the state as an organism which is higher than the nation, whereas Nazism sees it as a machine which is subordinate to the organic nation: the primary totality. True to its anti-democratic inspiration, the Nazi-Fascist state rejects the notion of the sovereignty of the people and denies the electorate a free choice of representatives who are accountable and removable. Instead of a multiplicity of competing parties, a single party monopolises power and the party leader is head of the state. The chain of responsibility moves in an upwards, not a downwards, direction.

No exposition of the Nazi creed should overlook its religious element. The alliance of a Protestant church with the Nazi Party and the mixing together of theology and racialism produced a species of German Christianity which displayed, at first, remarkable affinities to Afrikaner Christian-Nationalism. Two historical factors should be borne in mind. First, German Protestants are, for the vast majority, Lutherans, with a tradition of rendering unto Caesar what belongs to Caesar and leaving politics to the politicians. The German system, where ministers were virtually servants of secular authority, was a dramatic contrast to Kuyper's insistence on the strict separation of church and state. Second, German Protestantism was politically conservative, anti-liberal and anti-socialist. Among the most important precursors of Nazism was Adolf Stocker, the Berlin pastor who held the official appointment of 'Court Preacher' and who founded the Christian-Social Party in 1878. Although a Lutheran, Stocker may be described as Germany's version of Abraham Kuyper, with those methods and concepts he had much in common. Stocker's brand of religious conservative nationalism underwent a revival in the Lutheran church towards the end of the 1920s, when many church leaders saw possibilities for a religious growth in an alliance with the awakened Nationalist spirit. Out of this alliance emerged German Christian-Nationalism, a creed condemned by the great twentieth-century theologian, Karl Barth.

The essence of Nazi Christian-Nationalism was summed up by the Nazi youth leader, Baldre von Schirach, in 1936:

One cannot be a good German and at the same time deny God, but an avowal of faith in the eternal Germany is at the same time an avowal of faith in the eternal God. For us the service of Germany is the service of God. If we act as true Germans, we act according to the laws of God.[12]

The chief tenets of this creed held that the German people were divinely created and blessed by the Almighty; that their political leaders were divinely selected instruments; that the German nation had a divine task to build up the true church; that the maintenance of the nation, especially of its blood purity, was the will of God; and, therefore, that the policy of National Socialism was to do the will of God.

German Protestants saw in an awakened nationalism an opportunity to restore its links with the people and to build up a powerful national church. The founder of the German Christian movement was the Reverend Joachim Hossenfelder, who joined the Nazi Party in 1929 and later became Minister of Church Affairs in the Nazi government. His vision was of a single, unified Protestant church under a national bishop to replace the 29 quarrelling provincial churches, and to build a strong spiritually-centred Germany capable of fighting godless communism and rampant materialism. German Christians claimed to be completing the work of Luther, who had marked the emergence of the German people into the Christian world. Convinced that Germany was destined by God to play a leading role in Christian history, they set about creating a purely German church purged of foreign elements. In this new theology, the 'German' was more important than the 'Christian'.

In 1933 Hitler became Chancellor and set up the Third Reich. Appealing for church support, he declared that 'the national government sees in the two Christian denominations the most vital factors in the survival of our nationality. Their rights will not be touched.'[13] German Christian-Nationalists turned enthusiastically to Hitler, whose 1933 victory had been marked by a laudatory sermon from none other than Pastor Martin Niemoller. By the end of 1933 the German church had not only answered the call of Nationalism, but it had endorsed Alfred Rosenberg's anti-Jewish Nordic theology and canonised Hitler as a new Christian prophet. In the sober words of Karl Barth, it 'almost unanimously welcomed the Hitler regime with real confidence, indeed, with the highest hopes'.[14]

German Christian-Nationalism contains remarkable similarities to

Afrikaner religious thought. Both subscribe to the marrying of Bible and race; both see the church as an organ of Nationalist upliftment; both equate worship of God with nation-worship; and both stress the nation's God-given task among other peoples. At the same time, the differences are important. Whereas German Lutherans subordinated themselves to the state, party and leader, Afrikaner Calvinists sought to make themselves uppermost in the Nationalist movement. In Germany the church, spurred on by the party, 'nationalised' itself, but in South Africa there was an attempt to 'Christianise' the Nationalist movement. In Germany, the political leader was glorified and draped in semi-divinity, so that worship of Hitler became comparable to worship of Christ. In South Africa, however, the Calvinists firmly insisted on God's sovereignty, and generally avoided the cult of leadership. The subsequent development of German Christianity was marked by a deepening of these diverging tendencies, especially as the Aryanisation or Germanisation of traditional Christianity subordinated theology to the doctrine of the primacy of racial values and transformed it into an ultimate religious expression of a Nationalist culture.

After 1933 the 'Nationalist' component in 'Christian-Nationalism' began to absorb, sometimes selectively, sometimes unconsciously, relevant Nazi concepts: a process which continued right up to Hitler's defeat in 1945. During this time Nazi ideas furnished grist to the Christian-Nationalist mill. What emerged was a totally new substance with a distinctive Afrikaner flavour, but betraying the unmistakable colouring of Berlin. If the Afrikaner 'Christian' element was neo-Kuyperian, its 'Nationalist' partner was, for a time at least, neo-Nazi. Just as Afrikaner thought had natural affinities with Kuyperianism, so did it share much in common with Nazism. Nazism–Fascism, like Afrikaner Nationalism, repudiated the doctrine of inalienable human rights and the unity of humankind associated with the French Revolution. Instead, it put forward a creed which posited an absolute state or totalitarian *volk*, to which individual liberties were surrendered.

It is interesting to note that the nineteenth-century fathers of Nazism belonged to the same ideological family as Groen van Prinsterer, the initiator of the Dutch Christian-National movement, and his illustrious successor, Dr Abraham Kuyper. Both were dedicated counter-revolutionaries. Although their reaction was religious in origin and orientation, they sympathised with the Restorationist attack on the entire theory of natural rights and political democracy which had inspired the French Revolution. The works of van Prinsterer and Kuyper frequently quote the leading German proponents of an organic-hierarchical community, like Von Haller, Schlegel and Adam Miller. Van Prinsterer greatly admired Freiderich Julius von Stahl, the German conservative Nationalist, who in 1848 advocated a Christian state in which Jews would be treated as 'guests'.

Another possible link between the Dutch anti-revolutionaries and German precursors of Nazism was Paul de Legarde (1827–91) who contended that the nation based on race carried the essence of the human spirit. There was close agreement in concepts and methods between Kuyper and the pastor Adolf Stocker, who founded Germany's first Protestant Christian party in 1878, known originally as the Christian-Social Workers Party. An arch-conservative and Nationalist, Stocker sought to create an 'organic counter-movement' against rising liberalism, socialism and the theory of people's sovereignty and democracy. For him, the state was an organism which was willed and guided by God. Its object was to realise the nation's moral–cultural ideals, to protect the fatherland and the *volksgeist*. Stocker is frequently cited as an important element in the tradition which culminated in National Socialism.

Evolving independently of these European nineteenth- and twentieth-century anti-libertarian movements, Afrikaners developed a conservative Nationalism which similarly rejected the French Revolution's ideas. In the South African context the ideas of 1789 imply equal rights, liberties and brotherhood regardless of skin colour. They are therefore subversive of the Boer principles of authoritarian, hierarchical and racial dominance. The Great Trek was a direct protest against attempts by the British Colonial regime to democratise their structures. This event – which marks the first awakening of modern Afrikaner Nationalism – was enacted in defence of the principle of 'no equality'. Afrikaner Nationalism, though formed in a unique colonial experience, therefore flowed in the same ideological stream as German Nationalism. Its built-in rejection of the French Revolution's legacy of individual freedom and brotherhood, and its glorification of Nationalism based on race, created natural affinities with Nazism.

It would, however, be absurd to claim that Afrikaners acquired their views on race from the Nazis. These ideas were already part and parcel of the Afrikaner nineteenth-century tradition. Although Afrikaners did not produce trained ideologists before the late 1920s, their Nationalist theory partook of all these elements. What the Germans did was to furnish a respectable, internationally-known terminology to convey concepts and attitudes which had hitherto been intuitive, sub-verbal and part of *volk* tradition. The conservative side of Abraham Kuyper – particularly his organic concept, and his denunciation of liberalism and Marxism – also provided a doctrinal stepping stone to Nazi concepts. However, it should be constantly borne in mind that, despite a strong identity of viewpoints between German and Afrikaner Nationalism, their philosophical yardsticks are, in the final analysis, in conflict. For the German Nationalist, it is the race (whose wild spirit is embodied in an infallible, charismatic and irremovable leader) which is the justificatory authority. Among Afrikaners, this position is occupied by Calvin's sovereign God.

THE INCORPORATION OF NAZI IDEAS, 1933–9

From the early 1930s, identifiably Nazi and Fascist ideas began to occur in formulations of Calvinist Republicanism. Behind these demands for a South African totalitarianism lay the Broederbond's genuine disappointment with parliamentarianism which had, in their eyes, seduced the Nationalists into coalition and corrupted their principles. In its place they hoped to erect a single-party authoritarian system that not only expressed the numerical superiority of Afrikaners, but which also swept aside the liberal Anglo-Saxon constitutional concepts and ideological forms at the root of South African politics. In due course this led to the adoption of a philosophical critique of British imperialism, whose language, concepts and style originated in Europe.

Squaring Nazi ideology with Afrikaner tradition was the work of a number of Broederbond intellectuals, particularly the Potchefstroom radicals. Of those who contributed most to the incorporation of Nazi elements into the mainstream of Christian-Nationalism, the most outstanding were L.J. du Plessis, N. Diederichs, G. Eloff and P.J. Meyer. Du Plessis, a central figure because of his presence on the Broederbond Executive, his chairmanship of Volkskas, and secretaryship of the Calvinist Bond was one of the first sensitive antennae to pick up and echo the exhilarating new sounds from Europe. He was also, for a time, Deputy Leader of the Transvaal NP. As early as 1933 du Plessis suggested that South Africa ought to abandon its nineteenth-century multi-party system in favour of an authoritarian state which would preserve the organic character of Afrikaners. He proposed that all parties should be abolished, pointing out that none was permitted in Kruger's Republic, and that public representatives should be organised into occupational or vocational councils. The latter scheme seemed to owe something to Mussolini's programme for a corporate state in Italy.[15]

Some of du Plessis' ideas, as expressed in the above article – such as the *volk*'s organic character (race), the need to express unity of *volk* and state, recognition of pluralist-occupational groupings (the corporate society) and the prediction of the inevitable collapse of liberal parliamentarianism – have no genuine roots in South African conditions. They are clearly imported, and forced, a little awkwardly, into the context of the 1933–4 coalition crisis. In fact, far from undermining Parliament, fusion proved the ability of the Westminster system to express the consensus mood in South African politics. Equally, the *volk* state idea, which persisted in Broederbond and Christian-National thought until at least the end of the war, was just as 'foreign' as Westminster-style government. Such a state was meaningful, if at all, only in a country with a single nation, one language and a common culture, such as Germany or Holland. In South Africa it could only mean exclusive Afrikaner control over the state and the exercise of tyrannical power over everyone else.

Du Plessis' plan to replace parties with occupational representation influenced a small group of intellectuals but, as most of the Broederbond's leaders were gradually drawn into the NP's parliamentary struggle, interest waned in the corporate state. The idea was, however, powerfully revived by the OB in 1940 which, within a decade, was to embody most of du Plessis' key ideas. Du Plessis returned to his demand for a thorough and radical overhaul of South Africa's political system on Republican–totalitarian lines in December 1933, at the very moment when fusion seemed inevitable. He wrote:

> We firmly believe that a republican South Africa will be no Parliamentary democracy in the 19th century sense, but rather a State whose Government will be obliged to exercise its governing mandate autonomously of party-political dependence or manipulation for a period constitutionally stipulated, while contact with public opinion will be assured by a volks-council and an occupational council of sectoral representatives.[16]

An early example of the Nazi concept of organism (defined by the presence of a common blood in its veins, and distinctive physiological characteristics) may be found in an article by Potchefstroom's Professor of Philosophy, H. Stoker. He argued that 'the organic idea of nationalism' lay at the heart of Afrikaner nationalism: 'The organic unity of a nation flows from two parallel and related roots: (a) the vital-organic blood tie, and (b) the spiritual-organic cultural bond.'[17] The first gave individual members their distinctive physical characteristics, while the second was expressed in their culture, tongue, tradition and spiritual possessions. 'Just as body and soul formed a unity . . . so, too, the volk's blood-tie and cultural bond formed a unity, in which the deeper organic nature of the volk was realised.' Because English speakers lacked indigenous characteristics and identified themselves with people overseas, they could not form a nation with Afrikaners. Thus Stoker regards the Afrikaners as the only true nation in South Africa, and uses the organic concept – which occurs in Nazism and Fascism but also in Kuyperianism – to insist on their immutable differences. He concedes that at some date in the future an independently-evolved English-speaking South African people could form a broad national unit with the Afrikaners. But this 'new unity will also have to be organic, like two yolks in an egg . . . or two rose trees from the same root'.[18] The heavy stress in this article on the organic character of the nation (which is compared to a plant, tree or person), and its definition as a unit of blood or spirit, reveals the clear influence of Nazi and Fascist ideas.

An outspoken exponent of Nazi eugenics was Dr G. Eloff of the University College of the OFS, who contributed an article on 'race improvement' to *Koers* in 1933. He argued that 'society cannot today do without a number of inferiors . . . [who] must provide for its physical needs'. Strong, muscular and willing to work continuously without boredom, the non-highly-civilised persons had to be society's drawers of water and hewers of wood. Eloff proposed scientifically-planned marriages: church and state had to encourage marriage and birth 'among the superior persons', and to educate people to make 'an intelligent marriage choice'.[19]

The first full-scale book in Afrikaans pleading for an introduction of the Nazi system came from a former civil servant, A.J. Bruwer, who wrote *Capitalism, Party Politics and Poverty* in 1934.[20] This proposed the replacement of 'individualistic capitalism, which is ruining our volk in imperialism's interests, with a national-socialist system'. Government would be based not on party politics, but occupational (*eweredige*) representation, possibly leading to a dictatorship.

Of perhaps greater importance than the book itself was its review by L.J. du Plessis. Here he argues that, while 'individualistic capitalism is deadly for our volks-life' and should undoubtedly be replaced by a system of greater 'solidarism', this should not take the form of National Socialism: 'The driving force of solidarism must not be national socialism, because national-socialism is, in our case, un-national, and in any event un-Christian, but the basic principle of national reform can, with us, only be Christian-Republicanism.'[21] This reservation did not prevent du Plessis from continuing his attack on democracy and suggesting a one-party state for the purposes of national consolidation.[22] What his writings reveal is the selection of useful ideas and socio-economic devices from the rising Nazi-Fascist movement, but a reluctance, at this stage, to embrace wholeheartedly the system as applied to Germany. A limiting factor was undoubtedly Hitler's attitude to the churches, which divided Calvinist opinion in the Netherlands and in South Africa. Pointedly, du Plessis adds that only after Christ the King has cleansed the world of sin could a salvationist state be established.

Another important exposition of the principles of Nazism came in 1934 from H.G. Schulze, Professor of German at Potchefstroom. Nazism, he said, was not an isolated phenomenon, but merely an authentic German expression of a widespread spiritual movement. Contrasting with the liberal state, which recognised a plurality of outlooks, the Nazi state recognised only one world outlook. There was no contradiction between *volk* and state. Explaining anti-Semitism, Schulze stressed the Nazi concept of the *volk* being dominated by race. Since Jews belonged to a different race, they could not form part of the German *volk*. As guests in Germany, they could not be allowed to play a leading role in state, *volk* or church life.[23]

During the 1938 centenary celebrations of the Great Trek, speakers made much play of the Voortrekkers' blood purity, and used terminology strongly reminiscent of Alfred Rosenberg. The Reverend W.N. van der Merwe, for example, warned Afrikaners to avoid the road of 'degeneration and bastardisation' and to follow the Voortrekker principle of 'blood honouring and race improvement'. 'The pure Aryan blood of Hollanders, English, French and Germans, to name no more, which flowed together here on African earth, must be preserved', he exhorted.[24]

The eminent Afrikaner historian Gustav Preller echoes Nazi doctrine in his biography of *Andries Pretorius* (1937), the Trek leader. Preller sees history in simple racial terms, claiming that modern science has proved the existence of inherent and unalterable differences of quality, intellect and moral stamina between races. Following Hitler, he claims that some races posses original intelligence and are constructive, while others are merely imitative. Only developed races, Preller writes, can live by the ideas of liberty, fraternity and equality; for all others these concepts are fatal.

Nazi influence can be clearly detected in the sudden emergence of anti-Semitism in Christian-Nationalist thought. Traditionally, bonds between Afrikaners and Jews had been sympathetic, largely because of a common Old Testament orientation, and possibly because of their common exclusion from the Anglo-Saxon establishment. Many Jews had fought for the Transvaal in the 1899–1902 war, and one of Kruger's closest confidants was Sammy Marks, the Transvaal industrialist, benefactor and admirer of the Boer cause. But, following the Nazis, Christian-Nationalists – including such leading Broederbond figures as L.J. du Plessis, Dr Verwoerd, Dr Malan and Dr Dönges – introduced a form of anti-Semitism based on religious ('Christ-killers'), political ('Jewish money power' and 'Jewish bolsheviks') and racial foundations. This was accompanied by such slogans as 'British-Jewish capitalism', 'Jewish Marxists' and 'British-Jewish liberalism'.

In cartoons by Boonzaier featuring the character 'Hoggenheimer', the Jew was portrayed as a cigar-puffing, bloated capitalist. Clearly illustrating the influence of Nazi racial theories was the close correlation between the mounting intensity of Nazi persecution of German Jews and the frequency with which Christian-Nationalists began to raise the issue in South Africa, and to complain that Jews were threatening to 'murder Christian white South Africa'. To some extent anti-Semitism was an artificial and irrelevant importation into the Afrikaner context. Unlike Germany, there were no assimilated Afrikaner Jews who could influence Afrikaner cultural life from within and therefore from whom the *volk* had to be 'saved'. Moreover, South African Jews were distributed throughout all classes and occupational levels, and could not be said to hold a single, monolithic class or political position. But in so far as many Jews tended to support the non-Afrikaner movements for a more enlightened colour outlook, they formed (as a minority group) an easy and convenient target.

The only historical precedent for Afrikaner anti-Semitism can be found in Abraham Kuyper's attack in 1878 on Jews as carriers of liberal ideas, to which his ARP was uncompromisingly opposed. But there was no indigenous Boer tradition of anti-Semitism. In 1929, for example, General Hertzog testified fulsomely to the Jew's patriotism and his close fraternal bonds with the Afrikaner.[25] Dr Malan also paid tribute to the Jews in 1930 when he welcomed their full participation in the national life of the country and mentioned his appreciation of 'what the Jews have done for South Africa'.[26] Under the influence of Nazi thought, Afrikaner Nationalists soon reversed their policies and adopted anti-Jewish measures, based on the doctrine of Jewish non-assimilability. Economic reasons were found for branding Jews as a threat to Afrikanerdom. The annual congress of the Calvinist bond in July 1935 held a special discussion on the 'Jewish Question'. Dr Verwoerd helped organise a mass protest against the influx of Jewish refugees from Germany in 1936, and in 1937 he wrote a lengthy article entitled, 'The Jewish Problem Regarded from a Nationalist Point of View: A Possible Solution: Proportional Distribution in Trades and Businesses the First Great Necessity'.[27]

In October 1937 the Transvaal NP decided to exclude Jews from membership, an example later followed by the OFS and Natal NPs.[28] Demanding that Hertzog stiffen the Aliens Act, the Nationalists proposed a series of measures to prohibit Jewish immigration and to close certain professions to Jews and other 'non-assimilable' races.[29] Although the amendment to the Aliens Act was defeated, the Nationalists continued to stress that Jews were undesirable because they allegedly dominated the world of business and were propagators of communism.[30] In April 1937 the OFS NGK resolved that Jews were not God's chosen people and, in 1939, Dr Malan accused Jewry of having 'robbed the population of its heritage so that the Afrikaner lives in the land of his father, but no longer possesses it'.[31] A good summary of the Christian-National position is given by the Reverend C.R. Kotzé in his article 'The Jewish Question'.[32]

Afrikaner anti-Semitism was closely related to the Christian-National struggle against internationalism, non-racism, liberalism and socialism. As an identifiable minority group, Jews could easily be located in the business and professional world that Afrikaners were entering, and in the broad anti-Nationalist liberal alliance. While Afrikaner anti-Semitism could be doctrinally related to the rest of Christian-Nationalist theory, its force rested upon evidence that the Jew was hostile to Nationalism's racial aspirations and, like the Indian, was an economic competitor. In this respect, it is illuminating to compare Nationalist anti-Semitism with its anti-Asian propaganda. Both appealed to poor whites (allegedly the victim of foreign economic exploiters) and the new Afrikaner business class which was obliged to engage in competition with Jewish and Asian small shopkeepers, and much play was made of the non-Christian religious character of these two groups. One hesitates to say that Afrikaner anti-Semitism was entirely Nazi-inspired, but there cannot be the slightest doubt that many of the crude, anti-Semitic charges were drawn directly from Nazi propaganda and were, to that extent, imitative.

From the above discussion it may be seen that Afrikaner Nationalism recognised in Nazism a powerful companion movement and they borrowed from its vocabulary of concepts. Thus during the 1930s there were a number of attempts by Afrikaner intellectual leaders to graft on to the Afrikaner tradition new elements (for which there was doubtful or little historical precedent), such as an authoritarian dictatorship, the abolition of parliamentary democracy, the idea of the nation as an organism, the corporate system and a virulent form of anti-Semitism.

There were, however, serious differences among Christian-Nationalists on the question of Nazi-Fascism. While Afrikaner Nationalism felt refreshed by the dynamic spirit of Berlin, Afrikaner Calvinism found the Nazi tendency to glorify leader, race, blood and nation hard to swallow; the subordination of the German Protestant church to a totalitarian secular state stuck like a fishbone in their throats. Enthusiastic worship of leader, race and state could be seen as a disguised manifestation of humanism and smacked of the sin of idolatry. The upshot was that two schools of thought emerged during the 1930s among Christian-Nationalist theoreticians. On the one hand, a prominent figure like L.J. du Plessis went so far as to promote a partyless authoritarian dictatorship and the total destruction of liberal capitalist democracy. On the other hand, writers like A.H. van der Walt and J.D. Vorster – although delighted by Nazism's assault on liberalism – were disappointed by its idolatrous tendencies which they regarded as anti-Calvinist. Equally offensive to them was Nazi tampering with the Bible, which for Christian-Nationalists represented the infallible, inspired and literal Word of God.

Dr Verwoerd summed up the latter school of Christian-Nationalist thought by conceding that, while Nazism and Fascism had performed wonders for their countries and deserved approval as anti-liberal movements, it would be fatal to import them into an Afrikaner context. The Afrikaner possessed his own autonomous creed and should eschew foreign models. When talks for an alliance between Nationalists and Greyshirts collapsed, Verwoerd commented:

> The negotiations broke down on grounds of fundamental disagreement. The Grey Shirts stand for what they call a unitary state, with the abolition of political parties and their replacement by group representation and the appointment of a Leader. However one may play with words, this means nothing else but that they want to follow the Nazi or Fascist systems . . . with their dictatorships . . . the National Party did not accept the hand of friendship from a movement which by its very character would attack it and try to destroy it.[33]

Early misgivings about the Nazi and Fascist ideas of the state were voiced by A. van der Walt, Professor of History at Potchefstroom, in *Koers in die Krisis*, published in 1934. In an article entitled 'State Authority and Peoples' Freedoms', he expresses sympathy with the totalitarian reactions to the 'disintegrative and levelling' effects of liberalism, with its negation of all stable authority and all worthwhile freedom. Nazism and Fascism, he concedes, 'can bring about good' in specific circumstances, but warns that it could lead to an intolerable suppression of conscience and the abolition of the authority of various organic plural groupings within their own spheres. While welcoming Nazism's rejection of the legacy of the French revolution, van der Walt is critical of the doctrine's subordination of all life, including religious life, to the 'racial culture' of the state. This brought it into conflict with Calvinism's rejection of absolutism, replaced the Word of God with other norms, and gave the state or race the upper hand over the community's sovereign circles.

Although he does not directly attack Nazism or Fascism by name, the remarks of J.D. Vorster in the 1935 edition of *Koers in die Krisis* also seem to be critical of certain tendencies in the new totalitarianisms:

> Humanism limits God's sovereignty and makes Him in lesser or greater measure dependent on man. Human functions or qualities are here absolutised and given greater significance than allowed

[*bepaal*] by the Word of God. We find in Humanism a deification of human authority, of his reason, of his feelings, of his will, of his nature; particularly do we today find a tolerance which rejects the absolute authority of God and His Word, a preoccupation [*dwepe*] with human greatness and with human achievements, a glorification of human leadership, an authoritarian madness, a mindless following of persons, a man-worship.[34]

Though oblique, these remarks could well be seen as a Calvinist criticism of the deification of the Aryan race, worship of its noble qualities and achievements and the glorification of Hitler and the leadership principle. In a more obvious reference to Nazism and Fascism, Vorster deplores 'the theories of volks-sovereignty, of race-sovereignty, and of State-absolutism [that] reject the sovereign and absolute authority of God and place it in man'.[35] In this passage Vorster brackets Nazism and Fascism with the humanistic heritage of Rousseau.

Another obvious obstacle was the Afrikaner Calvinist belief that the Bible was the authoritative, infallible and inspired Word of God. Professor C.J.H. de Wet delivers a sharp attack on the practice of biblical criticism and biblical mistake-finding in *Koers in die Krisis* in 1935. Such tendencies are tantamount, he says, to placing the authority of science and human intelligence above the word of the Bible. This standpoint was irreconcilable with the Nazi practice of re-editing the Bible and its rejection of the Old Testament to stress Christ's role as an Aryan warrior.[36]

Yet even those Christian-Nationalists who found the whole of Nazism unpalatable were caught in a dilemma. From 1938 to 1943 Hitler was a hero to most Afrikaner Nationalists and sympathy for German Nationalism was widespread at all levels. It is not without significance that the NP frequently declared its friendliness towards Germany in the war's early years. Criticism of Germany's struggle (as distinct from Nazism) was not easy in the pro-German Afrikaner climate of the early war years: it automatically stamped the critic as pro-Allies, and therefore a Smuts supporter. But, although (as the next section shows) Germanophilism reached unprecedented heights for five years, it should be remembered that within the DRC there always remained latent reservations about Nazi ideas.

As a postscript, it should be noted that the deeply ambivalent attitudes of neo-Calvinists to Nazi ideas were very much evident in Holland too. During the 1930s there was indeed considerable sympathy amongst Dutch Christian-Nationalists towards Nazi ideology. To a large extent, this fed directly off the deeply conservative aspect of Kuyperian thought. Kuyper's successor as leader of the Dutch ARP was Dr Colijn, who served as Prime Minister for various periods between 1925 and 1939, and led the party until his death in Nazi detention in 1944. Under Colijn's leadership, the ARP followed a conservative policy during the early 1930s and displayed a conciliatory attitude towards the Fascist regime in Italy as well as the new Nazi government in Germany.

From the 1930s there was sporadic, but increasing, support within Dutch Protestant circles for Hitler's revolt against communist internationalism. By 1932 a large number of ultra-Nationalist, pro-Nazi/Fascist groups had sprung up, including the Nationaal Socialistische Nederlandsche Arbeiders Partij, the Nationale Unie, De Fascistenbond, Het Nationaal Bond and the Orange Fascists. The most important of these was the Nationaal Socialistische Beweeging (NSB) under the leadership of Anton Mussert. The NSB was, as its name implied, a movement rather than a party. In many respects it was a predecessor of, and counterpart to, the OB in South Africa. Indeed, a comparison between the two bodies might yield illuminating results. Founded by Mussert in 1931, the NSB was closely modelled on the Nazi Party and Mussert boldly emphasised his ideological links with Kuyper. Religion and Nationalism were the keynotes of the NSB's message, and it proposed to reorganise Holland as a corporate state. The NSB frequently cited the Afrikaner racial outlook as evidence that the Dutch religious character favoured Hitler's attitudes to race. Its programme, adopted in 1931, referred to the Boers as an overseas part of the Netherlands (Dietse) Volk. The Afrikaners were referred to as 'our kinsmen in South Africa'.

A major boost for Nazi influence among Dutch Christian-Nationalists came in 1934 with the publication of H. Diemer's *Het Duitsche Nationaal Socialisme*. Diemer was a prominent leader of the ARP and also a contributor to *Koers in die Krisis*. He was the first ARP leader of note to bring out into the open points of agreement between the conservative side of the ARP and Nazism, and his book was the first comprehensive work on the subject. Diemer summed up his impression of Nazism in one word: 'Order'. He praised Hitler as the embodiment of Germany's *volkscharacter*, and Nazism as a bulwark against godless communism.

In 1935 Professor Hugo Visscher resigned from the ARP to form his own extreme right-wing party, the Christelijke Nationale Aktie. Although in the Hervormde Kerk, Visscher had been a protégé of Kuyper and a theology professor at Utrecht since 1904. He was a tireless champion of the Christian authoritarian state and may well have exercised an influence on the OB tendency in South Africa. In 1938 Visscher cited the racial and religious attitudes of the Boers as an example of the fact that God had created races and commanded them to keep their blood pure.

Dr Colijn, who contributed an enthusiastic foreword to the three editions of *Koers in die Krisis*, sent a special message to the 1938 Voortrekker centenary celebrations. 'Our youth knows of the heroic deeds of Piet Retief, Hendrik Potgieter and President Kruger', he wrote, 'and they are familiar with the history of Pretorius, the murder of Retief and the punishment given to the Zulus'. Aside from this fulsome message of support, Colijn sent a special emissary, Dr F. Beelarts van Blokland, to represent the Dutch government at the celebrations. At the unveiling of the Voortrekker Monument he told the crowd, 'South Africa has a place in the heart of every Netherlander.' Beginning with the visit of H.H. Kuyper to South Africa in 1924, the rapport between the Afrikaners and the Dutch Calvinist establishment reached a new level of intimacy during the 1930s, exceeding anything that had gone before or would follow.

Close contact between the Dutch Christian-National movement and their Afrikaans counterparts was maintained until the Germans overran Holland in 1940. After that, however, the two countries took quite different paths. Among the first Dutch Calvinists to raise the anti-Fascist and anti-Nazi alarm were Dr J.J. Buskes, a dynamic pastor in a working-class area, and Professor Anema of the Free University. In November 1932 Buskes, who had been one of the pallbearers at Abraham Kuyper's funeral, warned that 'Christian Fascism is a greater danger to Protestantism than godless Bolshevism.' Professor Anema depicted Fascism as God-denying and man-glorifying.

During the 1930s many Dutch Calvinists became increasingly concerned about Hitler's use of violence, his establishment of an authoritarian state, the materialistic quality of German national life, and Nazism's worship of the nation. The deepest misgivings were aroused by Hitler's take-over of Austria in 1934, his occupation of the Rhineland in 1936, the growing violence against the Jews and the subjugation of the Protestant church. This last factor, and the racialist flavour of German Christianity in particular, stimulated the belated growth of Dutch Calvinist opposition to Nazism. Calvinism had always emphasised freedom of conscience and the state's toleration of dissent. Although sections of Dutch Protestantism continued to sympathise with Nazism, the Dutch Gereformeerde Kerken censored Nazism in 1936 and displayed an ever-growing repugnance to German Christianity. By contrast, solidarity among Afrikaners with Germany grew as the war drew nearer.

Hitler invaded Holland on 10 May 1940. After $4\frac{1}{2}$ days of resistance, the Dutch government surrendered. Any doubts which the ARP and the Gereformeerde Kerken's rank and file may have harboured about the evil character of Nazism were dispelled within a few months of the occupation. Reformed resistance to the Nazi occupation flared up with the first anti-Semitic measures of September to December 1940. The joint appeal by all six Dutch Protestant churches in October to withdraw these measures marked a turning point in Dutch Protestantism's relations with Nazism. Whereas there had been some sympathy within Holland for Germany's discrimination against the Jews in the mid-1930s, this now became the central issue on which Protestant Hollanders finally decided to defy the Nazis.

The early support in Dutch Protestant circles for Nazism indicates that Kuyper's divided legacy also divided the heart of the orthodox 'core of the nation'. But, despite their promising affinities, the Dutch *gereformeerdes* played a prominent role in the resistance. Though the members of the Dutch Reformed Christian Churches formed only 8–9 per cent of the Netherlands population, they yielded some 19 per cent of the resistance movement's casualties. Proportionately, only the communist and Jewish losses are comparable. The Nazi experience completely altered the course of Reformed Holland's twentieth-century development. Dutch Protestantism stepped back from the Fascist abyss and reaffirmed those basic virtues of Calvin – such as democracy, brotherhood, freedom of conscience and individual liberty – which were in danger of being suffocated by the extreme right-wing counterblast to the spirit of 1789. The Second World War ended the honeymoon of the Dutch and Afrikaner *gereformeerdes*. Though tempered to some extent by Calvinism, Afrikaner Nationalist support for Germany ended all real rapport between these two sections of Kuyper's followers.

7 Republicanism and the Struggle for Leadership within the Christian-Nationalist Camp, 1940–8

In South Africa, the outbreak of the Second World War led to an almost exact re-enactment of the 1914 scenario. Once again the two white sections were split into pro-British and pro-German factions, bringing Empire Loyalists and Republicans to the brink of civil war. As in 1914 the Afrikaners were plunged into domestic strife over how and when to exploit the war in order to overthrow the British connection. The war was both a windfall and a setback for the Broederbond. On the one hand it destroyed the Hertzog–Smuts regime which had ruled since 1933, opened the way for a clear-cut struggle between Republicans and anti-Republicans and greatly accelerated the upsurge of popular Republican sentiment among Nationalists. But, on the other hand, it released conflicting tendencies within the Nationalist-Republican camp, especially over the questions of National Socialism and methods of struggle. This had the effect of dividing brethren into bitterly antagonistic groupings, each jockeying for dominance within the movement.

The Broederbond worked energetically behind the scenes to reconcile differences, to co-ordinate efforts and to establish unanimity on final objectives but, for a time (notably during 1941–3), it seemed helpless to prevent cat-and-dog disputes between Dr Hans van Rensburg's OB and Dr Malan's NP. Indeed, as the Broederbond Chairman pointed out in 1943, the struggle 'had raged, in the very midst of the organisation which had given itself up to sacrifice and brother-love', causing 'the worst and most dangerous storm in its history'.[1] Fortunately for the Broederbond's leadership – a majority of whom supported the NP – the OB was weakened by state repression and Hitler's decline, thereby solving a problem which might otherwise have dealt an enduring blow to its influence.

The chief points of friction lay in different conceptions of the kind of organisations and strategy of struggle required to overthrow the imperial factor, and on the extent to which the future Republic should approximate to Nazi doctrines. The main questions centred around whether the struggle should be a primarily constitutional one in which the NP would seek changes by electoral and parliamentary means or whether the accent should be on the efforts of extra-parliamentary, paramilitary mass organisations; whether the tactics should be violent or non-violent; whether English-speaking consent should be sought for a Republic in which they would enjoy equal status and cultural rights, or whether they should be treated as second-class aliens; and to what extent Nazi doctrines could be reconciled with Calvinism in particular, and Christian-Nationalism in general. These disputes were dramatised in the public rivalry between the NP and the OB, the first being a parliamentary party employing constitutional methods, the second a mass *volks* movement which rejected the concept of a parliamentary struggle and leaned strongly towards militarism.

The AB entered the war in a powerful position. The mood of rank-and-file Afrikanerdom crystallised by the 1938 centenary celebrations favoured unity, militancy and Republicanism. With the formation of the RDB a powerful new sector of the *volk*, the new urban middle class, had joined the Nationalist struggle. Most importantly, the Broederbond had gained the allegiance of the Afrikaner youth, wide circles of the intelligentsia and communicators, and a big section of the urban workers. Thus by 1939 brethren were installed in leading positions throughout the Nationalist political structure. In the extra-parliamentary sphere, brethren likewise controlled most key positions in Afrikaner Nationalist life. The Broederbond network was therefore well placed to rouse large sectors of Afrikanerdom to concerted action. Its objectives during the war were, first, to formulate clearly the constitutional and ideological foundations of the forthcoming Republic and to ground it firmly in Christian-National principles; and second, to bind together all Afrikaner Republican elements into a single united force.

The war concentrated Afrikanerdom's thought on the possibilities of achieving a Republic. No longer was that aim a distant dream; as long ago as 1934 L.J. du Plessis had pointed out that any weakening of the British Empire, or a German victory, would favour the Republican cause. Behind the scenes the Broederbond played an extremely important part in arousing Republican sentiment and reconciling, where possible, the differences between various bodies. Although it failed to contain the Nationalist–OB rivalry, the

Broederbond succeeded in maintaining a united front of organisations in the initial war years, and it was instrumental in fashioning unanimity on ideological matters. That all Nationalist bodies committed themselves to the same basic pattern for a future Republic was entirely due to Broederbond efforts.

In 1939, as in 1914, General Hertzog argued that Britain's overseas wars were not South Africa's concern and he denounced the view that South Africa was automatically linked to Britain in her quarrel with Germany. This insistence on neutrality was strongly tinged with support for Germany, a country which he did not regard as being intent on world domination. In a dramatic parliamentary debate on the question of neutrality in September 1939, Hertzog was surprisingly defeated by a narrow majority of 87 votes to 67. Defending himself, the Premier cried angrily: 'The German people have been trampled upon and ground down until they said: so far and no further. Who can say that I am wrong, especially I who went through the same as these people?'[2]

Immediately following the parliamentary debate Hertzog resigned as Premier. He was followed by 37 MPs including Havenga, and joined Dr Malan in the parliamentary opposition. Hertzog's resignation repeated the pattern of 1914, when he split from the SAP on the issue of war and formed the NP. But Hertzog was no longer a lone voice in the wilderness; a powerful Nationalist movement already existed, which cautiously welcomed back the old leader who had abandoned them in 1934. Where Hertzog would fit in among his enemies of the past eight years was a delicate question. Nevertheless, his breach with Smuts had destroyed fusion and opened up the possibility for a mammoth reunification of Afrikanerdom. In the attempt to forge unity the Broederbond took the initiative and played an energetic part; but underneath was a fixed determination to root this unity on uncompromising Republican principles.

It was Dr Malan who held out the olive branch. Congratulating Hertzog, he said, 'I never doubted the Prime Minister's honesty and conviction and am happy that he passed today's heavy test and had the strength to survive it.' Generously assuring him of the NP's support, Malan said, 'It is not an unacceptable idea for Afrikaners that the German is attempting to gather together in his Empire what belongs to his race and speaks his tongue.'[3] The implied condition to this support was that Hertzog, the anti-Republican, should now support the Republic. As Malan declared, 'We are travelling non-stop on course to a single goal: the Republic of South

Africa – the only status under which we as a country can genuinely exercise self-determination . . . The end of this affair will be republican independence.'[4]

Acting with great speed, the Broederbond/FAK network organised a great 'Volks Reunification' rally at the Monument Koppie only five days after Hertzog's resignation in order to bring his supporters together with those of Dr Malan. The gathering was officially sponsored by the FAK and the appeal issued in the names of its Chairman, I.M. Lombard, and Secretary, Dr Meyer. On 9 September, 70 000 Nationalists gathered at the spot which had witnessed the climax of the Voortrekker celebrations a year before to applaud emotional unity appeals from Hertzog, Malan and Totius. The leaders grasped hands and solemnly swore that Afrikanerdom would never again be divided. With the return of the Hertzogite section to the fold, it seemed that the Broederbond had at last realised its tenacious dream stretching back to 1920: *Volkseenheid*, or pan-Afrikaner unity.

In 1940 Malan and Hertzog agreed to form a new party called the HNP (Reunited Nationalist or Peoples Party). It was pledged to fight for a 'free independent republic, separated from the British Crown and Empire' and to remove 'step by step, all anomalies which hamper the fullest expression of our national freedom'. So far as it went this was in accordance with the Broederbond's vision. But militant leading brethren such as Hendrik Verwoerd, N.J. van der Merwe, C.R. Swart and J.G. Strydom were dubious about the Hertzog-inspired qualifications to this goal. These were that the Republic would only be instituted after a special referendum rather than by the vote of a parliamentary majority, and that Nationalists who did not believe the Republic to be the overriding immediate issue would not be debarred from membership of the party.[5] These provisions both seemed to water down the Republican resolve and they renewed suspicions that Hertzog remained, at heart, a lukewarm Republican and compromiser.

To eliminate any backsliding, the Broederbond militants now launched a campaign (in which Malan apparently did not participate) to force Hertzog into a more radical posture. On 20 July 1940 the OFS Nationalists, led by van der Merwe and Swart, organised a mass rally at the Vrouemonument for women who died in the Boer War concentration camps 'to take active and immediate measures, on constitutional lines, to bring about a republic'. The mass meeting resolved that the 'time had come for the creation of a free and independent South African republic on the basis of Christian-Nationalism and the maintenance of White civilisation'. In a hint that Hertzog and Havenga had not finally severed their former unsavoury ties, Dr van der Merwe warned the meeting that 'a certain British-Jewish influence which played an important part in the fashioning of fusion . . . is again at work'.[6]

This meeting marked the start of the Broederbond-inspired campaign to drive Hertzog out of the reunited party. Dr Verwoerd's *Transvaler* began to suggest that Hertzog was being indecisive and timid over Republicanism and angrily accused him of pettiness in refusing to meet a Committee of Action chosen by the Bloemfontein rally.[7] A whisper smear campaign was started against Hertzog to the effect that he was secretly in league with Freemasonry to turn South Africa into a Republic within the Empire. Hertzog believed that his rumour originated with C.R. Swart.

The Broederbond's drive against Hertzog came to a head on 5 November when the OFS HNP Congress, led by Swart, rejected Hertzog's demand that the future Republic would guarantee full equality of status and political rights for the English.[8] Humiliatingly turned down by his own provincial party, Hertzog resigned and Swart was forthwith elected leader of the OFS HNP. The final breaking point came when, spurred on by brethren, the Transvaal HNP Congress laid down that the Republic would be brought into being by a parliamentary majority, debarred Jews from party membership and urged the other provinces to do likewise. This was too much for Hertzog. Charging that the OFS and Transvaal Nationalists were acting in bad faith, he cut his remaining ties with the Party and in December 1940 resigned from Parliament. This marked the end of Hertzog's political career and opened the way for Dr Malan, supported by the Broederbond machine, to take command of Nationalist Afrikanerdom. In January 1941 a group of ten loyalist Hertzogite MPs formed the Afrikaner Party under the faithful Havenga, but the moderate Republican policies of Hertzog had been clearly defeated. Indeed, of the 37 MPs who followed Hertzog in September 1939, 25 decided to remain in the HNP under Dr Malan.

When Hertzog died in 1942, a broken and forgotten man, many said that the Broederbond had deliberately hounded him out of politics in revenge for his embarrassing exposés of 1935–6. Whether the Broederbond drove him into the wilderness in fulfilment of their revenge oath cannot be determined. Indeed there is some doubt whether this oath forms part of standard procedure. Nevertheless, it is clear that many of the young brethren could not have viewed with any comfort the prospect of serving under the leadership of the old conservative who had tried to destroy Republicanism, whom they had reviled as a traitor for eight years, and who had made such a point of discrediting and exposing the Broederbond in 1935. Quite aside from personal motives, the Broederbond had strong political motives for liquidating Hertzogite moderation: he was neither a Christian-Nationalist nor an advocate of Afrikaner domination, and must therefore have been seen as an obstacle. Indeed, even at the height of the crisis, Hertzog clung to the unfashionable concept of co-operation and equality among the two white sections and displayed an unpopular concern for English speakers' status and rights.

THE RISE OF THE OB

Having neutralised the Hertzog moderates and consolidated its parliamentary front behind Dr Malan's HNP, the Broederbond suddenly found the newly-forged unity among Republicans imperilled by an outbreak of domestic conflict within the Christian-Nationalist camp. This was triggered off by the spectacular rise of the OB (Brigade of Ox-wagon Sentinels), a paramilitary, ultra-Nationalist mass movement formed in 1939. It led to some of the bitterest fratricidal in-fighting among Afrikaners since the 1914 rebellion, which not only shook the Broederbond's authority but also threatened to destroy its internal cohesion.

Like the RDB, the OB was the fruit of the 1938 Voortrekker centenary celebrations. Both were, in their different ways, attempts to translate the spirit of the celebrations into concrete action; both were Christian-Nationalist bodies; both accepted that Afrikanerdom had now entered its Second Great Trek (the trek from the *platteland* into the alien cities) and both sought to arm the *volk* for the coming struggle to conquer the English-dominated urban centres. Yet there were important differences. Although the RDB idea came from the octogenerian *Volksvader*, J.D. Kestell, the movement was conceived and led by brethren. In its practical form the economic movement was, from start to finish, a highly efficient Broederbond-controlled operation. By contrast the OB began, obscurely and spontaneously, as a genuine mass movement designed to perpetrate the atmosphere of Afrikaner solidarity which marked the celebrations.

The OB sprang from two roots: the upsurge of Republican Nationalism released by the Monument Koppie celebrations, and a strong identification with Nazism which, it was believed, would end the British Empire's world supremacy and thereby create conditions for Afrikanerdom to restore the nineteenth-century Boer Republics. The symbolic hero of the 1938 festivities was the God-fearing Voortrekker, who singlehandedly conquered the black barbarians to bring Christian civilisation to the interior and to find a resting place for his apartheid-based Republics. It was to maintain and honour the whole of this Voortrekker heritage that the OB was formed. To emphasise its embodiment of these memories, the OB draped itself in Boer symbols: the ox-wagon badge, the wearing of beards and Voortrekker clothes, and the Commando form of organisation.

The OB was more than a backward-looking folkloric society: it aimed to recover the Republic that the trekkers had lost. Moreover, its members identified themselves with the trek into the cities. Just as their forebears had 'civilised' the interior, so would they 'Afrikanerise' the new cosmopolitan urban areas. In 1838 the enemy had been Dingaan's Zulu impis; now, a century later, the foe was 'British-Jewish capitalism' and the subtle, but dangerous, forces of urbanisation and secularisation. The answer was a mobile *laager*, a unified *volk*, moving with closed ranks and linked arms into battle. Their vanguard would be the ox-wagon sentinels, the guardians of the trek.

The OB was exceptionally influenced by the rise of Nazism in Europe's political firmament. The romantic-heroic appeal of Nazism harmonised with the mythology of the Voortrekker tradition. Both tendencies stressed the '*volk*ish' character of the nation; both stressed activism, the *volk*'s rootedness in the fatherland's soil, and the cult of the super-man or super-race. As the drum-beat of war grew louder, the OB revived their ancestor's frontier mentality and saw in Nazi Germany – with its militarist virtues and its frequently proclaimed mission to save the Christian West from the Asiatic–Bolshevik danger – a modern version of what the Voortrekkers had stood and fought for. It viewed the Nazis as a contemporary manifestation of their own struggle to maintain white civilisation and the colour bar against communism and liberalism. The movement quickly outgrew its original cultural objectives and adopted a paramilitary form. Its leader was given the title Commandant-

General, and local chairmen were called Generals.

Unlike the NP, the OB was not committed to using the constitutional and economic procedures of the established system and found it easy to adopt the Nazi critique of parliamentarianism, democracy, capitalism, communism and liberalism. Drawing equally on the Voortrekker heritage and Nazi ideas, its battle texts were the Bible and *Mein Kampf*, its heroes Paul Kruger and Adolf Hitler. The OB organised itself as a vast Boer Commando in SS-type uniforms, and its ideal was a Nazi-Calvinist Republic. Not surprisingly, its emblem was an ox-wagon surmounted by a Nazi eagle.

The OB did not, however, begin as a Nazi organisation. Rather, it was a vigilante 'cultural' body, based on the commando idea, whose members would actively maintain the Afrikaner spirit everywhere. Its aims were identical to the objectives of the Broederbond, which gave the organisation its blessing and assisted it into the public arena. But its form was novel: neither a political party nor a pressure group, it was a broad *volksbeweging* (peoples' movement), embracing all Afrikaners regardless of sex, class, party political affiliation or region. The inaugural meeting of the OB was held in Bloemfontein in February 1939 and attended by C.R. Swart, the Deputy Leader of the OFS NP. Officers were sworn in at a local DRC consistory.

The founder-leader of the OB was Colonel J.C.C. Laas, a retired military officer, who encouraged the use of the trek idiom, the ox-wagon symbol and the wearing of beards. A somewhat limited figure, Laas was unable to cope with the organisational and ideological problems posed by the OB's spectacular expansion, and was forced to resign in October 1940. Colonel Laas saw the OB's aims in the following terms:

The perpetuation of the spirit of the ox-wagon in South Africa; maintaining, amplifying and giving expression to the traditions and principles of the Dutch Afrikaner; fostering patriotism and national pride, and harnessing and uniting all Afrikaners, men as well as women, who endorse these principles and are prepared to make energetic endeavours to promote them . . . The *modus operandi* is as follows: celebrating Afrikaans national festivals and our heroes' birthdays, erecting memorials, laying wreaths at monuments, locating and keeping in repair places of historical interest as well as the graves of Afrikaners who perished on the

'Pad van Suid Afrika' [Path of South Africa]; organising gatherings such as target-practice, popinjay, and vulture shooting, playing jukskei etc.; doing folk dances and singing folk songs, holding processions, regular gatherings of an educational and social nature, dramatic performances, lectures on our history, literature . . . debates, camps for men and women etc.[9]

The above passage suggests that the OB was, like the Broederbond, a non-political, cultural organisation with an all-embracing field of operation. What the innocuous original objects do not disclose, however, is the founders' intense Republicanism and latent Nazism. Neither do they indicate the extent to which the OB would encroach on the NP-controlled empire, which was constituted as a *laager* served by a single political organ (the HNP), a single cultural organ (the FAK), and a single economic organ (the proposed RDB). Ignoring all categories and barriers, the OB began to trespass on their territory and assume some of their functions.

Understandably, the NP hierarchy showed early signs of anxiety at the new movement. Although certain Nationalists – such as C.R. Swart, Eric Louw and M.D.C. de Wet Nel – joined the OB, others were wary of the new organisation. For one thing, Colonel Laas was not, apparently, a member of the Broederbond and too many young Nationalists were flocking to its banner. In August 1939 Dr N.J. van der Merwe, the Chairman of the FAK, attacked the OB as a potential source of disruption in the cultural field. He also firmly dissociated himself from suggestions that the whole party-political system be abolished.[10] *Die Vaderland*, the only pro-Hertzog Afrikaans daily newspaper, branded the OB as 'a scorpion's nest of unhealthy extremist activity', which was formed 'without informing Dr Malan by a group of political hotheads in his party, of whom a few were known for their Nazi sympathies'.[11]

The first year of the war strengthened pro-German sympathies and pro-Nazi tendencies among all sectors of Nationalist Afrikanerdom. Hitler's dramatic successes in Belgium, Holland and France after the May 1940 offensive generated further admiration for Germany and seemed to confirm the belief that the downfall of the British Empire was imminent. The effect on the OB was to sharpen its militancy, and wild hopes were raised that the final day of reckoning with Britain was at hand. Surprisingly, the Nazi invasion of Holland and the sorrowful capitulation of the Anti-Revolutionary government aroused no sympathy amongst Afrikaner Nationalists; least of all was there sympathy among the OB's Christian-Nationalists.

Illustrating the strong attraction of Nazi ideas was a booklet entitled *The New South Africa – The Revolution of the Twentieth Century*, by Dr Otto du Plessis, the NP's 'enlightenment' (information) secretary.[12] Published in 1940, soon after the fall of France, it proclaimed that Western democracy was doomed and hailed the emergence of the Nazi New Order, which had worked wonders for all who adopted it. The emergence of a New Order in South Africa was inevitable, though this might have to be modified to meet local conditions. Du Plessis maintained that a new, disciplined state under one party and dictator would have to be established. All unnational elements would be obliterated, and mining capital would be used in the interests of the 'older established population group'. Greater emphasis was placed on the undiluted nation than on the Christian-National character of the proposed Republic; nevertheless, du Plessis denied that the New Order would conflict with religion.[13]

Despite Nationalism's political sympathies with Germany and the outspoken support of some of its leaders for the New Order, and despite the Broederbond's hopes for an axis victory, Malan's NP refused to identify itself openly with Nazism. One possible reason is that the party was sensitive to Government allegations that it was a Nazi fifth column. As a legal parliamentary party, led by an ex-Cabinet minister, it was closer to the establishment than the youthful OB and more aware of the need for legality and constitutionalism. In reply to the OB the Nationalists therefore stressed their independence from all 'foreign' doctrines and increasingly drew a distinction between Christian-Nationalism and National Socialism. The chief exponent of Christian-Nationalism's indigenous properties was Hendrik Verwoerd, editor of the *Transvaler*. Having drawn a careful distinction between Christian-Nationalism and Fascism since 1937, Verwoerd again urged Afrikaners not to lose their sense of perspective. In an editorial in January 1940 he wrote: 'The Afrikaner will have as little to do with German National Socialism as with British imperialism . . . he will be as little a tool of Hitler as of Chamberlain.'[14]

In 1940 the OB began to organise for a new rebellion. The 1914 uprising had been crushed because of poor preparation, lack of co-ordination and inadequate links between the army and the population. Determined to avoid these errors, the OB set up the machinery for a *putsch* and formulated secret plans for a Nazi-style Christian-Nationalist dictatorship. In order to condition its members for a possible third Boer War, the OB held a major rally to celebrate the defeat of the British forces at Majuba in the Anglo–Boer War. Addressing the rally on 24 February 1940, Colonal Laas described the OB as a 'Boer organisation' whose essence was 'the presentation of the traditions and language of the Boer nation'. He made a point of stressing that Jews were absolutely excluded from membership.[15]

A secret military arm of the OB was formed, known as the Stormjaers (stormtroopers), based on the Nazi SS. Many policemen were clandestine members. The Stormjaers subsequently launched a campaign of terror and sabotage: it blew up post offices, cut telephone wires and carried out assassinations. They were responsible for beating up opponents in the NP, like F.E. Mentz, the Transvaal Provincial Organiser, and for an attempted kidnapping of Dr Verwoerd. All members were obliged to swear an oath 'before Almighty God to accept unreservedly the sacrifices demanded . . . by the divine destiny of the Nation'. It was repeated while revolvers were pressed to the candidate's chest and back, the candidate's right hand being raised and the left hand resting on a Bible. Potchefstroom (where a trial in April 1940 revealed a secret band of 150 saboteurs) was a major centre of Stormjaer activity. Whether the OB leadership was officially involved in their activities is not clear, but it is certain that Stormjaers were recruited from OB ranks and that they carried out OB policy.

An early clue to the OB's Republican plans was given in the 'Freedom Manifesto' of the ANS (which was, in effect, the OB's youth wing) issued on 1 July 1940. 'We feel that we have reached the point where we must boldly demand the transformation of the Union of S.A. into a Republican State', declared the introduction. 'To reach this goal we shall not hesitate to take all necessary measures.' The draft constitution envisaged the abolition of the Westminster-style system of party-political government. Instead, it provided for an authoritarian president, elected by the *volk* for a fixed period and responsible to God alone, assisted by an Executive and a *Volksraad* (Parliament) of occupational and area representatives. The state would distinguish between citizens, subjects and visitors. Its policy would stem from 'the traditional Afrikaners' Christian-National life outlook'.[16] As with subsequent OB draft plans for a Republic, this manifesto seemed to reveal the thoughts (if not the hand) of L.J. du Plessis and P.J. Meyer and possibly Diederichs as well. The document made no reference to Nazism, although a member of the Studentebond was later reported as saying that 'they were proud to be called Nazis'.[17]

The first and frankest manifestation of the pro-Nazi spirit in the OB came from the Reverend J.D. Vorster, the DRC minister and influential figure in the *Koers* confessional movement. Vorster, it will be remembered, had repudiated both Nazism and Fascism in an article on 'humanism' in 1934, because of their rejection of the absolute sovereignty of God. Now an OB general, he saw nothing incongruous in wholeheartedly commending Hitler. Addressing a meeting of the Afrikaanse Studentebond on the first anniversary of the outbreak of war, Vorster reportedly urged the youth to follow Hitler's example. He said that he had just read *Mein Kampf* and that it illuminated the path of South Africa. Attacking capitalism, Vorster went on to say that a new economic system should be devised which would prevent Hoggenheimers exploiting Afrikaners. No non-Afrikaner should ever be permitted to grow rich in South Africa. Vorster called for a Republic in which Afrikaners would 'dictate the terms to the Englishman who will be compelled to accept them'. He foretold of a new trek in South Africa: of aliens like Jews and jingoes (itinerary patriots) departing from the Afrikaner Republic. According to Vorster, the liberal democratic system was no longer acceptable. A Christian-National Republic should be built which would obey the rule of blood and not of the ballot box. Never again should elections be held in South Africa.[18]

Details of the OB's blueprint for an Afrikaner-dominated Christian-National dictatorship were made public in a 'Declaration on the Boer Republic' in 1940.[19] Like the Studentebond draft, it shows the influence of L.J. du Plessis and Meyer, and sought to replace the Westminster system of government with a mixture of constitutional ideas drawn from Kruger's South African Republic, the Nazi doctrine of the *Volk* state, and Mussolini's corporate system. Its ideas were characteristic of contemporary Broederbond thinking: an authoritarian Head of State with apparently unlimited powers, exclusive Afrikaner domination, subjection of English speakers, racially restricted citizenship, one official language, abolition of the monarchy and occupational representation. Commenting on this draft constitution, the United Party newspaper, *Die Suiderstem*, charged the OB leadership with planning to set up a full Nazi state. The only differences were the substitution of President for Führer, a *Burgherraad* for the *Reichstag*, *Raadslede* for *Gauleiters*, Republic for *Reich* and Christian-National for National Socialist.[20]

By November 1940 the OB had swollen to some 200 000 members.

Its rapid development into a neo-Nazi paramilitary, Republican movement worried the government. 'The OB must be watched sharply', said the Premier, General Smuts, 'because it is an organisation similar to that which brought Hitler to power in Germany. Its methods are similar and its aim is to introduce the Nazi system by underground methods.'[21] In November 1940 the German Consul in Lourenço Marques reported the receipt of a request from the OB for German help and support. However, this was not forthcoming and Berlin evinced a certain measure of caution, judging that the OB could achieve little and fearing that the Boers would blame the failure of a rebellion on Germany.[22]

THE CRADOCK AGREEMENT AND THE RISE OF J.H. VAN RENSBURG

The OB's spectacular growth also worried the NP and threatened to divide the Republican forces. From the middle of 1940 the Broederbond began efforts designed to maintain a united Christian-Nationalist Republican front. These culminated in the Cradock Agreement of 29 October 1940, by which the NP undertook to support the OB should it be persecuted, and the OB promised not to encroach on the political field. 'The whole of Afrikanerdom applauds this from its very heart', commented Dr Verwoerd in *Die Transvaler*.[23] Dr Malan declared that the two bodies had agreed to co-operate 'in the highest interests of the Afrikaner nation', and on the basis of non-interference in each other's affairs.[24]

Having failed to nip the OB in the bud, Dr Malan's Nationalists had no option but to co-operate with a movement which exercised genuine attraction for the Nationalist rank and file. Notably, three senior Nationalists (C.R. Swart, M.D.C. de Wet Nel and Eric Louw) were serving on OB provincial committees at this time. Eric Louw summed up the feeling of Nationalist militants in a speech at Beaufort West, when he told constituents:

> The establishment of the OB will contribute especially to the co-ordination of Afrikanerdom's fighting forces. The Afrikaner struggle is being fought on three fronts – the political front, the economic front and the language and cultural front. All three of these fronts are part of the struggle which has been waging for a century against powers and influences from without . . . There must, however, be co-ordination or co-operation between the

forces of struggle on all three fronts. The OB offers the means for such a co-operation.[25]

Coinciding with the Cradock alliance, the NP launched a heavy right-wing attack on democracy. Two days after the meeting Dr Malan forecast a frankly authoritarian Republic:

> Our greatest aim is now a Republic and *we shall try to obtain it as a result of the war*. To work out a system of government remains an academic matter. The Republic must first be obtained and the Republican Government will have to have *absolute authority* for a time in order to establish the Republic.[26]

Echoing him, Eric Louw declared, 'Without doubt radical changes will take place in the political as well as the economic and social spheres. New world conditions have brought *to light defects in the democratic system and a certain measure of rot has set in.*'[27] In December, J.G. Strydom developed a similar theme. Addressing a meeting in Pretoria, he said that the coming Republic 'will be very different from the Union of today. The cancer of British-Jewish capitalism will be completely uprooted. Our state system will be entirely our own, fashioned after our own system.'[28]

These statements suggest that there was not much to choose between the policies of the OB and the Nationalists at this time: both desired an Afrikaner-dominated Christian-Nationalist Republic which would exercise authoritarian rule over the other white sections, discriminate against Jews and be anti-capitalist. Both rejected the British connection, and both repudiated the democratic system. The major difference was that the NP was prudently constitutional and not overtly pro-Nazi. The OB, on the other hand, seemed bent on an extra-parliamentary and extra-constitutional struggle, and its leaders, such as J.D. Vorster, made little secret of their admiration for Hitler's doctrines.

An electrifying new element was introduced into the situation by the dramatic decision of the Administrator of the OFS, van Rensburg, to relinquish his post and step into the OB's vacant leadership in 1941. Dynamic, charismatic and a capable organiser, the 43-year-old van Rensburg seemed to embody the militant mood of resurgent Afrikanerdom; particularly its high hopes that a heroic New Era was at hand which would consign the British Empire and liberal-capitalism to oblivion. Van Rensburg was not, like many of his colleagues in the Broederbond, a fervent Nationalist in his youth.

As a 16-year-old he was a member of a Government Commando which fought a group of Boer rebels near Winburg in 1914. The tragic sight of Boer fighting Boer converted van Rensburg to Nationalism. He began at this time to read German, and found solace in the works of Oswald Spengler.

Van Rensburg's rise in public life was meteoric. After taking a law degree, he became private secretary to the Minister of Justice, Tielman Roos, in 1924. He then rose rapidly through the Civil Service, becoming Under-Secretary for Justice in 1930. Oswald Pirow, the Germanophile and fanatical anti-communist who succeeded Roos as Minister of Justice, adopted van Rensburg as his protégé and appointed him Secretary for Justice in 1933. It was during this time that van Rensburg acquired his mentor's admiration for Europe's new right-wing totalitarian movements, and he became a fluent German scholar. In 1936 van Rensburg, still only 38, was appointed by the Hertzog government to the Administratorship of the OFS.

At the first opportunity van Rensburg visited Germany, where a brief but deeply impressive meeting with Hitler moved him to compare the Führer's emergence to the miracle of Joan of Arc. He also met other top Nazis, including Goebbels and Goering. Ambitious, and convinced that a revolutionary new era was at hand, van Rensburg felt immobilised by his capacity as Administrator of the OFS. Shortly after war broke out he called a meeting of the officers of the Fourth Brigade, of which he was Commander, and told them that although he thought the war was wrong and admired the Germans, he would carry out his officer's duties. But there was one order he would never execute: 'I will not shoot my own people. I did that once, as a boy of 16 – and that was twice too many!'[29] Duly relieved of his command, van Rensburg also decided to relinquish his administratorship, in order to 'devote myself to other duties – more specifically the cause of my own flesh and blood of my own Afrikaans speaking Afrikaners'.[30]

Van Rensburg revitalised the OB and brought to it an aura of respectability which the eccentric and secretive Colonel Laas lacked. He was greeted in some quarters as the new saviour of Afrikanerdom, his advent being reputedly foretold by the famous Afrikaner mystic and seer, N.P.J.J. 'Siener' van Rensburg (no relation) who, only just before, had predicted that a man in a brown suit would suddenly emerge and lead his *volk* to its final salvation. On New Year's Day 1941, Dr van Rensburg accepted the post of the OB's Chief

Officer and Commandant-General. In a press statement the former Administrator and Secretary for Justice declared that the OB now stood in the front line of the Afrikaner struggle:

> That Afrikanerdom finds itself in a position of need and crisis as never before since October, 1899, must be perfectly clear even to a blind man; that dangers external as well as internal threaten our whole existence is equally unmistakeable; and at the focal point of these dangers stands the Ossewa-Brandwag . . . All the fire and venom of the enemies of Afrikanerdom – the capitalists, imperialists and their misguided followers – are being directed against this organisation. Because it sprang into the breach to protect and perpetuate the interests of the Afrikaner and his children and children's children in their own fatherland, its sentinels are now being threatened with imprisonment, with prohibition regulations, internment, spying, house-searching, assault and all the methods of intimidation which the enemies of Afrikanerdom have at their command in the Afrikaner's one and only fatherland. Against all these dangers and threats the Ossewa-Brandwag stands again in the breach; and it is an honour for me to be able to appear in the van and to share all those discomforts and dangers with them.[31]

Van Rensburg was formally installed on 15 January 1941. The following day, the *Transvaler* reported his views on totalitarianism:

> With democracy in its academic sense I have no special quarrel. In any case one should not speak evil of the dead. But I wish to add that a democracy or any other -cracy is not an end in itself, but merely a means to the end. The end is the nation. If I can serve my nation better by democratic action, I will do so, but if I have to choose between Afrikanerdom and democracy, then there is no other choice.[32]

Van Rensburg's remarks suggested that, notwithstanding the OB's Cradock pledge to refrain from politics, its aim was to take over the system and capture the state. This impression was strengthened by a statement from J.D. Vorster, who predicted that the OB would rule the country because it was the only purely South African movement.[33] Van Rensburg repeatedly told rallies that the OB alone could save the *volk* and that it was the only organisation that could achieve a Republic. He made it clear that he could not accept

Malan's thesis that the OB was a mere extra-parliamentary appendage of the NP. He presented Afrikanerdom with an alternative road to political power: extra-parliamentary, using violence if necessary, and taking sides with the government's enemy.

The advent of van Rensburg also led to a stepping-up of violence. His first public meeting in Johannesburg City Hall on 31 January 1941 led to two days of rioting, in which soldiers fought a running battle with armed bands of OB members in the city's main streets. The OB's clandestine militia, the Stormjaers, began to extend their campaign of sabotage and terror. After disturbances had broken out in Johannesburg and intelligence reports that the OB had recruited extensively within the Civil Service (especially the police), General Smuts acted speedily to forestall the possibility of a coup d'état. First, nearly 400 policemen were dismissed for pro-OB sympathies. Then, on 1 March, Smuts issued a decree forbidding civil servants from belonging to the OB on pain of prosecution. This was the first of a series of retaliatory measures by the state, which now saw the OB as its most dangerous internal foe.

Despite the OB's growing challenge, Dr Malan kept to his side of the Cradock Agreement. In February 1941, he warned Smuts to keep his hands off the organisation. 'The fact that already between 300 000 and 400 000 people have joined the Ossewa Brandwag', he told Parliament, 'proves what place it has taken in the hearts of the public, and I tell you that you must leave the Ossewa-Brandwag in peace'.[34] At the same time, he gently warned the OB to keep out of the NP's terrain, saying, 'The OB is a mighty organisation which wishes to discipline our people and make it easier for us to attain our national ideals. We need the OB on one side and the political party on the other.'[35]

Nevertheless, to safeguard his right flank, Malan began to move towards a radically anti-democratic stance early in 1941. Making allowances for differences in terminology and stress, it may be said that Malan adopted a position that was virtually identical to that of the OB. This was more than a simple tactical manoeuvre. By the end of 1940, it was already evident that the HNP subscribed to the same basic blueprint for a Republic as did the OB, even though they differed in the degree of their ideological commitment to Nazism. Behind this identity of viewpoint lay the work of a group of Broederbond intellectuals – particularly L.J. du Plessis, Nico Diederichs and P.J. Meyer – who had argued in *Ons Republiek* that the coming republic should be an Afrikaner-dominated, totalitarian, authoritarian and anti-democratic *volk* state. These men were also associated with a 'Commission for General Policy', on which was represented the HNP, OB and FAK, which had been set up (probably on the Broederbond's initiative) to consolidate all Afrikaner thoughts on the future Republic, and which had worked out a provisional draft constitution towards the end of 1940.

Ons Republiek is a revealing view of the AB's Republican plans in 1941. In a chapter by Diederichs, the chief themes of the secret organisation's thinking are elaborated.[36] These include:

1. the concept of the *volk* as an organic, natural community with a Christian-National character and life of its own, over and above that of the individuals who comprise it;
2. a Republican *volk* state, whose task is to preserve and embody the spirit of the *volk*;
3. exclusive Afrikaner control of the state with purposeful use of its machinery to Christian-Nationalise all aspects of life;
4. the state as a totalitarian and authoritarian machine, exerting strict control of press and radio, and prohibiting political parties whose principles are contrary to the fundamentals of church and state;
5. creation of a group of European second-class citizens (presumably Jews), banning of 'miscegenation', between first- and second-class persons, and limiting their access to the professions;
6. nationalisation of the banks, mining and key industries.

THE PEOPLE'S FRONT AND THE HNP'S PLAN FOR A BOER REPUBLIC

The high point of OB–HNP collaboration was between October 1940 and March 1941. Thereafter the OB's growing incursions into the political field, its ill-concealed disdain for the HNP's constitutionalism and van Rensburg's bombastic claims that the OB alone could bring about a Republic, began to erode the Cradock Agreement. As relations began to deteriorate, the Broederbond launched a new initiative to prevent an open schism. It stepped into the dispute with a plan for a monolithic People's Front composed of all Christian-Nationalist and pro-Republican bodies. Whereas the Cradock Agreement had been an attempt at achieving unity through the demarcation of fields of activity, the People's Front represented an attempt to establish a common ideological basis for co-operation. The public organ through which the Broederbond worked was the FAK's 'Provisional Committee of National Unity', a 'non-political' body set up at the outbreak of war to draft a constitution for a Republic. Represented on this Committee were the FAK, the RDB, the OB and the three DRCs. Almost all the representatives were brethren.

On 2 June 1941 the Provisional Committee issued a 'Declaration on Behalf of Volks-Organisations' to settle the question of the Republic's form, and to provide a basis for united action by parliamentary and extra-parliamentary organisations. Its objective was 'a free, independent republican, Christian-National State, based upon the word of God, eschewing all foreign models . . . with a Christian-National education system . . . and the strongest emphasis upon the effective disciplining of the people'.[37]

This important document was underwritten by an impressive list of organisations. The signatories to the Declaration were: I.M. Lombard (as Chairman of the FAK), J.F.J. van Rensburg (as Commandant-General of the OB), L.J. du Plessis (as Chairman of the FAK's Economic Institute) and N. Diederichs (as organisational leader of the RDB). The Reverends J.P. van der Spuy (Chairman of the DRC Council), I.D. Kruger (Chairman of the Inter-Church Commission of the DRC) and D.F. Erasmus (Vice-Chairman of the Calvinist Bond) signed in their private capacities.[38]

Two weeks later the NP accepted the Declaration, thereby completing the monolithic Christian-National front. After the NP's Union Congress approved the formulation, early in June 1941, Dr Malan publicly announced that the whole of the HNP and its leaders in all four provinces accepted the Declaration, the ideas of which were 'in full accord in letter and spirit' with the Party's proposals'.[39] With this endorsement, the Broederbond's Christian-Nationalist Republican front was complete.

Now augmented by NP representatives, the Provisional Committee began to promote the Declaration and a Draft Constitution, of which the Declaration was apparently a summary. With the incorporation of the Nationalists it was renamed the Afrikaner Unity Committee, and was destined to play a key role in trying to reconcile OB–HNP differences. The new Committee was again a creation of the AB and contained a majority of brethren. It became the focal point of the Broederbond's attempts to 'bring about reconciliation between the leaders of the opposing Afrikaner political bodies', and arranged for both the OB and the NP to have three representatives each.[40]

Coinciding with the Declaration of the Provisional Committee (now the United Front), the NP issued its own policy statement on the Republic. Called 'The Republican Order' and published by the Party's Federal Council during the 1941 mid-year Party congress, it elaborated on some of the ideas propounded by Malan in March.[41] Malan had made his Republican views known in an address to the NP's highest organ, the Federal Council, on 24 March 1941. This document attempted to steer a middle course between Nazism and British democracy, by making it clear that the Republic would be thoroughly Boer and not imitative of foreign models.

The determination to create a Christian-National totalitarian Republic, cast in a Boer, rather than a Nazi or British, pattern, was also expressed by Dr Verwoerd in August 1941: 'Countries can learn much from each other, but none with any honour would renounce what is their own creation to please another. The Afrikaner has his own ideas of the State, born out of a history of suffering and oppression. That is his Christian-National Republicanism.'[42] With this sentiment the OB would doubtless have agreed. The problem was how to interpret and give content to the idea of Christian-National Republicanism. The Broederbond's answer is to be found in the Draft Constitution, published by the NP in January 1942.[43] Designed to distil the best of Christian-Nationalist thought on the Republic's structure and content, the Draft had been prepared by the Broederbond-controlled FAK's Commission for General Policy, which contained experts from the HNP, the OB and the FAK. The final Draft was made available to van Rensburg and Malan in June 1941, who were asked for their comments and endorsement.

Malan was enraged when the OB issued 100 000 copies of a pamphlet on 3 July 1941, containing the 'Declaration on Behalf of Peoples Organisations' supplemented by portions of the confidential Draft, which had been privately submitted to the two organisations as a basis for discussion. Consequently, the Nationalists only formally accepted its principles and outline some six months later and relations between the OB and the Nationalists continued to worsen. Malan regarded the OB's premature publication of part of the Draft Republican Constitution as a breach of faith and a Broederbond attempt to steal a march on the NP. In his view it was a blatant incursion by the OB into the political field.

The growing rivalry between Malan and van Rensburg for political and ideological leadership of Afrikanerdom came out into the open in the second half of 1941. Hardly had the Unity Committee begun to function before they removed their gloves for bare-fisted combat. Malan responded to the OB's publication of part of the Draft Constitution by making his first open denunciation of the OB and the New Order's sympathy for Nazism. 'We differ from Nazism', he exclaimed on 4 August, because it demands a 'compulsory single party system' with an irremoveable leader.[44] On 12 August, Malan publicly accused the OB of violating the Cradock Agreement, and put to them a series of challenging questions.[45] He bluntly asked van Rensburg whether he still regarded the Cradock Agreement as binding, whether the OB proposed to confine itself to non-political matters, and why the OB had issued its Declaration while the Draft Constitution was still under discussion.

On 23 August van Rensburg replied at a rally in Brakpan, flatly denying that the OB was interfering in party politics, either by supporting Pirow's pro-Nazi New Order faction in the NP or in any other manner. He said he still regarded as valid the Cradock Agreement of October 1940 and confirmed that the two organisations had agreed not to interfere in each other's affairs. Van Rensburg categorically denied that he or the OB intended to transform the organisation into a new political party in competition with the NP. Regarding the allegedly premature publication of the Draft Constitution, he admitted that its contents were not intended for publication at this stage and had perhaps contained unnecessary particulars.[46]

During September and October the struggle between the HNP and the OB became more vicious. An unexpected token of support for van Rensburg now came from the disillusioned General Hertzog who, having been rejected by both the United Party and the Nationalists, emerged from semi-retirement to announce his conversion to Nazism. Addressing the Head Committee of the Afrikaner Party, which had been formed by a small band of faithful followers, he said in October 1941:

> Never again and under no circumstances will I again take part in a political system calculated only to satisfy the vanity, greed and lust for power of individuals at the expense of national interests. I am still willing to save my country, but apart from the morass of party politics. I regard National Socialism as suited to the moral and religious outlook of the Afrikaner; indeed, I consider

that the Constitution of the Old Free State Republic was based on it. There the question: 'Am I my Brother's keeper?' was always answered in the affirmative. Liberal Capitalism, with its unrestricted economic competition was responsible for the destruction of the Boer Republics and the impoverishment of all Germany.[47]

Hertzog's support notwithstanding, van Rensburg's sympathies were now becoming a source of embarrassment to some of the OB's supporters, and led to the Reverend C.R. Kotzé's shock resignation as Chairman of the Groot Raad in October 1941. This was a severe setback for the OB, which relied heavily on the blessing of neo-Calvinists, and it outweighed the propaganda value of Hertzog's statement. Fortunately for van Rensburg, Potchefstroom's three influential OB professors – du Plessis, Stoker and van der Walt – remained faithful, although they were now to express subdued reservations about certain aspects of Nazism. Professor Stoker, for example, stated categorically that Christian-Nationalism could not accept the deification of state or race. Van der Walt noted that van Rensburg made no secret of his strong attraction to National Socialism, adding that there was nothing in the Commandant-General's ideas which ran counter to Calvinism, provided that the sovereignty of God was humbly recognised.[48]

The resignation of Kotze (who, ironically, was replaced by the Reverend S.J. Stander, a former Christian-Nationalist critic of Nazism) marked the real start of the OB's decline. Harassed by Smuts, outmanoeuvred by Malan, unable to bring off the lightning *putsch* which it had led Afrikanerdom to expect, and with doubts rising as to whether Hitler would win the war, the OB lost some of its former glamour and the aura of high promise which had initially drawn Afrikaners to its bandwagon. Soon after Kotze's resignation, the last vestiges of OB–HNP collaboration disappeared. A final meeting between van Rensburg and Malan took place in November 1941; in January 1942 Malan broke off all negotiations, knocking a final nail in the coffin of the Broederbond-sponsored Unity Committee. Henceforth the two bodies were at daggers drawn; the OB mounted a propaganda attack on the 'foreign' system of party politics and Malan's role in playing the part of 'His Majesty's licensed Republican opposition'.

The Draft Constitution which the NP issued in January 1941 was the result of the collective efforts of a group of Broederbond draftsmen, and to that extent it may be regarded as a Broederbond document. Originally, it appeared in a highly provisional form as a basis for discussion (prepared by the FAK's Commission for General Policy) towards the end of 1940. Members of the Commission – among whom were representatives of the HNP, OB and FAK – undertook to spread its ideas, with a view to finally submitting the Draft to political leaders.[49] Dr Verwoerd expressed some of the ideas in this Draft in an article in *Stryd* of September 1940. The broad principles on which the constitution was based were contained in the Declaration on behalf of *Volks* Organisations and some specific details were disclosed in the disputed OB pamphlet of July 1941.

According to Meyer, who had a hand in preparing the Draft Constitution, the document produced 'a very great measure of agreement among Afrikaans leaders in the political and cultural fields with regard to the republican ideal and policy'.[50] Appearing in *Die Transvaler* and *Die Burger* on 22 and 23 January 1942, the text of the Constitution was introduced by an explanatory note. This explained that the Constitution was being published on the authority and with the assent of Dr Malan, leader of the NP, although it left room for amendment on certain points. After coming to power in 1948, NP leaders claimed that the Draft Constitution was purely a basis for discussion, not part of party policy, but this claim is belied by evidence which suggests that, subject to minor changes of detail, it represented the Nationalists' blueprint for a Christian-National Republic.

Several illuminating points emerge from the Draft Constitution. Its provisions are not only, as the preamble tells readers, in conformity with previous NP utterances and Dr Malan's Republican resolution to Parliament, but corresponds closely to other Broederbond-sponsored documents. Despite differences in style and phraseology, there is an extraordinary close resemblance between Dr Malan's and Dr van Rensburg's Republican plans, given the bitter relationship between them.[51] Indeed, both the NP and the OB were agreed on the following points.

1. The Republic would be an independent sovereign state outside the Empire.
2. It would be an Afrikaner-dominated *volk* state.[52]
3. Ideologically, the state would be Christian-Nationalist and recognise the sovereignty of God. All moral creeds, such as

liberalism, socialism and secularist doctrines, are forbidden.
4. The state would be totalitarian. All media, and certain important aspects of the means of production and distribution, would be state-controlled.
5. All British symbols would be effaced and replaced by Afrikaner symbols: the Head of State would become the President; the old Transvaal flag, the *Vierkleur*, would replace the Union Jack and the Union Flag; the national anthem would be 'Die Stem'.
6. Considerable authority is vested in the President, who is elected for five years. He has the power to appoint and dismiss the Prime Minister and Cabinet, and is responsible to God alone.
7. A corporate element is introduced into the machinery for electoral representation; in addition to Parliament, there is a Community Council with advisory powers composed both of official nominees and elected spokesmen for various social institutions, spheres of activity, occupations and interest groupings.
8. Non-whites are strictly segregated and encouraged to develop separately, although not in such a way as to disturb the availability of labour.

The only major difference of principle between the NP and the OB with respect to their Republican ambitions is that whereas Malan was prepared to tolerate a multi-party system (provided that all parties stood on Christian-Nationalist foundations), van Rensburg advocated the total abolition of parties in favour of the Volksbeweeging. The OB were also anti-parliamentarian and laid more emphatic stress on the authoritarian leader and the principle of corporate representation. Nevertheless the astonishing identity between the OB and the HNP, at a time when they were locked in mortal combat for leadership of the forces of Christian-Nationalism, can only be explained by the fact that the Broederbond was itself agreed on the basic principles listed above.

THE AFTERMATH

Germany's star waned after 1942, and so did that of the OB. This was, to some extent, a symptom of the declining chance of achieving a Republic arising out of a German victory. Significantly, the Republican upsurge had reached its peak in 1939–42 when there seemed a real possibility of the British Empire's imminent disintegration. The United Party's impressive General Election victory in 1943 also demonstrated that the electorate stood solidly with the Allies and would resist any attempt to foist a Republic upon them. Not only did the Government's police apparatus harass the OB but its erstwhile ally, the NP, kept up a constant broadside. Caught between the two fires and identified with a weakening Germany, the OB began to lose ground from late 1941.

One of its earliest casualties was J.D. Vorster, who was convicted for obtaining military information about the Simonstown naval base of use to the enemy in February 1941. He was sentenced to three years' hard labour. In June 1941, Robey Leibbrandt, a former South African Olympic boxer who had joined the Nazi paratroops, was secretly landed in South West Africa by a German submarine. His mission was to help organise a rebellion, but six months later he was arrested, and an incriminating list of Stormjaers was found on his person.

Dr Malan himself publicly denounced the Stormjaers in November 1941, when he dramatically disclosed that they were planning an armed rebellion. This was followed by a wave of arrests and the arraignment of 52 Stormjaer officers on charges of high treason. A furious van Rensburg accused Malan of conniving with Smuts to destroy the Stormjaers and blamed him for the arrests. In 1942 Smuts began to intern OB activists. Among those held in Koffiefontein detention camp were B.J. Vorster (brother of J.D. Vorster and Prime Minister of South Africa from 1966 to 78 and H. Stoker of Potchefstroom University, who completed *Stryd om die Ordes* on the eve of his arrest. Stoker later became Rector of the camp school and honorary president of the Calvinist Study Bond, which was formed in the belief that Calvinism was the 'eternal source of the volk's power and guide for the future'. Vorster lectured on law in the camp school and attended courses on philosophy and sociology, given by Stoker, and on genetics, given by Dr G. Eloff. He also belonged to the Calvinist Study Bond.

Surprisingly, Smuts did not intern key figures in the OB like van Rensburg, du Plessis and Meyer. But robbed of its activists, disrupted by harassment, and its hopes betrayed by Hitler's reverses, the OB gradually ceased to be a threat. So confident was the Government that it released many internees, including B.J. Vorster, in 1944. Although the OB toned down slightly on its outspoken enthusiasm for the Nazi creed, it continued doggedly to be pro-Germany and stuck to its claim to represent in South Africa what

Germany stood for in Europe. Claims that the tide had turned against Germany were dismissed as British-Jewish propaganda.

Tensions between the OB and the HNP occasionally flared into violence, as when F.E. Mentz, the Nationalist MP for Westdene, was almost beaten to death by four members of the OB in July 1944. Until 1948, the OB kept up its attack on the parliamentary system and political parties, denounced democracy, and demanded a Republican volk state. While Holland's Christian-Nationalists celebrated the downfall of the Third Reich, the OB went officially into mourning. General J.A. Smith, the OB's Deputy Commandant, said that his organisation would honour the indestructible legacy of Hitler. He had bequeathed the concept of an organic *volk* state based on the principle of 'one for all'. Together with Mussolini he had initiated a world reformation and a revival of living values. But an alliance of communism and capitalism had killed the two leaders.[53] Somewhat mercurially, du Plessis offered an apology in May 1945 for the OB's use of Nationalist Socialist ideas, insisting that the OB's policy was based on divine principles rather than on Nazism.[54]

Van Rensburg, however, remained unrepentant and reaffirmed the OB's commitment to National Socialism and Christian-Nationalism in the double struggle against capitalism and socialism. Outlining the OB's post-war policy, he deplored the tragic elimination of the German heart of white-skinned Europe. Inevitably, power was now shifting to the East and Asia: it was moving from whites to non-whites.[55] The OB would now devote its energies to fighting communism. In April 1946 the Bond of Former Internees and Political Prisoners was set up with van Rensburg as honorary president and B.J. Vorster among the executive council members. Its aims were the preservation of comradeship, provision of work and aid for former internees and their dependents, fund raising, and the publicising of the OB's wartime history. The very establishment of such a body was a sign that the OB, having gambled all on a Nazi victory, was a spent political force.

Although a few die-hard members remained irreconcilably opposed to the parliamentary system, van Rensburg and his close colleagues now realised that the struggle for a Christian-National Republic could only be fought through conventional political parties. Accordingly, the Commandant-General and his wife joined Havenga's Afrikaner Party, which was absorbed by the Nationalists in 1951. In 1948 B.J. Vorster attempted to gain NP nomination in the General Election, but his candidacy was vetoed by Malan. In due course, however, all the remaining OB leaders were reintegrated into the NP, a process of unification of all Christian-Nationalist Republicans which the Broederbond helped accelerate. These included P.J. Meyer, J.D. Vorster, L.J. du Plessis, G. Cronje and Hennie Coetzee, all of whom played a considerable role in the development of Christian-Nationalism in the 1950s.

The AB was itself a victim of the conflict, whose roots lay in a profound crisis in the nature of Christian-Nationalist ideology and over the best methods and agencies for attaining Afrikaner unity and a Republic. When the OB developed a dynamic of its own, the AB lost control of the situation and, despite tireless efforts and ingenious formulae, failed to create a genuine enduring People's Front. Nevertheless, the Broederbond was not permanently weakened by the in-fighting. An overwhelming majority of its Executive Committee and membership supported the NP, which eventually gained the upper hand over the OB and swept to victory in the 1948 General Election. Moreover, despite the apparently irreconcilable political–ideological differences between the OB and the HNP, the Broederbond's theoreticians were able to keep the debate within a strictly Christian-Nationalist context and to ensure a surprisingly close measure of agreement regarding the type of Republic envisaged by both bodies.

The fact that the HNP and OB draft constitutions shared, beneath the veil of differing terminologies, a common set of provisions, is probably attributable to the Broederbond's consolidation of Republican concepts. In reality, the sole point of disagreement was over the continued existence of political parties. This is not to deny the importance of the OB–HNP debate over Nazism. To some, it was a crucial issue of principle but, in my opinion, it was largely produced by tactical and terminological differences. All elements in the Broederbond were pro-Axis and pro-German; those Nationalists who rejected Nazism as a creed nevertheless hoped for a German victory and incorporated, perhaps unwittingly, Nazi concepts into their creed and blueprints. Conversely, the OB's Broederbond theoreticians never accepted Nazism unconditionally and openly rejected those emphases and orientations which conflicted with Calvinism's dislike of idolatry. The major determinant of the HNP's attitude towards Nazism was the outcome of the war. As long as Germany held the initiative, Dr Malan and his followers demonstrated support for Nazism and Fascism. Only the OB refused to compromise on its pro-German and pro-Nazi sympathies, remaining desperately loyal until the bitter end.

8 General Smuts Attacks the Afrikaner Broederbond

SURVEILLANCE OF THE BROEDERBOND, 1940–3

As Prime Minister, General Smuts showed remarkable restraint and tolerance in dealing with right-wing pro-German subversion. This was not only due to his phlegmatic temperament. Remembering, perhaps, how his suppression of the 1914 pro-German rebellion had fed the latent fires of Nationalism, Smuts was sensitive to the danger of escalating the domestic conflicts of 1940–3 into a full-blooded civil war. While South African volunteer troops were fighting a life and death struggle against the Axis in the Western desert and later in Italy, he permitted the official Nationalist parliamentary opposition and its affiliated religious, economic and cultural organisations to oppose the war effort openly, and to express sometimes blatantly treasonable support for Nazi Germany. Smuts even allowed the OB to function throughout the war as a crypto-Nazi, pro-violence, mass organisation.

Only when the OB's military arm, the Stormjaers, launched a wave of bomb attacks and personal violence and seemed to be planning a Munich beerhall-type *putsch* did Smuts take action. Under the wartime National Security regulations, in March 1941 he prohibited civil servants and policemen from belonging to the OB and interned a number of the organisation's leadership, although by no means all of them. Despite his apparent indifference, Smuts secretly established a special division of Military Intelligence to investigate the activities, membership and propaganda of subversive anti-war elements early in 1940. One of these investigations was headed by E.G. Malherbe (later the Principal of Natal University College) and was concerned with psychological warfare. This division, assisted by the security services of the police and the Department of Censorship, placed the AB under surveillance in 1940. The following year it began to submit reports to Smuts and produced mounting evidence that the Broederbond was the hub and focal point of Nationalist, Republican resistance to the war.

These Military Intelligence reports – of which the Broederbond knew nothing – gradually revealed the enormous ramifications of the secret organisation's operations and influence, its empire of inter-linked bodies, and its role in building a United Afrikaner Front in favour of a separate peace with Germany and a Republic. As a result of the intelligence reports Smuts decided to prohibit brethren from serving in the Civil Service in December 1944. It was a major setback for the Broederbond, being the only time in its history that its members had ever been penalised by authority. Although the Broederbond claimed that it was being restricted only because it was nationalistic, the evidence suggests that Smuts' reasons had everything to do with the security of the state.

One of the earliest reports was an Interim Report of 11 November 1941 which revealed in detail 'the subversive character of the Afrikaner Broederbond and its long term plans to overthrow the Union'. The report also stressed that the Broederbond was 'in complete control of the Ossawa Brandwag' and hinted at the existence of disloyal elements within the police force. Shortly afterwards, a list of secret AB members covering the years 1938–41 was compiled. Among the names are several Nationalist MPs, many clergymen and several leading civil servants.

As part of its psychological warfare against the Broederbond, the DMI 'leaked' news about the society's activities to the press. An example was the newspaper report of the Broederbond's annual Bond Council in October 1942, detailing attempts to arrive at unity within the Nationalist opposition.[1] A further DMI report was submitted to the government on 30 September 1943, of which we unfortunately possess only an appendix relating to the composition of the Broederbond's Groot Raad. Yet another DMI report was submitted on 8 November 1943, but sadly we have no record of it.[2] The growing body of information presented to the government indicated that the Broederbond network was at the heart of anti-war opposition, and that brethren occupied leadership positions in both the NP and the OB. These impressions were abundantly confirmed by a major intelligence coup: the secret monitoring of the proceedings of the Broederbond's twenty-fifth anniversary conference.

The ostensible reason for the presence of Broeders in Bloemfontein was the occasion of a large *moedertaal* (mother-language) conference in the City Hall. At a secret meeting over the same period in a building belonging to the OFS, Department of Education delegates gathered on 13 and 14 December 1943 for the Broederbond's silver jubilee conference. But, unknown to them, a hidden listening device transmitted a full report of their deliberations to the DMI. The transcript of the proceedings sheds such a fascinating light on the methods, style and atmosphere of the Broederbond that it seems useful to present a summary of its proceedings.[3]

The meeting began with a welcome from the Chairman, J.C. van Rooy. Before the formal proceedings began he asked delegates to submit themselves to a security check. All were to show their credentials to the Chief Secretary, I.M. Lombard, and each delegate had to examine the accreditation of the men on both sides of him. These precautions having been taken, a prayer was said. The Chairman announced that L.J. du Plessis of the Executive Committee was unable to attend and that his place would be taken by Max de Kock of Cradock. The proceedings were then formally opened.

Speaking on behalf of the Executive Committee, Dr Verwoerd introduced the first item on the agenda, namely a proposal to absorb the Trekmaats, a young people's version of the AB, consisting of 400 members in 34 country-wide divisions with an average age of 21. It was resolved that the Executive Committee would investigate more fully the possibility of the amalgamation. Next, Dr Diederichs reported on the Broederbond's efforts to ensure that the spirit of Pretoria University's Medical Faculty should be wholly Afrikaans. The Broederbond had already voted a donation of £1 000 to the faculty, but its Vigilance Committee was not yet fully satisfied that the faculty met with its requirements and was therefore withholding the money. Together with the DRC, the RDB and the Transvaal Teachers' Association, the Broederbond's Vigilance Committee had formed an *ad hoc* committee which had asked the University's Rector, Council and Senate for certain assurances. These were, in effect, that not only should the medical faculty's language be Afrikaans, but that its character should embody the Afrikaans religious tradition. The University's reply was evasive on the religious aspect, and for this reason the Vigilance Committee had recommended withholding the donation.

The third item referred to Helpmekaar, a nationalist education movement which raised funds to assist young Afrikaners. The subject was introduced with a series of dramatic revelations by David van Zyl about British imperialist plans to wean Afrikaner students from their own people through the medium of scholarships. He alleged that the originators of the British Empire Building Scheme were the

British Freemasons, who had in turn been influenced by an English-Canadian named Parkin, the Derby family and Lord Roseberry. One of the products of their work was the multi-million pound Rhodes Scholarship scheme which, he alleged, created British fifth columnists throughout the world. Promising young Afrikaners were sent to Oxford, forced to attend all lectures glorifying the British empire, introduced to English homes and, if possible, married off to English girls 'so that their homes would never be without a dictator ready to spout British imperialism at all times'. To counteract this tendency, van Zyl proposed that the Broederbond should make funds available so that Afrikaner students could study at their own universities without having to travel overseas.

After debating this issue, the meeting adjourned for lunch and the Chairman again emphasised the need for secrecy. After the meeting reconvened, the Chairman asked members to examine the membership cards of their neighbours in accordance with the fixed security procedure. Next on the agenda was the newly-created Engineering Faculty at Stellenbosch University, the first such faculty at any Afrikaans university. A Cape Town member (probably J.H. Conradie, MP) said that the faculty had been investigated and that its atmosphere and orientation was eminently satisfactory. He proposed that the Broederbond should make a donation of £1 000 and that £3 000 be allocated for study loans, with preference to be given to the sons of Broederbond members. A resolution for the adoption of these proposals was moved by a Mr Thom (almost certainly Dr Thom, who later became Principal of Stellenbosch University, Chairman of the FAK and Chairman of the Broederbond) who expressed his gratitude to the Broederbond on behalf of Stellenbosch. Thom stressed that it was not enough that Afrikaners should hold key administrative posts: they should also gain control of important technical posts. He also expressed reservations that sons of brethren should receive preference irrespective of their academic progress. The motion was passed unanimously.

Hennie Herbst, treasurer of the Broederbond and chief accountant of *Die Transvaler*, then delivered a financial report. He revealed that the Broederbond had invested £5 000 in Federale Volksbeleggings (the investment house established as a result of the FAK's 1939 Volkskongres). He stressed that the investment had helped Federale Volksbeleggings to sponsor new Afrikaner businesses. Dr Diederichs disclosed that the Broederbond had invested money in the Park Lane Nursing Home, Johannesburg. For the sum of

£7 000 it had converted a totally English institution (including matrons and nurses) into a wholly Afrikaans institution which was now under its effective control.

After approving the financial reports the conference reaffirmed the grant of Extraordinary Powers to the Executive Committee for the duration of the war. I.M. Lombard told the meeting that it had not so far been necessary to invoke these powers, but that the need might arise at any moment for the Executive to do so. The next item reveals the Broederbond's interest in gaining entire control of the Afrikaans sport of *jukskei*. Mr Liebenberg explained how this indigenous Afrikaans sport kept youth out of mischief and helped, both morally and physically, to build up the Afrikaans nation. It was imperative for the Broederbond to control all *jukskei* in the country, and to this end a special meeting would be held in the course of the congress to co-ordinate plans for carrying out this operation in various parts of the country.

Having disposed of Trekmaats, Helpmekaar, the financial report and *jukskei*, the conference now turned to an outline of Broederbond policy for the following year (1944). This was delivered by Dr Verwoerd, who spoke on behalf of the Executive Committee. The theme of Verwoerd's address was that Afrikaners should give each other mutual support in the economic field in order to build, brick by brick, a powerful Afrikaner monolith. The Broederbond's ultimate aim was to gain control of every key point in public life and, to this end, members should follow an aggressive policy of promoting their fellows into positions of authority. Unfortunately, Afrikaners were showing an insufficient degree of solidarity among themselves. The Executive Committee was most perturbed by evidence that Afrikaners, including brethren, were failing to support each other economically. Owing to the vigilance of the Postal Censor, it had not been possible to issue written directives to members regarding the support of Afrikaner ventures, or to convey information as to which firms were actually controlled by the Broederbond or else by reputable Afrikaners.

Verwoerd mentioned, *inter alia*, that Afrikaner medical and dental practitioners did not enjoy the support of their fellow countrymen: one dying Broederbond member had even chosen to be treated by a Jewish doctor when a local Afrikaner practitioner was available. He also mentioned the disgraceful case of a DRC minister and Broer who had sold his parsonage to an Indian. Verwoerd went on to summarise crisply the Broederbond's strategy:

It was not sufficient merely to support each other. It was the calculated policy of the Afrikaner Broederbond to gain control of as many key-points as they could. Members of the Afrikaner Broederbond should help each other to become members of school committees, village committees, town and city councils, in short, the Afrikaner Broederbond must gain control of everything it could lay its hands on, and must not refrain from pushing its members into any key-point whatsoever.[4]

To commemorate the twenty-fifth anniversary of the Broederbond its Secretary, I.M. Lombard (who joined in 1919), then gave a resumé of its history.[5] Lombard painted a picture of a small, dedicated band of patriotic Nationalists who had acted as the conscience of Afrikanerdom for a quarter of a century. He explained how the Broederbond had been born at a moment when Afrikanerdom's fortunes were at a low ebb. During the 1920s the organisation had steadily expanded, despite the crisis of 1924 when the Nationalists made a pact with Labour. In the 1930s it survived another crisis, this time caused by General Hertzog's attack. It had gone on to accomplish important achievements in the cultural and economic fields. Amongst these were the establishment of the FAK, the conversion of Pretoria University into a wholly Afrikaans institution, fostering the Afrikaans language, and gaining recognition of 'Die Stem' as the Afrikaans national anthem. Through the FAK the Economic Institute had been formed, and out of it various funds for the rehabilitation of the Afrikaner had been established. The Broederbond either controlled, or had an important state in, Volkskas, Unie Winkels, SASBANK, Federale Volksbeleggings, Saambou and the Park Nursing Home. Politically, the Broederbond was responsible for the organisation of the 1939 meeting at Monument Koppie and the formation of the Eenheids Front. Through this initiative, the Broederbond was attempting to maintain unity in order to strive for the Christian-National Republic. Lombard was reported as saying:

> All these things had been achieved because the A.B. had tackled each problem systematically and methodically, and shown patience where necessary until its goal had been reached. Lombard spoke very eloquently on the great value of brotherhood among the members and showed how the A.B. had weathered all storms because they were imbued with brother love and love of country which alone could spur them on [etc., etc.][6]

Lombard was followed by the Broederbond's Chairman, thought to be J.C. van Rooy, who said that the organisation had fully justified its existence in the economic and cultural fields. However, much work still needed to be done to bring about Afrikaner unity. The chief obstacle was the bitter dispute between the HNP and the OB, which raged not only in the public arena but also in the heart of the Broederbond itself. But, despite the perpetration of unbrotherly acts, the Broederbond had weathered this, the most dangerous in its history, and was still the mainstay of Republican Afrikanerdom. The Broederbond, he warned, would have to face grave challenges in the future, especially from 'their old enemies the British-Jewish capitalists'. Large-scale British immigration, communism, dual-medium schools, and so on would have to be fought. Above all, internal dissension had to be combated and ranks would have to be closed in order to win the Republic. Only after the attainment of a Republic should they argue about the nature of its character. The Chairman concluded with a reminder that the Broederbond was created by God to bring about his will; it fought not only for the Afrikaners but for the cause of God.

At the end of this speech delegates rose and sang the Free State Volkslied (the anthem of the former Free State Republic). On behalf of the Broederbond's foundation members, Henning Klopper called for redoubled Broederbond activity against its enemies, especially the British and the Jews. The meeting ended with the reading of a psalm and the offering of prayers by two DRC ministers. It is worth noting that the Broederbond anniversary conference – held in Bloemfontein on Monday, 13 and part of Tuesday, 14 December 1943 – coincided with the FAK's Volkskongress on dual-medium education, held in Bloemfontein on 14 December 1943. The Chairman of the FAK congress was J.C. van Rooy, and it is likely that most of the delegates to the Broederbond conference also attended the FAK congress (which, presumably, provided their alibi for being in Bloemfontein).

INVESTIGATORS PRESS FOR GOVERNMENTAL COUNTER-MEASURES, 1943–4

A confidential DMI report, probably issued in January 1944, provided detailed evidence of Broederbond infiltration into the teaching profession and Civil Service. It alleged that, of the 2 528 members of the Broederbond, about 40 per cent were either teachers in schools, colleges and universities, or *predikants* (priests) and members of bodies controlling schools and colleges. Moreover, the provincial education departments of the OFS, the Transvaal and even the Cape, were said to be under the control of the Broederbond. The report claimed that the special branch of the Broederbond in the government Union Buildings had been dissolved, probably because of the need for secrecy. This circumstance, coupled with the fact that senior officials were usually treated as *los broers* (that is, not attached to any branch), meant that it was almost impossible to reveal their identity. Nevertheless, a number of senior officials and departmental heads were mentioned whose names had come up 'by accident'.

Broederbond penetration of the state was detailed in the departments and ministries of Social Welfare, Posts and Telegraphs, Food Control, Justice, Education, Agriculture, Railways and Harbours, and Police. After analysing the all-pervasive grip of the secret organisation's octopus-like tentacles, it concluded with a plea – the first of several – for speedy government action. The report drew particular attention to the Broederbond's 'subversive character' and long-range revolutionary plans for the establishment of a Republic, as well as its undercover links with Nazism. It declared:

> In 1935, in full peace time, General Hertzog judged it necessary to destroy the Afrikaner Broederbond. Today, with better experience of its evil influence in war time, the need for action is much more urgent. If we are ever to dwell together in peace and sanity in South Africa, the Broederbond must be destroyed. The Government must act and act *now*.[7]

Backing up this plea, the DMI summarised the Broederbond's extensive penetration of the Civil Service structure and its key role in Republican Nationalist opposition to the war. This secret report was followed up with three memoranda, none of which bear any identifying marks of authorship of signatures. However, all the circumstantial evidence points overwhelmingly to a DMI origin. Each is written and set out in a similar style, summarising the Broederbond's origins and history using points and detail gleaned from the 1943 conference. Each document analyses the Broederbond's structure and aims and its ever-widening range of operations. Finally, each concludes that the Broederbond is dangerous, subversive and determined to wreck the Union.

In March 1944, the DMI issued possibly its most extensive analysis of the Broederbond: 29 foolscap pages dealing with the Broederbond's foundation, history, achievements and aims, conditions of membership and initiation, internal structure, its operations in the economic, educational and cultural fields, as well as in the Civil Service and the DRC, and its hand in the language medium agitation. To some extent, this repeats information contained in the memorandum of January 1944. Although it contains no identification of authorship, it clearly emanates from DMI sources. Again, the report lays heavy stress on the Broederbond's infiltration into the Civil Service and its clever work behind the scenes in obstructing government policy. Once more there is an urgent plea for Government action:

> If the *Afrikaner-Broederbond* is not similarly exposed [like the OB] and its strangle-hold eradicated root and branch – in particular its insidious hold on education – it WILL, AT ITS PRESENT RATE OF GROWTH, WITHIN A FEW YEARS DESTROY SOUTH AFRICA. Thus did the Nazi system, also starting with a small but powerful underground group, gain ultimate control, dragging the whole world into the most devastating war of all time. The potentialities, in the case of South Africa, are more dangerous. Germany's nemesis was disguised in the form of a humble and poorly educated house-painter. South Africa's equivalent is a university professor![8]

As a result of these disclosures, government spokesmen began to make open attacks on the Broederbond. In September 1944 a senior government MP, J.R.F. Stratford (the member for Parktown), described the Broederbond as a 'sinister organisation' which was sabotaging the war effort. 'Unless we can eliminate the influence of this organisation, the administrative efforts of the government and the task of reconstruction will become impossible. We must tackle the Broederbond with the glove off for if we don't, the United Party and all it stands for will be knocked out in the next few years.'[9]

In a strong attack on the Broederbond Harry Lawrence, the Minister of Welfare and Demobilisation, named Dr Verwoerd, editor of *Die Transvaler*, as a member and challenged him to confirm or deny his membership. Dropping all secrecy, Verwoerd replied under the rule which permitted brethren to disclose their membership in urgent circumstances. 'Certainly I am a member of the Afrikaner

Broederbond', he shot back in a press statement issued on 25 September 1944. 'Why did Mr Lawrence think it would take courage to admit it? I have never made a secret of it, and what is more, Mr Lawrence knew it for a long time.' Verwoerd added that the Broederbond was prepared to discuss its aims and activities 'just as openly and frankly as they were discussed with General Hertzog at a time when the latter was also under a wrong impression'.

As the propaganda attacks on the Broederbond mounted, the secret organisation began to brace itself for a possible governmental onslaught. This was discussed on 3 November 1944, when a hidden microphone again picked up the Uitvoerende Raad's deliberations. The Executive noted that there was 'considerable apprehension' among brethren in government employ, and expressed its own alarm at the concerted fire of government attacks. Dr Verwoerd admitted that the Broederbond would be weakened by the loss of its members in the public service, but warned against panic. He opposed the proposal that the Broederbond should make a personal approach to Smuts, and this was accepted. Dr Schumann thought it essential for brethren to remain in high posts in the Civil Service, implying that key members should be permitted technically to relinquish their Broederbond membership so that they could keep their positions. For the moment the Executive decided merely to tighten up on internal security. The major fear was of further leakages. It was decided to scrutinise all new recruits with the utmost care, to warn all divisions to be more careful than ever, and to impose a total embargo on sending important matter through the post. A new security measure saw the appointment of two Beskerm Broers (security officers) to each of the 18 regional 'circles' or branches.

These stringent precautions were carried out strictly. Lombard began to destroy the Broederbond's old records in November 1944. The climax to the intensifying attacks came at the United Party's Fourth Congress, held in Bloemfontein in early December. After a day of sharp criticisms of the Broederbond – of which the *Transvaler* of 8 December gave a rather jocular account – Smuts took the platform with a major statement. He lashed out at the secret society, calling it undemocratic, crypto-Fascist, deceitful and a plague on society. He expressed particular alarm at the Broederbond's secret infiltration of the Civil Service and wound up with the expected announcement of severe counter-measures: the Broederbond would be declared a proscribed political body for all civil servants, on

similar lines to the ban on the OB in March 1941. In his statement
Smuts said:

> I warn the people that there is something in their midst which
> conflicts with our better feelings and customs, affects the ethical
> character of our society, and in the long run is going to pollute
> our society. A small secret minority, or oligarchy, is working
> itself into a position of power. It is clear that the Broederbond
> is a dangerous, cunning, political, Fascist organisation of which
> no civil servant, if he is to retain his loyalty to the State and
> administration, can be allowed to become a member.[10]

Smuts' proposed purge was a most serious threat to the Broederbond and it caused considerable consternation within the Executive
Committee. Dr Verwoerd replied with a strong editorial on
9 December, denouncing Smuts for his attack on the Broederbond
and charging that he had been incited by Senator Andrew Conroy
to adopt this course. Two days later, Verwoerd threatened retaliation
when the Nationalists came to power.

> The jingo press rejoices over the new move for the oppression
> of Afrikanerdom. They rejoice too soon . . . They have not
> realised what this portends for their Sons of England, their Jewish
> Board, their Caledonian Society, their Freemasons, and all their
> aides who were always ready to oblige the English oriented
> governments in their fight against Afrikanerdom. The new
> nationalist government will know how to act.[11]

On the same day an emergency meeting of the Broederbond's
Executive Committee considered how to deal with the proposed
ban. The atmosphere was distinctly gloomy. Despite the Broederbond's high opinion of its services towards Afrikanerdom, it was,
in fact, cut off from the *volk* by virtue of its secrecy. Not only
was Afrikanerdom generally unaware of the benefits which the
Broederbond had secured, but some sections regarded it with a
certain suspicion. Precisely because of its elite and clandestine
character, the Broederbond lacked a popular place in the hearts of
Nationalists such as that occupied by popular and representative
bodies like the NP or the DRCs. As the shadow of the threatened
ban lengthened, the Broederbond Executive sounded out opinion
within the HNP, the DRC and teachers' bodies to see if they would
rally round the secret society. The response was disappointing. In

subsequent discussions the Executive took the momentous decision – the first in its history – to shed the mask of secrecy and to reveal to the *volk* the Broederbond's real character, in the hope of rallying Afrikaner opinion to its cause.

Verwoerd, who seemed to be the moving spirit behind the idea of press communiqués, outlined the approach. 'It must be pointed out to the nation', he is reported as advising the meeting on 11 December 1944, 'that the Afrikaner Broederbond had surely worked to further the interests of Afrikanerdom'. Thus the public should be told of the money paid out by the Broederbond, of its connection with the RDB and the FAK, so as 'to arouse the public into realising how much it owed the Afrikaner Broederbond'. J.C. van Rooy argued that it might be unwise to bring the Broederbond's 'children' (the FAK, DBR, and so on) into the picture, presumably to avoid exposing them to a security regulations ban. It was therefore agreed to play down the direct relationship between the Broederbond and its subsidiaries. Lombard suggested that stress be laid on the Broederbond's efforts to build the nation financially and morally.

Dealing with the defence of the Broederbond's secrecy, Dr Verwoerd reportedly said that the organisation:

> had maintained the confidential nature of its work simply because the nature of the Government demanded that this be so . . . If government servants were known to be working for Afrikaner ideals, the British imperialists would see to it that they were persecuted and victimised so that they would be retarded in their careers. Was the Afrikaner Broederbond, therefore, not justified in maintaining the confidential nature of its work?

The text of the proposed statements were discussed in detail at a meeting of the Executive Committee on 12 December 1944. Discussions were continued the next day, when Verwoerd drew an analogy between the secrecy of the Broederbond acting in the interests of the Afrikaner nation and the secrecy of the Cabinet. This form of justification, together with other points made in these discussions, later appeared in the Broederbond's published communiqués. One repeatedly gains the impression from DMI reports that Dr Verwoerd was chiefly responsible for drafting the communiqués. While the statements were being prepared, the *Transvaler* again hit back at the Government's 'unparalleled' attacks on the Broederbond. These, claimed an editorial, were proof of the

Broederbond's value to Afrikanerdom: 'The imperialist in South Africa has always picked those bodies or persons for strongest smearing for whom Afrikanerdom itself cherishes the highest regard.' A classic imperialist tactic, the editorial continued, was 'to shake the confidence of the oppressed in those who serve them most righteously'.[12]

On the same day the AB issued the first public communiqué in its 26-year history: an article on the organisation's character, signed by its Chairman, J.C. van Rooy, and Secretary, I.M. Lombard. This was published as the *Transvaler*'s page one splash lead story under a brave headline which proclaimed, 'Broederbond begins to put its case. Its high aim honourable service to Afrikanerdom.' But the Broederbond's offensive had begun too late. The machinery of government bureaucracy was already in gear. Next day General Smuts announced the ban. A statement from the Prime Minister's office at the Union Buildings in Pretoria on 15 December proclaimed the Broederbond as a political body under the National Security regulations promulgated in War Measure No. 4 of 1941, and gave all public servants and railway employees who belonged to the Broederbond 14 days to resign from it. Signed copies of their resignations had to be submitted to their respective ministers or administrators. Failure to do so within two weeks, without adequate excuse, would lead to prosecution.

Although the ban had been expected, its timing was a surprise. Many civil servants were on holiday, December and January being midsummer in South Africa. The ban caused widespread confusion within the Broederbond. There were differences of opinion on the best form of reaction. Some felt that civil servants and teachers should heroically refuse to resign and risk prosecution; but most recognised that, as wage earners, and as holders of key positions, they were more useful where they were in spite of the humiliating price imposed by Smuts. In any event, the Executive recognised that a call to stand firm regardless of the consequences was unrealistic and would be disobeyed.

Consequently, on 21 December 1944, the day before the ban came into effect, J.C. van Rooy issued an instruction to the Bond's civil servants in the form of a press statement in which the Executive Committee recommended that the majority of public servants, railway officials and teachers in the Broederbond should resign their membership, notwithstanding feelings of injustice and oppression.[13] This instruction was a tactical retreat: the Broederbond gave an honourable or technical discharge to its threatened members, so that they could retain their strategic points until the tide turned.

Never before had the Broederbond revealed so much of itself as it did in the three-week spate of public statements issued by van Rooy's Executive Committee. United Party critics of the Broederbond had made various accurate revelations; but none was so weighty and authoritative as those emanating from the Twelve Apostles themselves. In all, the Broederbond issued five explanatory communiqués about its nature and aims. I.M. Lombard made two press statements attacking the civil servants' ban, and prominent brethren, G. Moerdyk and Dr A. Stals, made fighting statements in favour of the organisation. The identity of a number of senior brethren in the Civil Service – such as Dr Wentzel du Plessis, Dr H. Mönnig and Professor Avril Malan – also came to light as a result of defiant resignations, prosecutions and dismissals.

The five communiqués were published in the *Transvaler* on 14, 21, 28 and 30 December; and on 4 January 1945. They were not pleas for mercy directed at Smuts, but rather attempts to explain to Afrikaners – who disappointingly showed total disinterest in the plight of the secret society – that the Broederbond was selflessly devoted to their best interests. While the communiqués constitute primary sources of the highest order, it must be remembered that they are essentially polemical documents. The Broederbond was defending its very existence; it was anxious to allay suspicions of nepotism; it had to answer allegations that it was an arrogant, underhand, sinister group of power-hungry men. Inevitably, these communiqués seek to place the Broederbond in a golden light, as a self-sacrificing benefactor of society which neither interfered in other organisations' affairs nor threatened anybody, and deprived no Afrikaner of his due.

There is not the space here to summarise the contents of the five communiqués. Whether they achieved their objects may be doubted, for the die had already been cast. Moving with great swiftness, Smuts had already prepared the banning order by the time the first statement appeared. Moreover, though their object was to arouse a mighty wave of Afrikaner opinion, there was in fact no red-hot upsurge of Afrikaner indignation, no enthusiastic rallying to the Broederbond's banner. Despite its anguished cries for help and thinly-veiled hints that it was being crucified, no spontaneous 'Hands Off Our leaders' movement arose. Though the communiqués aroused widespread curiosity and some sympathy, the only opposition seemed to come from the Broederbond itself, backed by Verwoerd's furious *Transvaler*.

EFFECTS OF THE BAN

The ban nearly crippled the Broederbond, caused considerable internal disruption and temporarily weakened its influence in the administration. Within three months virtually all the brethren in government service, numbering considerably more than 1 000 (or 40 per cent of its membership), had signed their membership. The withdrawal of so many civil servants and teachers almost brought the organisation's operations in these two strategic areas to a standstill. Moreover, the Broederbond suffered financially by being deprived of its subscriptions. But, despite their public indignation, Broederbond leaders took a philosophical view of their losses which it hoped were purely temporary. Indeed the Broederbond even held a jolly farewell banquet for some of its more distinguished resignees, and made discreet efforts to keep in touch with them.

On the Broederbond's urging, the HNP protested against the ban early in the 1945 parliamentary session and demanded that Smuts justify his actions. When the Broederbond issue came up in March 1945, there were strong exchanges between Smuts and brethren on the Nationalist front benches. Among the interesting disclosures were Werth's statement that the Broederbond had between 2 500 and 2 600 members and Dönges' admission that he had been a member since 1935.[14] On 21 March Smuts informed the House that the government had been notified of 500 resignations, but that eight officials had refused to resign. The government then took steps to maintain the law. Of the eight, two chose to resign as government officials, two were dismissed, and the cases of the remaining four were still being dealt with.[15]

The first civil servant to resign was Dr E.G. Jansen, a Director of the Land Bank. The report of his resignation (carried by the *Transvaler* of 29 December 1944) made no mention of his membership of the Broederbond; but it was clear from the context that the 'high standing citizen' preferred to give up his important government post rather than abandon the Broederbond. Jansen was certainly a person of considerable prestige. A founder of the Natal NP, he was a member of General Hertzog's 'National Independence Deputation' to the Versailles Conference in 1919. From 1924 until 1929 he was

Speaker of the House of Assembly, a post he held again between 1933 and 1944. Jansen had also served as Minister of Native Affairs in the Hertzog Pact government from 1929 to 1933. During his years as Speaker Jansen had demonstrated marked pro-Nationalist sympathies, and was Chairman of the Broederbond-sponsored General Monument Commission which was responsible for building the Voortrekker Monument. This distinguished record was spelt out in the *Transvaler* front page report. His nominal reason for resigning was that 'the United Party reveals a spirit which will not tolerate someone of another political conviction holding any state position'.

A few brethren followed Jansen's example. Dr H.O. Mönnig, a senior scientist at Ondersterpoort Laboratories, and A.J. Bosman, Under-Secretary of the Department of Commerce, let it be known publicly that they resigned in preference to giving up their membership of the Broederbond. Most, however, formally terminated their ties with the secret society. A few deliberately courted prosecution by defiantly informing their superiors that they would neither resign from the Broederbond nor from the Civil Service. In a news report headed 'Government starts campaign against Afrikaner Broederbond members', the *Transvaler* stated that a number of civil servants had refused to relinquish their membership of the Broederbond because 'they are fully convinced of the absolute groundlessness of the accusations against the Bond'.[16] The report claimed that departmental heads had 'begged' certain civil servants to resign from the Broederbond, on account of their great value to the state: 'It has been learned, however, that the members concerned are not prepared to accede to this request by the Departmental Heads, and would rather relinquish their posts, as a protest against the shameful and groundless actions by the Government against a high ranking Afrikaans organisation.'[17]

As the number of resignations began to mount, the Broederbond quietly attempted to soften the blow by keeping discreetly in touch with former members. According to Lombard on 12 February 1945, ex-brethren were not permitted to attend their branch meetings, but could nevertheless be invited to 'a sort of study circle or tea party'. Broederbond information could be given to them, but great care had to be taken to make certain that the former member had not, in fact, defected. Ex-members could still pay their subscriptions, but these should be paid to the branch secretary as gifts, and no receipts would be given. Widows of ex-brethren would receive payments from the Death Fund, with appropriate deductions. All branches should keep a watch on ex-members with a view to their eventual reinstatement. The Uitvoerende Raad, Lombard reportedly said, was very unwilling 'to lose conscientious Boers'. Finally, Lombard insisted that secrecy should continue to be strictly observed. 'Broers must not think that because certain revelations had been made public, that the Afrikaner Broederbond is now an organisation, the affairs of which may be discussed with every Tom, Dick or Harry.'

A farewell dinner was held in honour of 30 top-ranking resignees at the Johannesburg Station restaurant.[18] Addressing them, a senior Broer (thought to be Dr Jansen) said that the Broederbond was holding the banquet as a mark of esteem for those who had been forced to resign. He assured them that they had always been a credit to the Broederbond and that a place would always be kept open for them in its ranks. Proposing a toast, Jansen expressed the hope that they would 'always keep Afrikaner ideals on high'. In reply, an unnamed resignee said that the ex-brethren looked forward to the time when they could rejoin the organisation, and said that he was moved by the 'intense brotherly feeling' which prevailed that evening. A third speaker, thought to be Dr Albert Hertzog, said that future Broederbond meetings ought to commence with tributes to those who were being persecuted, adding that reunification would come. A further speaker (evidently a resignee) asked the remnant not to speak badly of the absentees and promised that the day was not far off 'when we shall arise'. The final toast was to 'Our Bond and Our Volk'.

By June 1945 there had been 18 prosecutions for failure to resign as government officials. An analysis of press reports show that six government employees were dismissed for failing to terminate their membership of the Broederbond. These were Jan Cloete, a senior clerk in the Department of Finance; Wentzel du Plessis, Head of the Division of Diplomatic and Consular Affairs; J. Combrink, Secretary of the National Housing and Planning Commission; B.J. de Klerk, Inspector of Agricultural Education in the Union Department of Education; B.G. Venter of the Department of Agriculture; and Professor Avril Malan, Head of the Division of Biochemistry and Nutrition at Ondersterpoort.[19]

Although the ban disrupted and temporarily incapacitated the Broederbond, bringing its work in the administration to a standstill, in the long run it was a relatively minor interruption to the organisation's growth. Unlike members of the OB, no brethren were interned. They were permitted to retain their official posts in the administration, and the Broederbond was able to carry on with its operations, albeit with even greater secrecy than before. The 1 000 or so brethren who resigned were not permanent losses. As early as March 1945 the Broederbond began to reconstruct itself, by putting into effect arrangements for keeping in touch with former members. In April 1945 a new recruiting drive was launched.[20]

With the war's end, the DMI was closed down and the issue of pro-enemy subversion fell away. The demobilisation of thousands of soldiers provided the Broederbond with an opportunity to exploit post-war discontent, particularly over the housing shortage and services. More importantly, the Broederbond turned from the Republican question to the colour issue with the policy of 'apartheid'. This was first given a wide airing at the FAK's Volkskongres in December 1944, and in theoretical works by Professor G. Cronje, the Pretoria University sociologist.

9 Post-War Developments and the Birth of Apartheid

Although the bitter quarrel between the NP and the OB, followed by Smuts' purge of brethren in the Civil Service, had nearly crippled the AB, it speedily recovered after Germany surrendered and the War Regulations fell away. In effect, the purge lasted only six months, for the Broederbond had left behind a considerable 'fifth column' with the Civil Service who merely resigned 'technically' and so the organisation retained its control over senior posts. The government lacked sufficient time to root all brethren from key positions in the administrative apparatus. Indeed, soon after hostilities ceased the DMI disbanded, Dr Malherbe became Principal of the University of Natal, and virtually all surveillance of the Broederbond ceased. Most of the records were destroyed, although Smuts kept some in his private possession (extracts of which appeared in United Party propaganda until 1953). Meanwhile, the Broederbond quietly began reinstalling loyalists who had been forced to resign, in the process passing over those who had proved unstable in the crisis. A heavy recruiting campaign was launched among the youth.

To the Broederbond's relief the split among the Republic Christian-Nationalists now simmered down. Hitler's downfall led to the final disintegration of the OB as a mass organisation, which now limped weakly along, robbed of the hopes which had kept it alive. When van Rensburg, loyal to the bitter end, publicly lamented the deaths of Hitler and Mussolini, he was also intoning the funeral rites of his movement. Soon, to his followers' dismay, he resigned to join the Afrikaner Party.[1] This was more than an admission of defeat in the struggle of Volksbeweeging versus Party: it was a capitulation to the Broederbond's line. In 1946 most of the OB's former activists formed themselves into an organisation of former internees and political prisoners, and van Rensburg was elected Honorary President. Notably, some of its aims – such as the rehabilitation of victimised members and defence of their record – were strikingly similar to those of the ex-Nazi organisation, ODESSA.

With the end of the war the NP once more dominated the political field. Gratefully freeing itself from its pro-German position, it began to concentrate on bread-and-butter issues, such as the cost of living and ex-soldiers' grievances. Mercifully for Malan, the unprofitable war-time disputes over Nazism were laid to rest. Nevertheless, the party did not relinquish its right-wing stance: Afrikaner Nationalism's opposition to liberalism and equality was not derived from the Nazi example and this aspect of its ideology remained undiminished by the extinction of the Axis powers. Afrikanerdom had merely lost the chance, by courtesy of a Nazi victory, of winning a Republic on the cheap. What had been gained was (as the HNP correctly gauged) a simpler reformulation of the terms of the local struggle with South African liberalism and internationalism; these political forces had emerged greatly emboldened from the war. The central issue now was African rights: that is, the question of the equality of mankind. Consequently the party began to focus its attention, above all on the colour issue.

The chief impetus for this switch of emphasis came from Broederbond intellectuals who, developing the themes of the 1944 FAK Volkskongres, began to formulate a long-term answer to the question of relations between the races. The Broederbond's sensitive antennae had already picked up and decoded the dangerous implications of the post-war humanitarian resurgence in South Africa. During the war the Western Allies committed themselves to a new liberal spirit, which was set out most cogently in the Atlantic Declaration. This, coupled with the South African economy's need for labour, had led to a relaxation of the colour bar, an increase in the urban African population, and a rise in the level of African skills. The Communist Party, which flourished during the war, was now working actively to organise the urban Africans for industrial action. Growing African militancy was reflected by the massive 1946 mineworkers' strike in particular.

Alarmed by the huge influx of Africans into the cities, Smuts asked Mr Justice Fagan to examine the situation and his report, published in 1948, indicated an increased rate of economic integration. It now seemed clear that African urbanisation would pave the way for a measure of political and social integration. All this was grist to Malan's mill. With a general election looming, the *swart gevaar* (black danger) seemed to be an ideal slogan. This was by no means an entirely new Nationalist theme; in 1929 General Hertzog had fought a general election on the 'black peril' issue. But whereas Hertzog was, to some extent, whipping up an artificial and exaggerated panic, Malan's decision to use a variation of the same slogan had the ring of topicality and urgency. A special Party commission was appointed to formulate a colour policy for the election.

Broederbond intellectuals played an important role in arousing Afrikaner agitation to the new dimensions of the 'colour problem', as articles from 1944 to 1947 in the FAK's organ, *Inspan*, show. From the pen of the Broederbond intellectual, Cronje, there came three pioneer works on apartheid.[2] Perhaps the most influential of these was *Regverdige Rasseapartheid*, which he wrote together with Dr William Nicol, a founder of the Broederbond, and E.P. Groenewald, Professor of Theology at Pretoria University (and also a Broederbond member). The book sets out lucidly and authoritatively a race policy founded on territorial segregation, and is solidly based on Christian-National concepts as set out in the 1926 Dingaan's Day pamphlet, *Koers* in the 1930s, and Strydom's article in *Koers in die Krisis* in 1941. One of the most remarkable features of Cronje's *Regverdige Rasseapartheid* was the advocacy of racial segregation in every sphere.

In *Voogdyskap en Apartheid* Cronje wrote:

> The Christian standpoint boils down to the belief that it is God's will that there should be a variety of races, volks, and cultures, and that every human group, whether race or volk, has its own task and calling, and further, that the self-realisation of every race or volk must tend to the glory of God. If this concept is valid [*juis*] then it is axiomatic that the glorification and maintenance of such variety, regarded from a Christian viewpoint, is justified and moreover can be taken as obedience to the will of God. If all of mankind degenerates into one mixed 'race' with one hodge-podge 'culture' – as the liberals desire in South Africa, in any event – then it would decidedly be an impoverished, uniform, one-tone humanity, because the variety of races and cultures can be characterised as a *rich* diversity.[3]

Taking a long-term view Cronje predicted, somewhat daringly, the inevitable demise of white trusteeship: 'Insofar as guardianship means that the Bantu must develop under the guidance of the White man, it must be realised that the logical development of this will eventually end in emancipation, maturity and self-determination.'[4]

This provocative idea was reflected in Dr Malan's famous 1948 election manifesto which committed the Party to 'the ultimate ideal of total apartheid' and spoke of the reserves as the 'true fatherland of the natives'. In fact, Afrikaner Nationalism was far from ready for the grant of separate political territories to Africans as proposed by Cronje. The 1948 manifesto did not speak of 'self-determination' and was silent on how the 'fatherlands' should be developed. Judging the electorate's mood correctly, Dr Malan used the emotional slogan of 'Apartheid' (separateness), to sum up the Afrikaner backlash against creeping black integration.

Like Malan, Strydom feared that the white electorate would shrink away from a policy that smacked of conceding rights of any kind, anywhere, to Africans. On an earlier occasion he had said,

> Our policy is that the Europeans must stand their ground and must remain *baas* [master] in South Africa. If we reject the *herrenvolk* idea, and the principle that the White man cannot remain *baas*, if the franchise is to be extended to the non-Europeans . . . how can the European remain *baas*? . . . Our view is that in every sphere the Europeans must retain the right to rule the country and to keep it a White man's country[5]

Facing up to the threats of liberalism, communism and black equality in the post-war world order (whose democratic spirit was epitomised in the United Nations Charter of Human Rights), the Afrikaner's response was a return to nineteenth-century Boer values. In the term 'apartheid' was contained a coherent, simple and direct answer to the Fagan Report's complexities and ambiguities, to Smuts' so-called *laissez-faire* integration, and to the post-war liberal ethos. This pungent slogan was to bring the Nationalists to power, and it contained all the negativeness, the yearning for *volk*ish purity and the search for self-isolation from dangerous world-wide trends of thought. The Christian-Nationalists were perhaps no longer talking about the dangerous spirit of 1789; but their repudiation of fellowship, equality and rights for Africans showed that counter-revolution was still uppermost in their thoughts.

When the 1948 election results were announced on 26 May 1948, it turned out to be something of a landslide, with the Nationalists gaining 36 new seats. On his triumphant journey from Cape Town to the Union Buildings, Malan jubilantly told his cheering supporters: 'Today South Africa belongs to us once more. For the first time since Union, South Africa is our own. May God grant that it will always remain our own.'[6] Symbolically, the dying Premier, General Smuts, was defeated at Standerton by Wentzel du Plessis, the civil servant who was dismissed from government service in 1945 for refusing to resign from the Broederbond.

Malan's promise of a firm solution to the 'native problem', coupled with government bungling over demobilisation and widespread post-war disillusionment, had brought the Nationalists a majority of seats, although not a majority of votes. The Nationalists, benefiting from the system of rural vote 'loading', had in fact won only a minority of the white vote and ruled with a razor-fine parliamentary majority. Still, it was an exclusively Afrikaner regime, the first in the Union's history. The Nationalists were helped to victory by their alliance with Havenga's Afrikaner Party which gave them a combined sum of 79 seats as against the opposition parties' 71. Even so, the combined NP-Afrikaner Party alliance polled 140 000 fewer votes than the opposition.

It may safely be assumed that behind this pact was the Broederbond, which had used the post-war period to heal divisions in the Afrikaner political front. A sign of the new honeymoon was the collaboration of Broederbonders Cronje (a former OB General) and Nicol (a Nationalist) in the joint work, *Regverdige Rasseapartheid*. Yet the alliance ran into difficulties when a section of the OB's leadership (notably Dr van Rensburg and his wife), joined Klaas Havenga's Afrikaner Party. Given the cautious and undoctrinaire version of Nationalism to which Havenga subscribed the combination is difficult to explain, except on the basis of van - Rensburg's old ties with General Hertzog who, it will be recalled, embraced National Socialism on the eve of his death. But, although Malan was willing to work with his old colleague Havenga, there was still bad blood between himself and van Rensburg.

Signs of the still rankling bitterness manifested themselves when B.J. Vorster, a former OB general, sought the HNP nomination in Brakpan in 1948. So resentful were the Nationalists of the OB and its war-time opposition to parliamentary politics that Dr Malan himself vetoed Vorster's nomination: a move strongly supported by Dr Verwoerd, the prospective candidate for Alberton, and Ben Schoeman, Chairman of the NP on the Witwatersrand. Undaunted, Vorster stood as an independent and was only narrowly defeated. Yet in 1962 the same Vorster was chosen by Verwoerd as Minister of Justice, and in 1966 he defeated Schoeman to become party leader and prime minister.

Despite these lingering conflicts, the 1948 victory meant that the Broederbond was, through the NP, in a good position to control the levers of state policy. The party it had fathered as Afrikanerdom's sole political front, and to whose pre-eminence within Afrikanerdom it had contributed more than any other factor, had emerged triumphant. True to the crusade against the spirit of 1789, the Broederbond regard the new situation as a vital opportunity to erase finally all traces of liberalism in South Africa. Dr Diederichs, one of the most important Broederbond members, issued a stirring call to battle in his maiden speech to Parliament on 19 August 1948:

> What is at issue [between the United and Nationalist Parties] is two outlooks on life, fundamentally so divergent that a compromise is entirely unthinkable . . . On the one hand we have nationalism, which believes in the existence, the necessary existence of distinct peoples, distinct language, nations and cultures, and which regards the fact of the existence of these peoples and these cultures as the basis of its conduct. On the other hand we have liberalism, and the basis of its political struggle is the individual with his so-called rights and liberties . . . This doctrine of liberalism that stands for equal rights for all civilized human beings . . . is almost the same as the ideal of communism.[7]

In his speech Diederichs completely ignored the fact that the United Party (which stood for white trusteeship and the colour bar) was hardly an instrument of liberalism, let alone communism. But Broederbond theory recognised only one antithesis; the collective, organic, Christian nation, versus the liberal, arithmetical aggregate. In faithful Kuyperian terms, it defined the coming struggle in the language of the nineteenth-century *Kultuurkampf*. The major tasks now facing the Broederbond were to widen the sphere of Afrikaner unity to include the 250 000 Afrikaners who voted for General Smuts in 1948; to frame projects for the 'Afrikanerisation' of South African life; and to mobilise Afrikaner opinion for the clash with awakening African Nationalism and the forces of communism.

Of the 12-member 1948 Cabinet a high proportion were brethren.[8] Somewhat surprisingly J.G. Strydom, leader of the Transvaal Nationalists and 'Lion of the North', was given the relatively junior portfolio of Minister of Water Affairs. His conspicuous downgrading seemed to indicate Malan's determination not to be a prisoner of the militant northerners (and, it could be argued, of the Broederbond, the headquarters of which were in the Transvaal). Certainly there seemed to be a disproportion of Cape Nationalists, who filled seven of the twelve portfolios in the Cabinet. These were men whose loyalty Malan could be totally sure of.

Several brethren were elected as MPs, including A.J.R. van Rhijn, J. du Pisanie, A. Hertzog, A.I. Malan and W.C. du Plessis. Outside Parliament, W. Nicol was given the important post of Administrator of the Transvaal. Elsewhere, the new regime quickly set about consolidating the hold of brethren on key posts in the state, Nationalist civil servants were quickly promoted over the heads of their English-speaking superiors, despite public protest. In 1950 W. Marshall Clark, the youthful General Manager of the Railways, was forced to retire (and given a substantial sum of public money in compensation). He was replaced by Broederbonder Willie Heckroodt. Only three years later Heckroodt himself retired and was succeeded by D.H.C. du Plessis, one of the founders of the Broederbond. Coupled with similar attempts to secure the Civil Service for Afrikanerdom was the release of political prisoners. One of the government's first acts was to free men serving sentences for war-time crimes against the state. These included the captured agent Robey Leibbrandt and Erich Holm, who had been responsible for broadcasting Nazi propaganda to South Africa on radio Zeesen. Defending his release of those imprisoned for fifth columnist and treasonable offences C.R. Swart, the Minister of Justice, said it was necessary to heal the wounds created by the war.[9]

After 1948 the focal point of decision-making moved to the Cabinet, where Dr Malan (though still a loyal Broeder) had made it clear from the start that power would reside with the government and the NP, rather than the Broederbond. Nevertheless, the Broederbond comprised a clear majority in the Cabinet and it remained the largest and most powerful single pressure group within the party. Malan was neither a prisoner nor a pawn of the AB, but he was completely encircled by its zealots and depended on its goodwill and extensive network of power. While the Broederbond could not issue directives to Malan (and neither is it conceivable that it presumed to do so) the secret organisation was nevertheless able to mobilise opinion both inside and outside Parliament in order to ensure that its wishes prevailed.

Just before the 1948 election the *Sunday Express* had claimed that 60 of the NP's 93 candidates were brethren.[10] Within the Cabinet the proportion of brethren was at least as high, despite Malan's preference for including loyal Cape Nationalists who were not close to the centre of Broederbond decision-making. Nevertheless, with T.E. Dönges (an immediate past member of the

Broederbond Executive and an intimate of the Prime Minister) holding the key Ministry of the Interior; with Verwoerd leading the Senate; and with brethren scattered in vital posts – from the Transvaal Administratorship, head of the SABC (Dr S. Pellisier), to newspaper editors, directors of finance houses, and leaders of Afrikanerdom's extra-parliamentary network – Malan was never free of Broederbond pressures. Little is known, however, about the degree of the Broederbond's influence amongst MPs or about any of its specific proposals during this period. Thus, in the absence of documentation, we shall have to deduce the Broederbond's role from the activities of its leading members.

THE BROEDERBOND'S EXTRA-PARLIAMENTARY ACTIVITIES

Amongst the most important activities with which the Broederbond was intimately connected during the term of the first Nationalist government were the establishment of the Institute for Christian National Education (ICNO); the establishment of the South African Bureau for Racial Affairs (SABRA); the FAK's Second Economic Volkskongres; and the DRC's formulation of the scriptural criteria justifying apartheid. All were attempts to pursue the Broederbond's long-term Christian-National policies in the fields of education, economics and colour policy. Some of these developments suggest that the Broederbond was more 'militant' than the regime in its pursuit of strict Christian-Nationalist goals.

A few months after the Nationalists' accession to power the FAK established the ICNO and in February 1948 it also issued a programme for CNE. This document had taken a decade to draw up and represented the final word on the Broederbond's aims in this field. The document deals with education from the nursery to the university and advocates a uniform ideological basis for the education of all groups which would be 'rooted in Christianity'. The ICNO's active promotion of its programme – whose extremism greatly embarrassed a government which was seeking to mollify the increasingly unruly English-speaking section – proved that the Broederbond was not only active, but that it was determined to act as a zealous pace-setter for the Cabinet, regardless of what English speakers thought.

Among the directors of the Institute were prominent brethren such as T.E. Dönges and E.G. Jansen (both of whom were members of Malan's Cabinet), G.F. de Vos Hugo, J.H. Greybe, Chris Coetzee and J. Meiring. Others included dedicated Christian-Nationalists like H.P. Wolmarans, E. Greyling, G.D. Worst and D.P. Laurie. Most, if not all, were Broeders.[11] J.C. van Rooy, then serving a second spell as Broederbond Chairman, wrote a preface to the programme in his capacity as Chairman of the FAK. He stated that the widest spectrum of Afrikaner interests had been consulted and warned against any slackening in the Christian-Nationalist struggle.

For reasons of space the document will not be summarised fully here; it is set out in full in the Appendix to Vatcher's *White Laager* and a shortened version is contained in Bunting's *South African Reich*. Nevertheless, four cardinal points should be mentioned.

1.   All white children should be educated according to their parents' world view. This means that Afrikaans-speaking children should have a Christian-Nationalist education, for the Christian and Nationalist spirit of the Afrikaner nation must be preserved and developed. By Christian, in this context, we mean according to the creeds of the three Afrikaans Churches; by Nationalist we mean imbued with the love of ones own, especially ones own language, history and culture. Nationalism must be rooted in Christianity.

(Article 1)

2.   As well as being founded on Christian theory, the content of all subjects should cultivate a spirit of Nationalism and the child should 'become an heir to and worthy carrier of the national culture' (Article 3). Thus, 'Geography should aim at giving the pupil a thorough knowledge of his own country and the natural objects pertaining to it, in such a way that he will love his country . . . and be ready to defend it, preserve it from poverty and improve it for posterity' (Article 6v). Similarly, 'History should be seen as the fulfilment of God's plan for humanity . . . God has enjoined on each nation, its individual task in the fulfilment of His purpose. Young people can only undertake the national task fruitfully if they acquire a true vision of the nation and of the direction of the national heritage' (Article 6vi). All education should be exclusively in the mother tongue, except in teaching other modern languages: 'Bilingualism cannot be the aim of education, and the second official language should

not be taught until the child has a thorough knowledge of his mother-tongue' (Article 6iii).

3. There should be no mixed schools. English and Afrikaans speakers should be educated in separate primary and secondary schools. 'In each there should be the right relationship between home, school, Church and State' (Article 8i). The basis of higher education should be same as for schools.

> The content should be scientific, but founded on the Christian Faith . . . University teaching should be thetic rather than anti-thetic, never purely eclectic and never reconciliatory. Science should be expounded in a positively Christian light, and contrasted with non-Christian science . . . It is all important . . . that the teaching staff should be convinced Christian-Nationalists.
>
> (Article 11ii)

4. The education of 'non-whites' should also derive from the Christian-National world-view so that they are inculcated with the principles of Christianity, separate identity and apartheid.

> The education of Coloureds should be seen as a subordinate part of the Afrikaner's task of Christianising the non-White races of our fatherland . . . The welfare and happiness of the Coloured lies in his understanding that he belongs to a separate racial group . . . and in his being proud of it. Coloured education must not be financed at the expense of White education.
>
> (Article 14)

> Native education should be based on the principles of trusteeship, non-equality, and segregation; its aim should be to inculcate the White man's view of life, especially that of the Boer nation, which is the senior trustee . . . Owing to the cultural infancy of the native, the State, in cooperation with the Protestant Churches, should at present provide native education. But the native should be fitted to undertake his own education as soon as possible, under control and guidance of the State. Native education should lead to the development of an independent, self-supporting Christian-Nationalist native community. Native education should not be financed at the expense of White.
>
> (Article 15)

This document indicates the far-reaching implications of the strategy to 'Afrikanerise . . . South Africa on Christian-Nationalist lines'. It was for these reasons that the ICNO pamphlet aroused a vociferous protest from English speakers. The formation of an Education League to oppose CNE became a rallying point for a rare upsurge of English-speaking Nationalism. In 1949 Dr Abraham Jonker, a United Party MP, told the House of Assembly that the country was anxiously awaiting the Government's response to the ICNO's programme. 'There is', he said, 'a nation-wide alarm over this threat to drag politics into our schools. It lies within the power of the present Government to stem the tide flowing . . . towards bitter racialism.'[12] At a public meeting in Cape Town S.J. Marais Steyn, MP, said that the ICNO policy aimed at inculcating the narrowest concept of Calvinism known in South Africa. 'It was the one thing the Nationalists could do for which there was no redress. The economic situation could never be restored, but the rape of the minds of impressionable children could never be undone.'[13]

In the face of sustained criticism the government attempted to play down the significance of the ICNO manifesto for CNE. In May 1949 Dr A.J. Stals, the Minister for Education, told the House of Assembly that the FAK document represented only a statement of policy and intentions on the part of individuals. Referring to allegations that the pamphlet emanated from the Broederbond, Stals denied that this was the case. Continuing, he argued that the pamphlet sought no greater rights for the Afrikaner than for the English-speaking youth.

Not only was the government on the defensive, but some of the exponents of CNE, like J. Chris Coetzee, began to explain that they had been misunderstood.[14] Nevertheless, criticism continued to mount. The South African Labour Party denounced the ICNO plan. It declared, 'This policy is the negation of the true teachings of Christianity; it is diametrically opposed to the best interests of true nationalism and has nothing in common with true education.'[15] So intense was the fury aroused among English-speaking academics and Afrikaans-speaking supporters of the United Party that the Government was obliged to give an assurance that the programme did not represent its official policy.

In 1950 Dr Stals was forced into making a major retraction when he promised English speakers that the Cabinet was not planning to impose CNE. Though merely tactical, this retreat was a sign that Malan's regime feared provoking English speakers into open rebellion. It demonstrated that, despite the power of the Broederbond (of which Stals was a member), the government was limited by the state of public opinion in the timing and manner in which the Broederbond's blueprints could be implemented. In the final resort decision-making lay with the Cabinet. Yet, although successive Nationalist regimes attempted to avoid outright confrontation with English speakers over Christian-Nationalism, the spirit of CNE was, step by step, introduced into the schools.

Ignoring criticism, the FAK at its biennial congress in Bloemfontein in 1950 asked the ICNO 'to give full practical effect to its policy in view of the fact that this policy is supported by religious organisations and also by Churches'.[16] Throughout the 1950s the ideas of CNE were propagated at DRC synods and at domestic Afrikaner functions. But at government level the question of CNE was handled with the greatest delicacy. The violent agitation it had aroused was an object lesson to the regime. Henceforth, the term 'Christian-Nationalism' virtually disappeared from the Nationalists' public vocabulary, although the term 'Christian' remained prominently in place. However, if the provocative term was abandoned the concept itself was retained and, spurred on by the Broederbond, the NP continued to rebuild South Africa on Christian-National lines. An example of the new circumspection was apparent when Prime Minister Verwoerd was interviewed about his plan for a new uniform educational system in 1959. Asked whether this would be a Christian-National system, the Premier replied: 'No, it will be Christian and national.'

Paralleling the rise of the NP was a remarkable expansion of Afrikaner economic power. During the 1940s Afrikaner capitalism emerged as a significant factor in the Nationalist movement and the South African economy. It will be recalled that the FAK's 1939 Economic Volkskongres deliberately set itself the task of gaining a larger share of business life for the Afrikaner as part of the process of 'capturing' the cities and 'Afrikanerising' the means of production and distribution. The spearhead of this campaign was the FAK's Economic Institute and the RDB movement. The success of organised Afrikaner economic Nationalism in its first decade can be illustrated by a few examples. An overall index of this economic growth is the fact that between 1939 and 1950 the Afrikaner's share of commerce rose from 8 per cent to 30 per cent, finance from 5 per cent to 8 per cent, and industry from 3 per cent to 6 per cent. Thus, although the absolute Afrikaner position was still extremely weak, the rate at which Afrikaner enterprises were growing was spectacular when compared with the economy as a whole. The total turnover of Afrikaans commercial concerns during this period rose from £38 million to £294 million, and of industrial enterprises from £6 million to £44 million.

Particularly notable was the Afrikaner breakthrough in the financial world. Federale Volksbeleggings, the Broederbond-sponsored finance company, increased its capital fifteen-fold between 1940 and 1952. SANLAM, the insurance company, increased its assets from £900 000 to £4 million from 1939 to 1949. Volkskas, the Broederbond-created bank, increased its control over all savings nine-fold between 1942 and 1952. During the same period the number of Afrikaans directors rose by 295 per cent, business managers by 208 per cent, and merchants by 213 per cent. Finally, Afrikaner earnings grew from £100 million to £350 million.

These dramatic examples of growth were no accident, and neither were they purely a by-product of the post-war boom or the natural growth of an Afrikaner urban entrepreneurial class. They were the result of a carefully-planned offensive by the FAK's Economic Institute and the RDB's mass propaganda and, by implication therefore, of the Broederbond's efforts to gain a grip on the economy. In October 1950 the FAK, the RDB, the Economic Institute and the Afrikaans Handelsinstituut organised a Second Economic Volkskongres to examine their balance-sheet for the past decade, and to plan for the future. Once again the sponsoring bodies and the conference itself was dominated by brethren. The conference chairmen were L.J. du Plessis, Chairman of the Economic Institute; J.C. van Rooy, Chairman of the FAK and the Broederbond; Dr M.S. Louw; and Dominee Jac Conradie. The Arrangements Committee consisted of L.J. du Plessis, N. Diederichs, H.P. Oosthuizen, I.M. Lombard, A.J. Visser, P.S.Z. Coetzee and A.F. Weich.

Speakers at the Volkskongres included Dr Malan, the Prime Minister; Nico Diederichs, who spoke on 'The Afrikaner's Economic Development during the past Ten Years and the FAK's Role Therein'; C.G.W. Schumann on 'The Afrikaner in Commerce'; and M.S. Louw on 'The Afrikaner in Finance'. A former pro-OB and Studentebond leader who joined the RDB at an early stage, Dr Anton Rupert (now head of Rembrandt Tobacco), dealt with 'The Afrikaner in Industry'. S. Pauw addressed the conference on 'The Afrikaner Entrepreneur, Consumer and Worker'; and L.J. du Plessis took 'A Look into the Future'.[17]

In the opening address Malan described the conference as the first milestone in the Reddingsdaad movement launched after the 1938 Ossewa Trek. The economic movement, he said, was born out of need since Afrikaners had for years lived in economic darkness, totally excluded from South Africa's commercial, industrial and general economic life. According to Malan, the Afrikaners' choice was stark: either to die or, relying on their inner energies, to propel themselves into the economic sunlight. Afrikaner backwardness for the most part was not due to an inferior calibre. Malan reminded his audience that their European ancestors had been at the spearhead of Western Christian civilisation just as the Voortrekkers were in South Africa. Moreover, the Afrikaner's Dutch forebears were outstanding traders whose genius in business was the world's envy.

In Malan's view the reason for Afrikaner economic decline was the fact that the Boer pioneers lived in relative isolation with few schools, and on large farms which did not require intensive cultivation or scientific methods. The Anglo–Boer War had ruined many financially. Consequently, it was others who possessed the skill and means to take advantage of the mining and industrial growth of the twentieth century, whereas the Afrikaners remained poor. Their migration to the towns was a trek backwards rather than forwards. Although the state gave sympathetic help to rehabilitate the poor Afrikaner whites, what was required was an act of self-help. This realisation sharpened after the 1938 celebrations when Afrikanerdom recovered its nerve and self-confidence in its own destiny. The economic achievements of the FAK in the past decade meant that Afrikaners could hold their heads up high. Malan closed by saying: 'Of one thing we are today certain. There is leadership; there is self-confidence; there is faith; there is hope; there is the firm will to persist until the end. The future lies ahead. And the future calls.'[18]

Dr Diederichs, in his address, conjured up echoes of the wartime claims of Dr Meyer and himself that the RDB was not a conventional capitalist body concerned with money-making, but rather sought spiritual ends. It was characteristic of the Afrikaner that he always 'attached more weight to the spiritual than to the material'. Thus the economic strengthening of the *volk* 'was never an end in itself, but was always seen purely as a means, and indeed essential means to the fulfilment of the eternal spiritual calling of our nation'.[19] Diederichs went on to discuss the RDB's achievements in industrial, financial and commercial life. In the field of mining, however (of which less than 1 per cent was in their control), Afrikaners had achieved very little. But they had begun to penetrate the gold and coal mining industries.

Reporting on the RDB's activities over the past decade, Jac Conradie drew attention to its role in organising the Afrikaner's buying and saving power. Apart from the great numbers of Afrikaans business undertakings which, directly or indirectly, came into being through its efforts, continual propaganda was made for the application of Afrikaner purchasing power. Another one of the RDB's 'most important functions' was the 'protection of the Afrikaner workers against foreign factory influences'. It had paid especial attention to the plight of Afrikaner workers and had rescued the White Workers' Protection League with funds when it could 'no longer stand on its own legs'.

Despite its achievements, Conradie revealed that there had been a disappointing falling-off in RDB membership and subscriptions. From its peak in 1946 (381 branches, 64 771 members and subscriptions totalling £16 255) it had dropped in 1950 to some 267 branches with 32 757 members paying only £9 009 in subscriptions.[20] A balance sheet issued by the Economic Institute detailed the various Afrikaner business concerns in which the Reddingsdaadfonds had invested. But the total amount collected in ten years – £183 325 – fell far short of the initial million pound target.[21]

With a large number of flourishing Afrikaner businesses now standing on their own feet, the need for a special mass body to organise Afrikaner consumers had, to some extent, fallen away. In any event, a Nationalist government could now give official aid in certain respects. The Volkskongres decided to convert the RDB from a mass organisation into an 'economic protection and development society' attached to the Economic Institute. The administrative and executive personnel of both bodies were therefore integrated. Essentially, this meant that the RDB had become merely a department of the Economic Institute and was to operate (on a much smaller scale than hitherto) only as a pressure group. In a sense the decline of the RDB was an index of the growth, between 1940 and 1950, in the number of successful Afrikaner houses which no longer required backing from a parapolitical mass body. The RDB continued to function, but its last annual congress appears to have been held in 1956. This suggests that its functions were gradually taken over by the Handelsinstituut, the FAK and its regional Skakel Komittees.

To formulate the new apartheid policies a group of Afrikaner intellectuals, including many brethren, formed the SABRA in 1948. This was the Afrikaner counterpart to the liberal South African Institute of Race Relations, a largely academic body founded in 1929, which expressed well-reasoned and soundly documented attacks on apartheid. Interestingly enough, SABRA was not formed at Potchefstroom, Pretoria or Bloemfontein, but at Stellenbosch: the prestigious Cape university which had produced Malan, Dönges, Louw, Sauer, Erasmus, Verwoerd and most of the Cape Nationalist intelligentsia. Until now, Potchefstroom and Pretoria intellectuals comprised the chief exponents and pace-setters of Afrikaner Nationalism. The emergence of Stellenbosch subtly reflected the shift in the internal balance of Nationalist power to the Cape, and a newly-found confidence among a slightly more pragmatic group of Afrikaner intellectuals who had been overshadowed for the past 30 years by the rigid theoreticians of the north.

To some extent SABRA was a more ambitious version and revival of the South African Bond for Racial Studies which, formed in 1935 (at the time when most of Nationalism's energies were absorbed in internal ideological disputes and the struggle against Anglicisation) gradually faded away. The emergence of SABRA seemed to portend that a slightly more flexible and human version of apartheid would be produced for the Party's consideration. In fact, SABRA contained many of South Africa's leading Christian-Nationalists and graduates of the Free University of Amsterdam, as well as a large number of brethren. While the emotional and belligerent frontier spirit was absent, the desire for boundaries was nevertheless strong.

Of the 19 founder members of SABRA (not all of whom were Afrikaners) at least 11 were brethren.[22] Six of the committee came from the Transvaal. Proof of the Broederbond's approval of the organisation was the presence among its founders of the Bond Chairman, J.C. van Rooy, and a Chairman-to-be, H.B. Thom. Other founder members of SABRA included two Broederbond Executive members, Albert Hertzog and Nico Diederichs. The formation of SABRA indicated that the Afrikaner intelligentsia were abandoning their central, almost myopic, preoccupation with the struggle for dominance with the English, and turning to the broader issue of relations between white and black. The inclusion among the founders of Colonel Stallard, a leading English-speaking (and strongly anti-Republican) protagonist of segregation, showed the Nationalists in their increasingly important role as champions of white mastery and the representatives of right-wing racial exclusivism. Having gained the means to impose their hegemony over the English, Nationalism's chief task, as many now saw it, was to settle finally the colour question.

SABRA was intended as a sort of unofficial Afrikaner Brains Trust to promote publicly and to develop the concept of separate development. It was to address itself to the three main problems posed by apartheid: defining the status of the 1 500 000 'coloured' people (the 'brown Afrikaners'); defining the rights of the 8 000 000 urban Africans; and working out schemes for the development of the reserves. Since it was independent of the regime, SABRA was also a relatively free clearing house for ideas and occasionally acted as a pressure group to force the government to accelerate the pace of apartheid. But the fact that successive Nationalist regimes were loath to grapple positively with SABRA's proposed solutions (and that its orientation remained relatively moderate) brought tbe Bureau into conflict with the Prime Minister, Dr Verwoerd. In 1960, with the assistance of the Broederbond, Verwoerd engineered a purge of SABRA to rid it of its reformist elements.

With the notable exception of J.C. van Rooy, it is significant that the initial composition of SABRA excluded a number of Potchefstroom professors like J.D. du Toit, S. du Toit, L.J. du Plessis, D.W. Kruger, A.H. van der Walt and Hugo du Plessis, who had frequently expressed themselves on the colour question. Also absent were former members of the OB, such as Geoffrey Cronje of Pretoria University, who had dramatically spotlighted the idea of separate development on the eve of the 1948 election. Another interesting feature was the fact that the word 'Christian-National' does not appear in SABRA's original aims or constitution. Only two DRC ministers and one member of the Cabinet were among its founders, though the DRC enthusiastically welcomed its formation.

The explanation of these unusual features in a Broederbond-sponsored body could lie in the fact that many OB supporters (like L.J. du Plessis, P.J. Meyer and G. Cronje) were not welcome in NP circles. Potchefstroom, too, had lost influence, partly because it had produced so many OB supporters whose manipulation of Christian-Nationalism and flirtation with aspects of Nazism had to some extent discredited the term. Indeed, a by-product of the war's end, the collapse of the OB, the emergence of the NP as the unrivalled champion of Afrikanerdom and the transfer of power to the Cape, was the decline of Potchefstroom as a force in Afrikaner affairs. It was regarded as being too extreme and had blotted its copybook by acquiescing to Nazism.

However, none of this impaired the influence of Christian-Nationalism, or the NP's link with the DRC; it merely meant that the dominance of a tightly-knit group of Potchefstroom professors over the rapidly expanding and diversifying nature of Afrikaner Nationalism (and thus of the Broederbond itself) was reduced. SABRA's direction tended to be monopolised by Cape intellectuals like Professors Nic Olivier, B.I.C. van Eeden, G.B.A. Gerdener, J.F. Bruwer, A.H. Murray and the Reverend J.C. du Plessis. It is worth noting that only in the mid-1950s did the name L.J. du Plessis appear above an article in SABRA's journal.[23]

THE DRC AND APARTHEID, 1949–50

Dr Malan's concept of apartheid was not a well worked-out one. It was an uneasy balance of two apparently conflicting principles: separate national self-determined homelands for Africans, and white *baaskap*. Both ideas were contained in the NP's 1948 election manifesto, but the Party's emphasis was decidedly on white mastery, a theme which remained popular at the hustings. Two factors forced the DRC to define its view of apartheid and to justify that policy on scriptural grounds. The first was the world Protestant community (to which the Afrikaans churches belonged) which asked the DRC to explain its attitude towards segregation in theological terms. The second factor was discontent among non-white members of the DRC who were affected by the rising militancy of the black liberation movement. There was also the question of the DRC's preparation for its part in celebrating the centenary of van Riebeeck's arrival, planned for 1952. The occasion was seen as having enormous religious significance, for it was van Riebeeck who first established Calvinism in South Africa.

The 1949 Synod of the Transvaal NGK, in reviewing the past 300 years, stressed that the planting of the *volk* in 1652 was an act of God's grace, and that His Kingdom should be established and expanded throughout southern Africa. This formulation raised a problem which began to nag at the DRC's troubled consciousness: clearly, God did not create or choose the Afrikaners for themselves.

On the contrary, he chose them to extend his Kingdom. But had the Afrikaner, in fact, seriously attempted to grapple with this task? Where was the evidence of concerted efforts to evangelise the heathen? Dominee P.J. Viljoen, Chairman of the Council of Churches, touched on these doubts when he said the Church should be self-critical for 'our refusal to show wholehearted obedience' to the divine instruction to make disciples of all nations. Many Afrikaners were opposed to missionary work, seeing 'in the Christianisation of the heathen, a danger for the apartheid idea'. According to Viljoen, the DRC had to support apartheid even though the Bible neither commanded nor forbade it:

> What the Bible commands is Christian guardianship . . . Whether we wish it or not we stand as guardian over Native, Coloured and Indian and God requires an account [from us]. We certainly have the right to watch over our own interests . . . But if we do this at the cost of the interests of the Coloured races, then we are untrue to our guardianship.[24]

In Viljoen's view apartheid could benefit both white and black provided that it did not lay too much emphasis on saving the whites. There should therefore be less talk about curbs and restrictions and more about the 'ideals and privileges of apartheid', for apartheid sought positively to develop each non-white group in conformity with its own character and capacity. Concluding his talk Viljoen refers back to the example of Israel. 'Without apartheid', he comments, 'the knowledge of the Lord would have disappeared rapidly from Canaan'. Consequently, 'we are convinced in our soul that it will be the end of Christendom, if the White is to play with the purity of his race. For us, this is the only manner that Christianity can achieve victory over heathendom.'[25] The implication here is that apartheid is more than a recipe for the autonomous existence of an Afrikaner Christian nation. It divided Christians into those born of Christian parents and those of heathen descent. In a true Christian state, neither Afrikaners nor Africans should govern: Christianity alone could rule.

Inevitably, Potchefstroom joined in the growing debate about the Church's attitude towards apartheid. Totius' son, S. du Toit of the Potchefstroom theological school, declared: 'It is urgently necessary to test our apartheid policy against the Scriptures.'[26] If apartheid failed to measure up, it had to be rejected. Du Toit argued that the Afrikaners were born in the eighteenth century under God's providential guidance. From the moment they became a nation they rejected the principle of equality. The principle of differentiation was not based upon skin colour but on the whole content and philosophy of life which pigmentation symbolised. Afrikaners realised that they were born as a nation in a miraculous way, and developed a sense of calling. They realised that they were the bearers of a Christian civilisation at the southern point of Africa and were convinced that they could fulfil their vocation only by protecting their identity. Voortrekkers lived according to the Bible and based their outlook on the scriptures. The question was whether this traditional outlook, crystallised as the apartheid policy, was justified by the scriptures. Du Toit went on to sum up the Christian-National position on race in the form of seven propositions. They do not bear repeating here for they contain little that is new (apart from the heavy emphasis on humankind's blood unity). Although he does not talk of the necessity for 'vertical' apartheid, this was very much part of the Potchefstroom perspective.[27]

The idea that true Christianity could not justify privilege based upon colour was the crux of a debate which broke out in late 1949 following the Cape NGK's adoption of its Synodal Commission report on race relations. This report staunchly defended apartheid, thereby aligning church, Afrikaner, nation and Party.[28] The Synod supported the government's policy of 'political and territorial segregation', disapproved of 'social equality', condemned the 'disregard of race and colour differences between white and black in daily intercourse', and expressed itself in favour of strengthening 'social differentiation to the benefit of both sections'. In these respects it identified itself with the mission policy expressed by the 1935 Synod of the Federated NGK.

The Synodal Commission emphasised the 'positive' aspect of apartheid, arguing that by a just application of 'separate, indigenous, development to independence' it did not endorse inferiority or oppression. In a passage which echoed the Christian-National standpoint of *Koers* since the mid-1930s and implicitly rejected naked white domination without the compensation of black autonomy, the commission said that the ultimate future relationship between the network of separately developed racial groups could only be gradually determined over the course of time. It added (with emphasis): 'In any event only "vertical" division can bring every group to its highest point, while the "horizontal" opinion, in this case, which obstructs the non-Whites' road to separate indigenous [*eiesoortige*] development to independence is rejected by your commission.'

The salient implication of this report is its expression of full approval of the Nationalist regime's colour policies. Nevertheless, its interpretation of apartheid laid far heavier stress on separate development to independence than the regime did. In other words, the DRC could only reconcile apartheid with Christianity if it were 'vertical' and not 'horizontal'. A further point which emerges is that the scriptural defence of ecclesiastical apartheid, while proving that the Bible recognises the existence of separate races, nowhere commands that they be compulsorily segregated. It does not give one Christian nation the right to dominate another, or forbid believers of different races to worship their common God together. All the report does is to provide some biblical justification for separate churches for different language and cultural groups.

These omissions led to a remarkable repudiation of the scriptural basis of apartheid by Professor Ben Keet, a graduate of Amsterdam's Free University and Head of Stellenbosch University's NGK Theological Seminary, whose pioneer attack on Church apartheid opened a new phase in the history of Christian-Nationalism. Keet's lone voice was the precursor of other Calvinist voices which, 12 years later, were to be raised against the DRC's association with Christian-Nationalism. His repudiation of the link between Christianity and Afrikaner domination paved the way for men of a younger generation – like Beyers Naudé – in the 1960s which plunged Christian-Nationalism into its deepest crisis.

In a series of articles published in *Die Kerkbode* in 1949 Keet replied to the Synodal Commission.[29] He rejected the Commission's argument that scriptural recognition of the existence of diverse peoples and races constituted a justification for ecclesiastical or constitutional apartheid. Nowhere in the Gospels was there justification for compulsory segregation of persons of different colours or races merely on the grounds of their pigmentation or ethnic origin. Keet said that it was dangerous to start with the existing practice of apartheid and then to consult the scriptures for confirmation of that policy. This was a mere rationalisation of a preconceived secular opinion. Satan, he pointed out, had on occasion used the Word of God for his own purposes. The correct approach was to examine the scriptures directly and without preconceived opinions. Practice had to be brought into conformity with the scriptures, not the other way around.

Keet denied that the scriptures lent themselves to direct judgements on national, biological, economic, cultural or other natural phenomena. They did not illuminate or comment on such questions; in the whole Bible there was not a single word about colour differences. The Bible was concerned with humankind's salvation, not culture. Much was made of the fact that Israel was always warned to keep itself segregated and pure from surrounding nations, but these injunctions flowed from Israel's extraordinary religious calling. It was not because the national existence of Israel was of great significance, but because God had entrusted to Israel, his chosen people, the revelation of the true God. And had Israel perished as a people the true religion would have vanished from the earth. Israel was therefore a special case. It could simply not be compared with any other people.

According to Professor Keet, apartheid (in so far as it stood for isolation and racial seclusion) conflicted with the spirit of the Old and New Testaments. He went on to demonstrate how the 'incorrect approach' of the NGK's Synodal Commission had produced 'false interpretations' of the scriptures. When Paul said in Athens that God made all the nations of mankind of one blood and established the fixed boundaries and times of their dwelling places (Acts 17: 20), he was not saying that there should be no intercourse among men. On the contrary, Paul was asserting the unity of mankind. Differentiation did not mean dissociation or cleavage. In Corinthians (1: 12) Paul spoke of the body's unity despite the diversity of its members. In effect, he was telling his audience that the Gospel had done away with the privileged position of the Jew as regards the heathen. 'Essentially', said Keet, 'the human race is one. God loved, in Jesus Christ, the whole world, not simply a specific people.'

Keet also attacked the Commission's attempt, by reference especially to the Old Testament, to justify its prohibition on marriages among Christians of different races. For example, the Commission quoted Nehemiah (13: 23) who condemned the intermarriage of Jews with foreign (Moabite) women. The NGK, Keet declared, had misunderstood the scriptures on this point. Nehemiah's strictures against the Moabite women had to do with their *heathenness*, not their race or culture. The sole kind of mixed marriage which the Holy Scriptures thought dangerous was between believers and non-believers. Once again, the example of Israel did not apply to the Afrikaner situation. After all, if race impurity was an index of sin, then the Afrikaners had been conceived to an extreme degree in sin, while the Chinese (whom the Bible did not even mention) were probably the most faithful to God's ordinances! The plain fact was that there were no pure races: Jesus Christ himself was not of pure Jewish origin.

In Keet's view, diversity of race, nationality, language and culture were gifts of nature through which people had to glorify God. This variety was the very hallmark of God's creation, yet it was underscored by unity. If exaggerated stress was placed on diversity it became an antithesis. Diversity did not mean that one's *volk* had to be divided from and opposed to her peoples. Total isolation led to madness. Keet recognised that the Afrikaner was conceived and born with a national mission. In the religious sense, this calling was clearly to bring the Gospel to the surrounding heathens and semi-heathens. But they had to execute this mandate, in the first place, as Christians. The fact that they bore a fixed character perhaps made it easier to fulfil this mission, but it was a great mistake to lay such stress on the concept of national calling that one forgot or distorted the Gospel as in National Socialism. Moreover, if there was any conflict – as there had frequently been – between the promotion of the Kingdom of God and the demands of the nation, the former had to take precedence.

In sum, Keet asserted that there was no theological basis for apartheid within the church, for the social segregation of believers or for the strict division of the lives of persons who subscribed to the same creeds and liturgy. Such policies were rooted in colour feeling, a sentiment which identified colour with civilisation and was rooted in the white people's fear of loss of their standards. He suggested that the NGK should acknowledge that the division which occurred in the ecclesiastical sphere sprang, in the first instance, not from unselfish motives, but from a strong colour consciousness. As an immediate step to bring the DRC's practice into conformity with the scriptures, Keet suggested that the NGK's (Coloured) mission church be represented on the Council of Churches, and that each church should exchange, on special occasions, official delegations which would attend the other's services and observe the Lord's Supper (*Nagmaal*) together. Why should the DRC be afraid of taking the lead, he asked. 'We avow to the same Lord, we acknowledge the same sacraments, we belong to the same Church, we stand in the same holy community.'

Keet's modest practical proposal made little impact upon the DRC which, linked by the AB to the NP, was in no mood to weaken Afrikanerdom's common front against its foes. Yet pressure built up for the DRC to reconcile its advocacy of apartheid with its crusade for non-white converts and for a just formulation of segregation. Already the NGK Commission had indicated the outlines of an ethical formula by suggesting the separate and indigenous development of each black group to independence. It had proposed that apartheid should be 'vertical', and it rejected the equation of apartheid with black inferiority. Although the Cape NGK was far closer to the NP than to Professor Keet, these proposals represented an important concession. They marked the beginning of an attempt to nudge the NP into paying greater attention to the 'positive' aspects of its apartheid manifesto.

So far the Nationalist government had refused to commit itself explicitly to the future of the African reserves, the rate of transition from 'horizontal' to 'vertical' apartheid, and the status of urban Africans. Malan's measures were purely restrictive with respect to African rights. It was clear that he intended to mount a step-by-step assault on the 'colour problem', beginning with the statutory abolition of all vestiges of 'liberalism'. This would precede the implementation of more expensive plans to convert the African reserves into homelands. Of great importance in the conversion of the NP to a programme of 'vertical' apartheid was the far-reaching decision of the 1950 Church Conference on colour policy. This reaffirmed with greater emphasis and authority, the decision of a DRC national conference in 1947 which urged more territory for Africans wherein they could achieve the right to govern themselves and advance to the highest positions.[30] There is some evidence to suggest that the Broederbond (whose intellectuals had urged the need for independent African Christian-National territorial units in the 1930s) were prominently associated with this development.

Meeting in Bloemfontein in 1950, together with its missionary off-shoots, the three DRC sister churches committed themselves categorically to total apartheid in its most radical form. The Congress rejected ultimate integration on the grounds that it would lead to unnecessary and dangerous clashes between the two races. Calling on Malan to define clearly the long-term constitutional future of Africans, the Congress declared: 'In his own areas, the Bantu must be guided, in accordance with his own national background [and] fertilised by Christian civilisation, to develop to full nationhood.' These proposals, with their novel overtones of African sovereignty and partition of the economy were, however, judged premature by the NP. While accepting it as a final ideal, Malan rejected total (territorial) segregation as economically impracticable. The 'white' urban areas – not to mention white farmers – would always be dependent on African labour. A further dash of cold water was thrown on the DRC scheme by the Transvaal Nationalist leader, Dr Strydom, who stressed that the party's single-minded goal remained 'the preservation of whitedom and its domination in South Africa'.

The unanimity of all the DRCs on Christianity and apartheid suggests that the Broederbond was lurking in the background. Whether the Broederbond actually controlled the DRCs cannot be stated with certainty. But this seems highly probable given the organisation's heavy representation in the ministries and top echelons of all the Afrikaans churches. The fact that all the DRC Synods had adopted nearly identical resolutions praising projects launched by the Broederbond in the 1940s indicates some degree of co-ordinated, behind-the-scenes pressure. Moreover, Smuts's DMI reports confirmed the Broederbond's domination of the churches during the war.

Criticism of the Broederbond – which reached sufficient intensity by 1949 to force Malan to praise the organisation as being an asset to society and to deny emphatically that it dominated his regime – had also grown within the Afrikaner churches. In 1949 (the year in which the DRC was working out its united front on apartheid) charges of Broederbond manipulation of the synods became so embarrassing that the NGK's Federal Council decided to set up a commission of inquiry into the operations of the Broederbond with special reference to its role – if any – in the church. The investigation was carried out by the Kommissie van Aktuele Sake (Commission for Topical Matters), and its report was adopted at the meeting of Council of the NGK on 17 May 1951.

The NGK Commissioners concluded that the Broederbond was a 'good organisation' and summaries of their report were carried in certain of the English-language newspapers.[31] Their report completely exonerated the Broederbond from the charge that it interfered with the churches and accepted the secret organisation's claim to be a non-political body. But, in the light of what is known about the Broederbond, it cannot be taken at face value. Within the DRC itself the impartiality of the report was questioned and it was suggested that a majority of the members of the investigatory commission were themselves brethren. In April 1963 Dr Barnard,

Chairman of the NGK's Synodal Kommissie van Aktuele Sake demanded a fresh inquiry into the Broederbond, claiming that it had only made a superficial investigation.

Perhaps the most important public repudiation of the NGK's decision came from a *predikant*, Dr D.J.J. de Vos, who had formed a small breakaway DRC. Speaking in Cape Town in April 1952 he said that he had studied the Broederbond's activities within the DRC for nearly 20 years. He claimed that there were nearly 356 *predikants* in the Broederbond and that there were more than 1 000 Broederbond cells in 1 000 parishes. Thus the Broederbond was not only deeply entrenched in the DRC but it was a key factor in South Africa's political life and was working to keep the NP in power.[32] There is no way of checking the accuracy of de Vos' figures and his attack was somewhat hysterical and therefore perhaps exaggerated, but there is no reason to doubt the substance of his accusations. These were to be repeated constantly by reputable and authoritative figures within the DRC for the next 20 years.

CONCLUSION

The years following the Nationalists' accession to power in 1948 were a climactic and heroic period in Afrikaner history. In 1961 the Nationalist aim of a Republic severed from Britain was at last achieved, and total Afrikaner paramountcy in South Africa was secured. In contrast to Afrikanerdom's bleak foreboding and despair in 1902, the Nationalists ruled the country with resolution and a high sense of morale. Acting from a position of strength, the NP attempted to broaden its white power base by including members of the English-speaking community in the Cabinet. Initially, at least, this did not represent a return to the conciliatory spirit of Louis Botha; on the contrary, it was part of a wider strategy to 'Afrikanerise' the English speakers and to consolidate white rule on the basis of Nationalist right-wing ideology.

In 1969 – the party's twenty-first successive year in office – a rift of potentially catastrophic implications appeared in its ranks as a result of this 'outward-looking' policy. It flared up among Nationalist Afrikaners, dividing the NP, the AB and the Christian-Nationalists into *Verligtes* and *Verkramptes*: a schism which in some respects, echoed those of 1933 and 1943. The dissidents were, to all intents and purposes, politically defeated when, in 1970, the breakaway

HNP under Dr Albert Hertzog was crushed at the polls. This internal upheaval did not detract from Nationalism's far-reaching transformation of South Africa since 1948. Dr Malan, though the second Nationalist prime minister, was the first to rule without any parliamentary support from English-speaking elements. Born in 1933–4, the splinter GNP had successfully challenged and smashed the Anglo–Boer political alliance which had ruled from 1910 to 1948.

The 1948 Nationalist victory represented, therefore, a historical transfer of political power within the white ruling class, from the binational Anglo–Boer alliance to Afrikaner uninationalist exclusivism. Apart from the short-lived eighteenth- and nineteenth-century Boer Republics, the indigenous Afrikaners had never been in a position to rule themselves. Moreover, their Republics had always been enclaves of independence in a territory over which paramountcy was claimed or exercised by metropolitan Holland or Britain. Even during a brief period of British indifference to the autonomous Voortrekker states, the Afrikaners' control was provisional rather than absolute. Using the politically integrative machinery of Union, Afrikanerdom had finally gained a victory over their English-speaking historical rivals by conventional parliamentary methods, rather than through war or rebellion. In this way they had achieved mastery over the whole of southern Africa.

It is notable that the Republic was inaugurated in 1961 with the country in a State of Emergency because of the danger of a popular uprising following the Sharpeville crisis. This illustrates the dominant fact of the post-war years: that while the Nationalists fought to confirm and consolidate their hegemony within the white group, they were also continuously engaged in a second battle, namely, the fateful confrontation between a white ruling caste and the black liberation movements centred around the African National Congress. Increasingly, Nationalist Cabinet ministers have referred to the new Battle of Blood River, faced by a sustained challenge from the black majority for a share in the white monopoly of political power and economic wealth. Whereas the English-speaking community – excepting the English-language press, the liberal universities and, to some extent, the Anglican church – soon surrendered to Afrikaner mastery, black protest movements confronted Afrikaner Nationalism with a determination and dynamism as fundamentally radical and intense as their own.

Unlike the Afrikaner variant, however, African Nationalism was neither exclusivist, narrow or racist. It was a universalist Nationalism, seeking a South Africa in which all, regardless of colour, would share equal political rights. Doctrinally, the clash between the racial Afrikaner nationalism and the supra-racial liberation movement (whose programme is set out in the 1955 Freedom Charter) represents the highest stage of the 150-year-old ideological conflict over the principles first proclaimed during the French Revolution. In this clash the Afrikaners emerge as the champions of authoritarian, aristocratic and privileged rule, a society in which pigmentation is the condition for, and guarantee of, political rights. Challenging this notion is a movement committed to the ideal of liberty, equality and fraternity for all individuals, regardless of skin colour.

The creeds of both Afrikaner Nationalism and the liberation movement have a long ancestry, going back to the first clash between Boer colour attitudes and liberal Europe's emancipatory principles in the early days of the nineteenth century. For the first time, however, the leaders of the cause for non-white emancipation were Africans, Indians and Coloureds themselves, rather than overseas missionaries, well-wishing whites or European philanthropists (although a small and courageous group of whites, chiefly Marxists and liberals, have identified themselves with and helped to consolidate the goals of non-racialism). This dramatic face-to-face confrontation has been largely provoked by the NP's concerted attempts after 1948 to resurrect in an industrial economy dependent upon black labour the nineteenth-century Boer principle of 'No Equality in Church or State'.

Committed to a programme of strict and rigid colour segregation in the cosmopolitan urban areas, the Nationalists have legislated since 1948 to extend segregation and to liquidate all remaining areas of unofficial racial contact. By virtue of its aspirations and traditions, Afrikaner Nationalism was the absolute antithesis of '1789'. It came to power only three years after the defeat of the Nazi-Fascist challenge to the democratic spirit, with the world hostile to master-race and anti-democratic doctrines. Not only were the Nationalists therefore advocating a discredited ideology, but the movements for national independence in Africa and Asia made the international climate hostile to its aims. Defying a censorious United Nations, the Nationalists intensified their application of apartheid until blacks, deprived of their legal organisations, resorted to extra-legal protest (such as sabotage) in 1961. This revolt was soon stamped out and the underground leaders like Nelson Mandela and Walter Sisulu were imprisoned on Robben Island. In April 1967, however, the first armed band of African guerrillas crossed Zambia on their way south.

Just when the Verwoerd regime seemed to have paralysed the internal machinery of non-racial opposition, a new form of protest against apartheid arose from within the very heart of Afrikanerdom in the shape of the Christian Institute, established in 1963 by prominent members of the DRC, including the Reverend Beyers Naudé (a former NGK Moderator) and A.S. Geyser (a former NHK Professor of Theology). Proclaiming that apartheid and Christianity could not be reconciled, they launched a vigorous attack within the Afrikaner establishment against the doctrine of Christian-Nationalism. It was the first time in 300 years that an organised group of DRC theologians repudiated apartheid as a violation of God's Word. This led in 1968 and 1969 to the entry of more Christians of other denominations into the struggle against apartheid, whose intervention in the 1970 General Elections caused the government acute embarrassment. The event was of historical significance: not since 1828 had a significant and organised group of Christian clergymen and laity campaigned for desegregation.

Coinciding with this left-wing dissent within the Calvinist community came an attack from hard-line Christian-Nationalist hawks, the *Verkramptes*, against Prime Minister Vorster's policies of a broader white unity and the normalisation of South Africa's relations with the outside world (especially with the newly-independent African states of Malawi, Lesotho, Swaziland and Botswana). For the years immediately ahead, the outlook is unclear. The AB, which reached the height of its power during Dr Verwoerd's regime, seems to have been weakened by the *Verligte–Verkrampte* dispute. Christian-Nationalism has been appropriated by the ultra-Nationalists as their own creed in the struggle within Afrikanerdom and is also in the throes of a crisis whose full dimensions cannot yet be measured.

Yet the two great themes with which this study deals – the Broederbond and Christian-Nationalism – remain in the forefront of the struggle. How they will shape it, and whether they will survive it in their existing form (indeed, whether they will survive it at all), are not questions that can today be easily answered. Without a knowledge of these two factors, however, it is certain that the gathering crisis within Afrikanerdom cannot be fully understood.

Notes and References

Preface

1. South African Institute of Race Relations, *Race Relations Survey 1934* (Johannesburg, 1935), p. 41.
2. *The Guardian*, 5 February 1937.

Introduction

1. Bloomberg is referring here to the Netherlands' Anti-Revolutionary Party (ARP) and its offshoot, the Christian-Historical Union. The position has changed somewhat since he wrote this passage: in 1979 the ARP merged with the Christian-Historical Union and the Catholic Peoples' party to form the Christian Democratic Alliance. In part, this reflects the secularisation of Dutch politics since the 1960s.
2. G.M. Carter, *The Politics of Inequality: South Africa Since 1948.*, 2nd edn (London, 1959), Appendix IV, p. 467.
3. Ibid., p. 471.
4. Ibid., p. 469.
5. Ibid., p. 126.
6. J.J. Van Rooyen, *Die Nasionale Party: Sy Opkoms en Oorwinning – Kaapland se Aandeel* (Cape Town, 1956), p. 38.
7. Van Rooyen, *Die Nasionale Party*, p. 317.
8. A. Hepple, *Verwoerd* (Harmondsworth, 1967), p. 133.
9. Ibid., p. 134.
10. *Sunday Times*, 25 January 1970.
11. *Sunday Times*, 6 August 1961.
12. *Sunday Times*, 4 May 1969.
13. *Die Burger*, 4 May 1969.
14. *Sunday Times*, 7 September 1969.
15. This figure, applying to 1984, is given by R. Davies, D. O'Meara and S. Damini, *The Struggle for South Africa*, vol. 2 (London, 1984), p. 270.

1 The Precepts and Tenets of Christian-Nationalism

1. P.J. Meyer, *Trek Verder: Die Afrikaner in Afrika* (Cape Town and Pretoria, 1959), p. ix.
2. Ibid.; see Ch. 1.
3. J.C.G. Kotzé, *Wie Beset Hierdie Bedreigde Huis?* (Stellenbosch, 1964).
4. J.D. Vorster, 'Etniese Verskeidenheid, Kerklike Pluriformiteit en die Ekumeme', in *Grense: 'n Simposium oor Rasse en ander Verhoudinge* (Stellenbosch, 1961).
5. A.B. du Preez, *Inside the South African Crucible* (Cape Town and Pretoria, 1959).
6. F.J.M. Potgieter, *Veelvormige Ontwikkeling: Die Wil van God* (Bloemfontein, 1956).

7. A.P. Treurnicht, 'Die Verhouding van die Staat tot die Kerk by Dr Abraham Kuyper, 1837–1920', University of Cape Town, PhD thesis, 1956.
8. N. Diederichs, *Nasionalisme as Lewensbeskouing en sy Verhouding tot Internasionalisme* (Bloemfontein, 1936), pp. 22–3.
9. Vorster, 'Etniese Verskeidenheid', pp. 66–7.
10. Vorster, 'Etniese Verskeidenheid', p. 69.
11. *SABRA Newsletter*, 21 (November/December 1956). See also Potgieter, *Veelvormige Ontwikkeling*.
12. A. Kuyper, *Pro Rege III*, p. 258, cited in du Preez, *The South African Crucible*, p. 60.
13. S. du Toit, 'Openbaringslig op die Apartheidvraagstuk', *Koers*, August 1949.
14. Vorster, 'Etniese Verskeidenheid', p. 66.
15. I have not been able to locate this precise quote, but see G. Eloff in 'Navorsing in Verband met die Fisiek-Antropologiese Einskappe van die Boer', in *Agter Tralies en Doringdraad* (Stellenbosch, 1953).
16. J.D. du Toit, 'Die Godsdienstige Grondslag van ons Rassebeleid', *Inspan*, December 1944, p. 13.
17. Vorster, 'Etniese Verskeidenheid', p. 69.
18. Address by B.F. Nel to the 1943 Mother-Tongue Education Conference, *Inspan*, January 1943, p. 10.
19. Diederichs, *Nasionalisme*, p. 63.
20. C.J. Hugo, 'Die Taak van die Kerk ten Opsigte van Rasseverhoudings', in *Grense*, p. 197.
21. *SABRA Newsletter*, 21 (November/December 1956).
22. H.G. Stoker, 'Die Idee van Nasionalisme', *Tydskrif vir Wetenskap en Kuns*, December 1931.
23. N. Diederichs, 'Die Republiekeinse Volkstaat van die Toekoms', in J.A. Coetzee *et al.*, *Ons Republiek* (Cape Town, 1941), pp. 125–9.
24. J.A. du Plessis, 'Kerk en Staat', in H.G. Stoker and F.J.M. Potgieter (eds), *Koers in die Krisis*, vol. 1 (Stellenbosch, 1935), p. 118.
25. See A.P. Treurnicht, 'Grense Tussen Kerk en Staat', in *Grense*.
26. J. du Plessis, 'Kerk en Staat', p. 120.
27. Cited in W.H. Vatcher, *White Laager: The Rise of Afrikaner Nationalism* (London, 1965), Appendix V.
28. Ibid.
29. D.F. Malan, *Die Burger*, 3 May 1937.
30. De Wet Nel cited in G.M. Carter, T. Karis and N.M. Stultz, *South Africa's Transkei* (London, 1967), p. 61.
31. H. du Plessis, 'Christianisering van die Bantoe-lewe met behoud van sy Bantoeiteit', *Koers*, February 1935.
32. *Summary of the Report of the Commission for the Socio-Economic Development of the Bantu Areas Within the Union of South Africa*, UG 61/1955, Ch. 40, para. 21.
33. Ibid., Ch. 14, para. 30.
34. Ibid., Ch. 40, para. 4.
35. Ibid., Ch. 40, para. 20.

2 The Anatomy of a Secret Society: An Overview

1. The Broederbond was never driven underground by oppression. As a result of its anti-war activities in 1944, however, the Premier, General Smuts, barred brethren from the Civil Service. See Ch. 8.
2. Charles Bloomberg made these estimates in the late 1960s. Compare with R. Davies *et al.*, in *The Struggle for South Africa*, vol. 2 (London, 1984), p. 267, which says 'Today it has approximately 12000 members, including almost every member of the South African Cabinet, senior state bureaucrats, military officers and businessmen.'
3. Justice D.H. Botha, *Report of the Commission of Inquiry into Secret Organisations* (Pretoria, 1964).
4. P. van den Berghe, *South Africa: A Study in Conflict* (California, 1967), p. 104.
5. Official AB statement to Southern Transvaal's NGK Synod in 1963.
6. Executive Committee, 9 November 1945.
7. *Rapport van die N.G. Kerklike Kommissie vir Aktuele Vraagstukke oor die Bestaan, Doel en Strekking van die Afrikaner Broederbond* (1951).
8. DMI Report, 'Twentyfifth Anniversary Meeting of the A.B. held in Bloemfontein on the 13th of December, 1943', p. 13.
9. DMI Report dated Pretoria, 29 March 1944.
10. Ibid., p. 18.
11. Ibid., p. 10.
12. Ibid., p. 28.
13. This section is dealt with in greater detail in Ch. 8.
14. Davies *et al.*, in *The Struggle for South Africa*, vol. 2, p. 270, claimed in 1984 that the FAK was composed of some 3000 affiliate bodies.
15. O'Meara gives the date for the RDB's official demise as 1957, though it was effectively defunct earlier. O'Meara, *Volkskapitalisme: Class, Capital and Ideology in the Development of Afrikaner Nationalism* (Cambridge, 1983), p. 151.
16. *Die Transvaler*, 30 December 1944.
17. S. Patterson, *The Last Trek: A Study of the Boer People and the Afrikaner Nation* (London, 1957), p. 269.
18. Charles Bloomberg does not indicate where these figures come from, but compare with the Table 10 in O'Meara, *Volkskapitalisme*, p. 201.
19. Note: Charles Bloomberg wrote this before the work of O'Meara, Moodie and Giliomee-Adam which all, to a lesser or greater extent, are sensitive to the links between Afrikaner Nationalism and the development of capitalism in twentiety-century South Africa. Interestingly, Bloomberg has a note at the end of this section on the RDB's role in the struggle for economic power which reads: 'The Afrikaner nationalist-economic movement has only been superficially touched on by writers on South Africa. No study has been made of it; and most of the information in this paper is published for the first time. Yet it is an integral part of the Afrikaner Broederbond's grand design for Afrikaner mastery, and its rise is certainly as important for an understanding of the growth of Afrikaner power, as is the rise of the Nationalist Party.

3 Birth and Early Years

1. Bloomberg refers to D.*A*.C. du Plessis, following the spelling used in secret reports by the Smuts government on the Broederbond. Other sources refer to him, however, as D.*H*.C. du Plessis.
2. 'History of the Inception and Development of the AB', report of an address by the Broederbond's Chief Secretary, I.M. Lombard, to the Broederbond's 25th anniversary congress in December 1943 (henceforth Lombard, 'History of the AB').
3. Louis J. du Plessis, *Letters of a Farmer* (Krugersdorp, 1951), pp. 3, 9.
4. President Steyn of the OFS used it in praising the Nationalist poetry of J.D. du Toit. The Afrikaans Studentebond's journal was called 'Young South Africa'.
5. Lombard, 'History of the AB', and official AB statement in November 1964.
6. The 1951 DRC Federal Commission of Inquiry into the Broederbond pinpoints the date of the Broederbond's formation as 9 December 1919.
7. Lombard, 'History of the AB'.
8. *Star*, 12 October 1948.
9. Ibid.
10. Lombard, 'History of the AB'.
11. W.H. Vatcher, *White Laager: The Rise of Afrikaner Nationalism* (London, 1965), pp. 76–7.
12. This supposition was apparently made by Arthur Barlow, MP.
13. B. Bunting, *The Rise of the South African Reich*, 3rd edn (London, 1986), p. 30.
14. Du Plessis, *Letters of a Farmer*.
15. O. Pirow, *James Barry Munnik Hertzog* (Cape Town, 1957), p. 131.
16. Ibid., pp. 131–2.
17. J.G. Strydom in *Die Vaderland*, 9 October 1923.
18. Hansard Debates, vol. 10, col. 2198, 15 March 1928.
19. L. Thompson, 'Afrikaner Nationalist Historiography and the Policy of Apartheid', *Journal of African History*, III, 1 (1962).

4 The AB's Christian-Nationalist Counter-Offensive

1. The phrase 'bigger son' was used by L.J. du Plessis at the Broederbond's 1932 Congress.
2. H. Stoker and F.J.M. Potgieter (eds), introducing *Koers in die Krisis, vol. 1* (Stellenbosch, 1935).
3. O. Pirow, *James Barry Munnik Hertzog* (Cape Town, 1957), p. 154.
4. L.J. du Plessis, 'Die Loop van die Dinge', *Koers*, December 1933, pp. 38–9.
5. Lombard, 'History of the AB'.
6. Pirow, *Hertzog*, p. 166.
7. A. Hepple, *Verwoerd* (Harmondsworth, 1967), p. 38, says that Verwoerd joined the Broederbond either in 1934 or else a few years earlier. Verwoerd himself disclosed that he was recruited in 1935.
8. J.A. du Plessis, 'Christelik-Nasionale Onderwys' and L.J. du Plessis,

'Die Loop van die Dinge', *Koers*, December 1934.

9. Ibid.
10. Quoted in W.H. Vatcher, *White Laager: The Rise of Afrikaner Nationalism* (London, 1965), p. 107.
11. Another member of the translation board was Ben Keet, who was later to arouse controversy by rejecting apartheid on theological grounds.
12. Lombard, 'History of the AB'.
13. J.A. du Plessis, 'Die Betekenis van die Afrikaanse Bybel vir Ons', *Koers*, August 1933, p. 4.
14. See S. Patterson, *The Last Trek: A Study of the Boer People and the Afrikaner Nation* (London, 1957), pp. 267–8.
15. Lombard, *Die Transvaler*, 30 December 1944.
16. Hepple, *Verwoerd*, p. 35.
17. Report of the 1934 Poor White Conference, p. 123. See also Hepple, *Verwoerd*, p. 28.
18. Report of the 1934 Poor White Conference, p. 31. See also Hepple, *Verwoerd*, p. 29.
19. L.J. du Plessis, 'Ekonomiese Reorganisasie van Ons Volk', *Koers*, August 1934, p. 18.
20. Lombard, 'History of the AB'.
21. *Volkshandel*, March 1941.
22. *Die Wagtoring*, June 1933. Farewell editorial by de Wet.
23. *Koers*, Editorial, August 1933.
24. H.G. Stoker and F.J.M. Potgieter (eds), *Koers in die Krisis*, (Stellenbosch, 1935), vol. 1.
25. Ibid., p. vi.
26. Ibid., p. 3.
27. Foreword by H. Colijn in ibid., p. 2.
28. G. Besselaar, 'Internasionale Calvinisme', in ibid., p. 68.

5 General Hertzog's Attack on the AB

1. *Natal Advertiser*, 29 October 1936, speech to 1936 United Party Conference.
2. General Hertzog's Smithfield address, 7 November 1935. Reprinted as Annexure B in J.H.P. Serfontein's *Brotherhood of Power: An Exposé of the Secret Afrikaner Broederbond* (London, 1979). Hertzog named Malan's cohorts as 'Dr van der Merwe, Adv. Swart, Dr C.W. du Toit, Adv. J.G. Strydom, Messrs. Werth, Haywood, Martins, etc.'
3. This suggests that the organisation's nature, structure and composition remained constant for the next 30 years.
4. AB Minutes, 21 October 1944.
5. *Natal Advertiser*, 29 October 1936.
6. Ibid.
7. W.H. Vatcher, *White Laager: The Rise of Afrikaner Nationalism* (London, 1965), p. 81.
8. A. Hepple, *Verwoerd* (Harmondsworth, 1967), p. 59.
9. *Rand Daily Mail* (*RDM*), 11 July 1937.
10. Ibid.

11. *RDM*, 10 June 1937.
12. L.J. du Plessis, 'Christelik-Nasionale Organisasie van Afrikanerwerkers', *Koers*, June 1937.
13. N. Diederichs, *Nasionalisme as Lewensbeskouing en sy Verhouding tot Internasionalisme* (Bloemfontein, 1936).
14. Ibid., p. 24.
15. Ibid., pp. 30–1.
16. Ibid., p. 55.
17. Ibid., pp. 22–3.
18. Ibid., pp. 62–3.
19. Hepple, *Verwoerd*, p. 43.
20. Hepple, *Verwoerd*, p. 45.
21. See, for example, Gustav Preller's *Andries Pretorius* (Johannesburg, 1937); *Day-Dawn in South Africa* (Pretoria, 1938); and Dr P. van Biljon's 1937 Stellenbosch doctoral thesis, 'Grensbakens Tussen Blank en Swart'.
22. Recently, the notion of the Calvinist origins of Afrikaner Nationalism and the Afrikaner claim to be a 'chosen people' has been brilliantly challenged. See André du Toit, 'No Chosen People: The Myth of the Calvinist Origins of Afrikaner Nationalism and Racial Ideology', *American Historical Review*, 1983. See also A. du Toit and H. Giliomee (eds), *Afrikaner Political Thought: Documents and Analysis*, vol. 1: 1780–1850 (Berkeley and Los Angeles, 1983).
23. *Gedenkboek van die Ossewaens op die Pad van Suid Afrika* (Cape Town, 1940).
24. J.D. Vorster's estimate in *Gedenboek*, p. 68.
25. H.F. Verwoerd, *Gedenkboek*, in 1 December 1938, Middelburg, p. 93.
26. *Gedenkboek*, p. 96.
27. *Gedenkboek*, p. 97.
28. J.H. Conradie, *Gedenkboek*, p. 117.
29. *Gedenkboek*, p. 732.
30. D.F. Malan's speech to 1934 Poor White Conference. Some of these quotes may be found in Hepple, *Verwoerd*, p. 28, and J.C. Coetzee, 'Die Volkskongres oor die Armblanke-Vraagstuk', *Koers*, December 1934.
31. For a detailed account of the Volkskongres, see E.P. du Plessis, *'n Volk Staan Op: Die Ekonomiese Volkskongres en Daarna* (Cape Town, 1964).
32. N. Diederichs, *Die Vaderland*, 31 August 1940.
33. N. Diederichs, *Die Transvaler*, 5 September 1940.
34. *Die Burger*, 18 December 1939, and *Die Vaderland*, 18 February 1950.
35. E.P. du Plessis, *'n Volk Staan Op*, p. 124.
36. *Die Transvaler*, 5 September 1940.
37. Ibid.
38. Ibid.
39. E.P. du Plessis, *'n Volk Staan Op*, pp. 114–15.

6 Christian-Nationalist Colour Policy in the 1930s and the Impact of Totalitarian Thought

1. L.J. du Plessis, 'Rasverhoudinge', *Koers*, October 1933.
2. P.J.S. de Klerk, 'Die Sending en die Onderwys van die Naturelle', *Koers*, October 1934.
3. H. du Plessis, 'Christianisering van die Bantoe-lewe met Behoud van sy Bantoeiteit', *Koers*, February 1935.
4. H. du Plessis, 'Assimilasie of Algehele Segregasie', *Koers*, June 1935.
5. Ibid.
6. L.J. du Plessis, 'Die Naturelle-Wetsontwerpe', *Koers*, April 1936.
7. *Rassebakens*, 1, 1 (1939).
8. J.G. Strydom, 'Die Rasse-Vragstuk in Suid-Afrika', in H.G. Stoker and J.D. Vorster (eds), *Koers in die Krisis*, vol. 3 (Stellenbosch, 1941), p. 244.
9. Ibid.
10. B. Bunting, *The Rise of the South African Reich*, 3rd edn (London, 1986).
11. *Race Relations News*, January 1939.
12. *The Times*, 29 July 1936.
13. S.W. Baron, *Modern Nationalism and Religion* (New York, 1947), p. 146.
14. Ibid.
15. L.J. du Plessis, 'Die Krisis van die Demokrasie', *Koers*, August 1933.
16. L.J. du Plessis, 'Die Loop van die Dinge', *Koers*, December 1933, pp. 38–9.
17. *Tydskrif vir Wetenskap en Kuns*, February 1932.
18. Ibid.
19. G. Eloff, 'Rasverbetering deur Uitskakeling van Minderwaardige Individue', *Koers*, December 1933.
20. A.J. Bruwer, *Kapitalisme, Party-Politiek en Armoede* (Bloemfontein, 1934).
21. Review by L.J. du Plessis in *Koers*, February 1935, pp. 39–40.
22. L.J. du Plessis, 'Konstitutionele Hervorming', *Koers*, June 1934.
23. H.G. Schulze, 'Die Duitse Nasionaal-Sosialisme', *Koers*, December 1934.
24. *Gedenkboek van die Ossewaens op die Pad van Suid Afrika* (Cape Town, 1940) p. 179.
25. Bunting, *The Rise*, p. 59.
26. Bunting, *The Rise*, p. 59.
27. *Die Transvaler*, 1 October 1937.
28. A. Hepple, *Verwoerd* (Harmondsworth, 1967), p. 223.
29. Bunting, *The Rise*, p. 62.
30. Bunting, *The Rise*, p. 63.
31. *Die Volksblad*, 11 July 1939.
32. C.R. Kotzé, 'The Jewish Question', in Stoker and Vorster, *Koers in die Krisis*, vol. 3, p. 230.
33. *Die Transvaler*, 3 November 1937.
34. J.D. Vorster, 'Humanism', in H.G. Stoker and F.J.M. Potgieter (eds),

Koers in die Krisis, vol. 1 (Stellenbosch, 1935), p. 373.
35. C.J.H. de Wet, 'Bybelgeloof–Bybelkritiek–Bybelfoute', in ibid., p. 374.
36. Ibid., p. 89.

7 Republicanism and the Struggle for Leadership within the Christian-Nationalist Camp, 1940–8

1. DMI Report, 'Twentyfifth Anniversary Meeting of the A.B. held in Bloemfontein on the 13th of December, 1943', p. 19.
2. P.J. Meyer, 'Politieke Verset teen die Oorlog', in *Agter Tralies en Doringdraad* (Stellenbosch, 1953), p. 24.
3. Ibid, p. 25.
4. *Die Transvaler*, 6 September 1939.
5. A. Hepple, *Verwoerd* (Harmondsworth, 1967), p. 79.
6. B. Bunting, *The Rise of the South African Reich*, 3rd edn (London, 1986), pp. 87–8.
7. *Die Transvaler*, 15 August 1940.
8. Hepple, *Verwoerd*, p. 84.
9. Bunting, *The Rise*, p. 83.
10. N.J. van der Merwe, 'Wat Omtrent Party-Politiek?', *Koers*, August 1939.
11. *Die Vaderland*, 14 August 1939.
12. According to Charles Bloomberg it is quoted in a 24pp., United Party publication issued by O.A. Oosthuizen, its General Secretary, entitled 'South African Nationalism', and issued before the 1948 election.
13. Bloomberg, says du Plessis, who later became Administrator of the Cape, was not speaking on behalf of the HNP leadership.
14. *Die Transvaler*, 13 January 1940. See also 22 February 1940 and 1 May 1940.
15. *Die Transvaler*, 26 February 1940.
16. A summary of the manifesto is given by Meyer in *Agter Tralies en Doringdraad*, p. 26.
17. *Sunday Express*, 2 March 1941.
18. *Die Suiderstem*, 16 September 1940.
19. A reproduction of the Constitution was published in *Die Suiderstem*, 28 September 1940.
20. *Die Suiderstem*, 29 September 1940.
21. *Trouw*, 18 October 1967.
22. *Die Huisgenoot*, quoted in *Trouw*, 19 October 1967.
23. *Die Transvaler*, 31 October 1940.
24. *Die Transvaler*, 1 November 1940.
25. *Die Burger*, 5 October 1940.
26. *Die Burger*, 31 October 1940.
27. *Die Burger*, 1 November 1940.
28. *Die Burger*, 2 December 1940.
29. J.H. van Rensburg, *Their Paths Crossed Mine* (Cape Town, 1956), p. 154.
30. *The Star*, 31 December 1940.
31. *RDM*, 1 January 1941.

32. *Die Transvaler*, 16 January 1941.
33. Ibid.
34. Hansard Debates, vol. 41, col. 2196, 4 February 1941.
35. W.H. Vatcher, *White Laager: The Rise of Afrikaner Nationalism* (London, 1965), p. 65.
36. N. Diederichs, 'Die Republiekeinse Volkstaat van die Toekoms', in J.A. Coetzee *et al.*, *Ons Republiek* (Cape Town, 1941). Contents summarised in *Sunday Express*, 26 October 1958, and *RDM*, 22 October 1958.
37. Bunting, *The Rise*, p. 105.
38. *Die Transvaler*, 13 June 1941, and Bunting, *The Rise*, p. 105.
39. *Die Transvaler*, 13 June 1941.
40. Lombard, 'History of the AB', p. 17. He also reveals that the AB created the Afrikaner Unity Front.
41. *Pretoria News*, 4 June 1941.
42. *Die Transvaler*, 8 August 1941; Hepple, *Verwoerd*, p. 213.
43. *Die Transvaler* and *Die Burger*, 22 and 23 January 1942.
44. Quoted in *Trouw*, 18 October 1967.
45. In an address to the Transvaal Congress of the NP in Pretoria, 12 August 1941.
46. *Sunday Times*, 24 August 1941.
47. *RDM*, 2 October 1941.
48. H.G. Stoker, *Stryd om die Ordes*, and A.H. van der Walt, *'n Volk op Trek* (Johannesburg, 1944), p. 25.
49. Meyer, 'Politieke Verset teen die Oorlog', (Stellenbosch, 1953), p. 27.
50. Ibid., p. 28.
51. Compare the NP's Draft in 1942 with the OB Groot Raad's blueprint of 1942; Diederichs, du Plessis and Meyer in *Ons Republiek*, 1941; Declaration of Volks Organisations, 1941; the ANS 'Freedom Manifesto', 1940; and Transvaal OB Republican Declaration, 1940; Dr Verwoerd in *Stryd*, September 1940.
52. A distinction is drawn between the *volk* (the people) and the *bevolking* (the population), between citizens and subjects. Only members of the *volk* are eligible for citizenship. To ensure that Afrikaners alone have exclusive access to political power, the Republic's political arrangements – such as the criteria for qualifying for civil rights, the franchise and the right to participate in politics – act to entrench the Afrikaners' constitutional dominance and exclude 'foreigners'. The importance of denying a say in political affairs to white 'aliens', especially Jews, was repeatedly stressed by Malan, Verwoerd, Strydom, Dönges and Louw. In addition, all 'unnatural elements' would be dispossessed of political influence and treated as subjects.
53. *The OB*, 9 May 1945.
54. *The OB*, 30 May 1945.
55. *Sunday Times*, 4 November 1945.

8　General Smuts Attacks the AB

1. See, for example, *Natal Daily News*, 7 October 1942.
2. Mentioned in Index to DMI Memorandum of January 1944.

3. 'Special Observation. Twentyfifth Anniversary Meeting of the A.B. held in Bloemfontein on the 13th of December, 1943'. The following account is drawn from this extensive document.
4. Ibid., p. 13.
5. Ibid., p. 17.
6. This account provided the skeletal framework for Ch. 2. We shall therefore not repeat the points already mentioned. The document is headed 'History of the Inception and Development of the AB', 13–14 December 1943.
7. The substance of this quote appears also in the DMI Report of 29 March 1944, pp. 28–9.
8. Ibid.
9. *Natal Daily News*, 12 September 1944.
10. Quoted in J.H.P. Serfontein's *Brotherhood of Power: An Exposé of the Secret Afrikaner Broederbond* (London, 1979).
11. *Die Transvaler*, 11 December 1944.
12. *Die Transvaler*, 14 December 1944.
13. *Daily News*, 21 December 1944.
14. Hansard Debates, vol. 52, cols 3854 and 3890.
15. *Natal Daily News*, 21 March 1945.
16. *Die Transvaler*, 26 January 1945.
17. Ibid.
18. DMI Report of 16 February 1945.
19. See *Natal Daily News*, 23 and 24 February 1945; *RDM*, 22 February 1945, 5 March 1945 and 13 April 1945.
20. DMI Report of 16 April 1945.

9   Post-War Developments and the Birth of Apartheid

1. *The OB*, 9 May 1945.
2. These were *'n Tuiste vir die Nageslag* (Cape Town, 1945) (A Homeland for Posterity); *Regverdige Rasseapartheid* (Stellenbosch, 1947) (A Just Racial Apartheid); and *Voogdyskap en Apartheid* (Pretoria, 1948) (Trusteeship and Apartheid).
3. Cronje, *Voogdyskap and Apartheid*, p. 40.
4. Ibid., p. 26.
5. Bunting, *The Rise*, p. 129, no date given.
6. S. Patterson, *The Last Trek* (London, 1957), p. 104.
7. Bunting, *The Rise*, p. 196.
8. C.B. says at least seven were Broeders. Wilkins and Strydom in *The Broederbond*, p. 119, claim that only N.C. Havenga and E.H. Louw were not brethren.
9. Bunting, *The Rise*, p. 131.
10. *Sunday Express*, 23 May 1948.
11. Bunting, *The Rise*, pp. 244–5.
12. *The Star*, 21 April 1949.
13. *Cape Times*, 23 April 1949.
14. *Inspan*, 24 May 1949.
15. *The Star*, 13 May 1949.

16. *The Friend*, 5 October 1950.
17. See *Verslag van die Tweede Ekonomiese Volkskongres (1950)* (Bloemfontein, 1950); *The Friend*, 5 October 1950.
18. *Verslag*, pp. 15 and 7–15.
19. Ibid., pp. 21, 22–3.
20. *Verslag*, pp. 161 and 159–71.
21. *Verslag*, p. 149.
22. Founder members named in *SABRA – Tydskrif vir Rasse Aangeleenthede*, no. 1, 1949.
23. 'Immigration: An Afrikaner's View', by Prof L.J. du Plessis, *SABRA*, January 1954.
24. P.J. Viljoen, Chairman of the Council of Churches, speech published in *Die Kerkbode*, 25 May 1949.
25. Ibid.
26. S. du Toit, 'Openbaringslig op die Apartheidvraagstuk', *Koers*, August 1949, p. 13.
27. By 'vertical' apartheid is meant total separation with blacks able to rise to any position in their own areas. 'Horizontal' apartheid conveys the idea that there is an absolute ceiling or colour bar, preventing blacks from engaging in certain sorts of jobs.
28. Report published in *Die Kerkbode*, 21 December 1949, and summarised in *Die Kerkbode*, 30 December 1949.
29. See *Die Kerkbode*, 'The Holy Scriptures and Apartheid', by Ben Keet, 7 December 1949; 14 December 1949; 21 December 1949; 30 December 1949.
30. N.J. Rhoodie and H.J. Venter, *Apartheid* (Cape Town and Pretoria, 1960), p. 164.
31. See *Natal Daily News*, 18 May 1951; *Cape Times*, 18 May 1951.
32. *Natal Daily News*, 8 April 1952.

Index

242 *Index*